# HISTORY OF THE EARLY SETTLEMENT INDIAN WARS OF WESTERN VIRGINIA;

# AN ACCOUNT OF THE VARIOUS EXPEDITIONS IN THE WEST, PREVIOUS TO 1795.

## WILLS DE HASS

# TABLE OF CONTENTS

# PREFACE.

It is sincerely regretted that circumstances should have arisen to delay the publication of the present volume beyond the time contemplated in the original prospectus. That delay, however, instead of impairing, will be found to have added to the merits of the work, by the opportunity which it has given to render more comprehensive its local character, and more accurate its general details. In the preparation of this work, we have encountered difficulties which at times appeared almost insurmountable. None but those who have attempted such a task, from so great a mass of apparently irreconcilable facts and statements as we have had to work upon, can form any conception of the labor and difficulty undergone. Starting out with the avowed determination to make the truth of history substitute the error, we soon found that the line drawn would be a difficult and painful one to pursue; for it necessarily compelled us to do violence to the feelings of some, and greatly disappoint the expectations of others. But, determined faithfully and impartially to discharge our obligations, we have strictly adhered to the course marked out, and enforced with rigid severity the rule adopted for our guidance. All statements of doubtful authority have been discarded, and no evidence received but that of the most unquestionable character. A few errors may, nevertheless, have crept into our pages; but these are believed to be unimportant as they were unavoidable. In the preparation of this volume, we have labored to present not a mere compilation of facts, but a history drawn from sources original and reliable. To accomplish this, the very best means have been adopted; public documents searched, private records examined; and the living witnesses who still linger among us, — sole depositories of many important historical facts, without which our annals would be incomplete, personally consulted. The labor has been difficult, annoying and expensive, as much of it could not be performed without considerable personal inconvenience.

The early history of the West is full of most lively interest to readers, both at home and abroad; and that which relates to Western Virginia and its borders is so in an especial degree. Here it was that Washington received those severe lessons in war which prepared him for the great achievements he so gloriously performed in after life, and here was struck the first great blow in the struggle for American Independence.

A distinctive feature of the work will be found in Part VII., containing biographical sketches of some of the prominent actors in our border wars; — the men who, amid dangers, privations and suffering, founded, in the depth of the primeval forest, the institutions of freedom we now enjoy. It is a matter of great regret that the prescribed limits of the work could not permit the insertion of all the memoirs contemplated in the original design. This omission it is hoped to supply in a subsequent edition.

Some other changes have also been made. The ground proposed to be gone over was found far too extensive to allow justice to be done each subject; and therefore, we determined to confine ourselves strictly to the three distinctive features of the work — History, Indian Wars, and Biography. This departure from the original plan cannot but render the volume more acceptable to the local as well as the general reader. That part which we proposed to embrace under the head of a Topographical description of the North-western counties, will either be given in a subsequent edition, or embodied in a separate work on the Present Condition, Resources and Statistics of Western Virginia. There are one or two references in the text to the county notices proposed to be given, which the reader will understand without further explanation.

In consequence of this departure from our original plan, some portions of the work have been prepared with considerable haste, and occasionally, the labors of others called into requisition. This course has been to a certain extent unavoidable; the Author having recently received an appointment under the Government, which will require and engage both his time and attention.

To the many kind friends who have furnished material and extended facilities in the preparation of the present volume, the Author returns his sincere thanks.

With these brief statements, explanations and acknowledgments, the volume is respectfully submitted to the public.

W. De H.

# PART I. GENERAL INTRODUCTORY HISTORY. 1492-1687.

# CHAPTER I. AMERICA ANTERIOR TO COLUMBUS.

Up to the close of the fifteenth century the vast continent of America was wholly unknown to European nations. How painful is the reflection, that previous to the discovery by Columbus, this great Western World is destitute of history or chronology! That it was inhabited centuries ago, by a people far superior to the uncivilized Red Man, found here by the Europeans, the evidences are too strong to admit the shadow of a doubt. We trace them in their vast and mysterious monumental remains, stretching from the far North to the extreme South; from the Atlantic on the East to the Pacific on the West.

But who were they? Whence came and whither went that race? Contemporary history furnishes no aid, for they were isolated from all the world beside. Alas, they have faded from the earth without leaving a vestige of their history behind: the remembrance of their deeds lives not even in tradition nor legendary song. One by one, they have, as a nation, risen, flourished and disappeared, beyond the remotest memory of man, with all their greatness, their glory and their pride. The beautiful apostrophe of Campbell, to a mummy in Belzoni's collection, frail relic of a once noble and intellectual being, can with much truth be applied to the ancients of America, —

Antiquity appears to have begun,

Long after their primeval race was run.

Phoenician, Scandinavian, British and Danish tradition, separately lay claim to an early acquaintance with the Western Continent; but their accounts are equally vague and hypothetical, and for all historical purposes, entitled to but little consideration. As to the Sagas of the Icelanders and Norwegians, about which so much has recently been written, we must receive them with every degree of caution, since they come to us in such a dreamy and unsatisfactory manner as to render them almost useless for the purpose of the historian. But, it is not our wish at this time, to enter into an inquiry upon the highly interesting subject of American Antiquities. At another time, and in another place, we may take occasion to refer to this matter more in detail.

As to the discovery and settlement of the continent anterior to Columbus, the character and limits of a work like this would preclude the possibility of saying much. It is enough at this time, to know that these immense regions were laid open to European enterprise by the genius and energy of that illustrious navigator. To him is due the credit of bringing to light a new continent, and changing the whole current of affairs on the old. Columbus, it is believed, availed himself of no information touching a former discovery. He knew nothing, it is asserted, either of the attempt, or alleged success of the Northmen. His frail barks ploughed the uncharted seas through which ships had never moved. His men despaired, but Columbus never lost confidence of success. He never spoke in doubt or hesitation, but with as much certainty as if his eye had beheld the promised land.

Who can contemplate the greatness and character of the services conferred upon mankind by this single achievement of the Genoese Navigator, without feeling lost in the grand scale of future probabilities?

Who can say what will be its ultimate influence upon the various nations of the earth? Who can estimate the extent and incalculable advantages it has already conferred on the Western hemisphere? The primeval wilderness, filled with fierce beasts and savage man, has become the chosen abode of more than twenty millions of freemen; the seat of vast Commonwealths, blessed with the joys, the comforts and the arts of civilized life, in all their shapes and varieties of refined intellectual existence.

# CHAPTER II. EARLY ENGLISH DISCOVERIES.

Before entering upon the subject of our local history, it may not be amiss to glance briefly at the earliest successive efforts of monarchs, adventurers, and discoverers to colonize the Western Hemisphere. It is not proposed to notice, in detail, the progress of cis-Atlantic discovery, as that belongs more appropriately to a History of the United States. We may with justice and propriety, however, claim to occupy a brief space in a preliminary survey of the efforts of France and England to effect footholds on the North American continent. This we deem essential to a proper elucidation of our subject, as most of the difficulties encountered by the people of the western parts of Virginia and Pennsylvania, undoubtedly grew out of the contending claims of those two powers for supremacy in the west. The earliest English claim to sovereignty in this country was based upon the discoveries of John and Sebastian Cabot, father and son, who, acting under a commission from Henry the Seventh, to "sail in tire Eastern, Western, and Northern Seas, to search for continents, islands, or regions hitherto unseen by Christian people," and to plant the flag of Britain upon any country thus discovered. Sailing with these instructions, they discovered the continent of North America near Labrador, on the 24th of January, 1497. Running along the whole extent of our coast, from the 38th to the 67th degree of North latitude, these English adventurers took possession of the country in the name of that monarch, with the privilege of holding it to the exclusion of all other persons. This patent, embodying as it did the very "worst features of colonial monopoly," was abrogated in the following year, and a new one, breathing a more enlightened spirit, issued in the name of John Cabot. Under this new grant extensive explorations were made by Sebastian Cabot, one of the most distinguished navigators of his age. Great, however, as were these discoveries, but little was done by the British Crown, during the next half century, to take formal possession, by actual settlement, of the newly acquired regions.

The first Tudor, so happily described as

"Proud, dark, suspicious, brooding o'er his gold,"

could see no propriety in diminishing the number of his subjects at home by sending them to distant climes; while Henry VIII., and his celebrated minister, Cardinal Wolsey, had quite enough to attend to, without allowing them either time, means, or inclination, to fish up continents from the "vasty deep," or "annex" unexplored provinces, peopled by savages, who had never heard of Harry, Luther, or Pope Clement VII.

It was not, indeed, until the splendid conquests of the Spaniards in the West Indies, Mexico, and South America had excited the cupidity of Elizabeth, that any effectual attempts, on the part of Britain, at further exploration or colonization were made.

In 1578, the attention of the English government was directed to the importance of colonization, by Sir Walter Raleigh, whose genius and enterprise were equal to any undertaking. He procured a patent for Sir Humphrey Gilbert, (half brother of Raleigh) who, in 1583, attempted a settlement upon the sterile coast of New Foundland; but, of course, was compelled to abandon it as wholly unsuitable for an English colony. A second expedition was fitted out in 1584, under a direct grant to Raleigh himself. This expedition sailed under the auspices of Sir Richard Grenville, a near relative of Sir Walter. It consisted of two small vessels, commanded by experienced officers, and sailed from London in April of that year. In July, a landing was effected on an inlet of North Carolina, (Wocoken, supposed to be the present Ocracock.) Here the party remained until September, when, becoming discouraged by reverses and disappointments incident to a settlement in an unbroken wilderness, they sailed for home, taking with them two natives, Manteo and Wanchese.

On their return, they gave the most glowing description of the country visited, representing it as a region where nature appeared clothed with the most brilliant colors, and abounded in fruit, game, fish, &c.

A third expedition was at once determined upon, and fitted out with the least practicable delay. It sailed under the broad pennant of Sir Richard Grenville, and reached Roanoke about the middle of June (1585). Out of this expedition, one hundred and eight men were left on the island, (Roanoke) with a supply of provisions for two years.

The new colonists embraced some of the most energetic and vigorous-minded men who had yet left the mother country.

Sir Richard, having appointed Ralph Lane, Governor of the Colony, returned to England. By this expedition, Manteo was restored to his friends, and became invaluable to the colonists as guide and interpreter.

A year's residence, however, in the unbroken solitudes of the New World, proved quite enough to cool the ardor of the colonists, and make them determine to leave by the first opportunity. They had no idea of being longer made instrumental in extending the "area of freedom." Shortly after, (1586) Sir Francis Drake arrived with his fleet, and despite his entreaties every soul left for England.

Scarcely had the colonists departed, when Sir Walter Raleigh, in company with Sir R. Grenville, Hariot, Cavendish, and other distinguished men, arrived at Roanoke. Sir Walter Raleigh was greatly disappointed and chagrined at the failure of their favorite scheme. Not discouraged, however, he succeeded in persuading fifteen men to remain on the island, while he returned home, and sent out (1587) a new expedition, under the command of Captain John White. On reaching Virginia, a party was sent to hunt up the men left on the island, but all was silent as the grave; naught, save the whitening bones of a single victim, gave any clue to their melancholy fate. All, it is supposed, fell a prey to savage cruelty.

White was made governor of the colony, and was assisted by twelve councillors. One of these (Annaias Dare) was White's son-in-law, and shortly after the arrival of the little band of colonists, was signalized an event not unworthy of note in the early annals of Virginia, — that event was nothing less, than the birth of the first white child in North America.

White having, as he supposed, comfortably secured the emigrants, returned to England, with the view of making further arrangements for increasing the little colony, and promoting the interests of those left behind.

White found on his return, the government and people full of anxious solicitude to meet the threatened Spanish invasion. But Raleigh, true to his purpose of securing a permanent settlement in Virginia, despatched White with two ships of supplies for the relief of the colonists. Instead of proceeding at once to the colony. White engaged in capturing Spanish prizes, until at last overcome, he lost all, and was compelled to return to England, to the great chagrin and disappointment of his noble and generous friend and patron.

"The Invincible Armada of Spain" had to be overcome, and the safety of England herself secured, before another effort could be made to succor the colony at Roanoke.

It was not until another year had passed, that White could be sent in aid of the colonists. On arriving at the seat of the colony, what was his alarm to find, as the only vestige of his people, a vague inscription pointing to Croatan as the place to which they had gone.

The fate of the colonists has never been satisfactorily ascertained. The presumption is, they all fell victims to savage power. Some have indulged the idea that they amalgamated with the Hatteras Indians; but while humanity may dictate such a hope, "credulity must entertain a doubt of the truth of the hypothesis."

White soon after returned to England, in hopeless despair of ever hearing again from his hapless friends or unfortunate daughter.

Sir Walter is said to have sent several times in search of his "liege men," but nothing satisfactory was ever ascertained.

Sir Walter, having forfeited his patent by attainder, James the First granted a new patent for all our territory, from the 34th to the 45th degree, under the general name of Virginia; a name previously conferred by Elizabeth in reference to her own unmarried state. The South Virginia division extended from Cape Hatteras to New York, and the first colonization of the new patentees was made at Jamestown, on James' river. May 13th, 1607.

The settlement of Jamestown, has by some, and with much truth, been termed the most important event since the era of the Reformation. Who can properly estimate the ultimate influence it is destined to exercise upon the future history of the world?

Within the entire range of recorded history, we know of no more grand and imposing spectacle than the landing of that little band of hardy pilgrims, with the determination, come weal or woe, to plant then and there, a colony that should be self-sustaining and self-relying.

The heroic Smith and his resolute companions then, laid broad and deep the corner stone, upon which has since been reared the proud temple of American Liberty. Aye, those men, seeking homes in the wilderness of the West, unconsciously planted the germ of a nation that was destined to spring forth in the fulness of its strength, and startling the tyrants of Europe in their seats of power, cause them to feel that the "divine right" no longer existed — that the young giant of the West had inflicted a blow which shook the foundations of their very thrones. Great have been the regrets of Britain at the success of the "American experiment;" but all such regrets will be more futile than even her efforts to roll back the flame of freedom, or check its mounting to meridian splendor! The fabric which has grown from the plantation of the colonies at Jamestown, at Plymouth, on the Island of Manhattan, on the banks of the Mississippi, and along the borders of our great inland seas, now stands the mark and model, the admiration and wonder of the world! The vicissitudes of five and seventy years, while they have shaken down the pillars of most of the corrupt monarchies of earth, have but proven to mankind the indestructible material of the plain temple of Republican Freedom.

Of the gallant Captain Smith, the most devoted of the chivalrous spirits at Jamestown, it might be expected we would say something. In consequence, however, of our circumscribed limits, we can only add, that his accomplished address, great skill, consummate bravery, indomitable courage, and devoted patriotism, mark him as one of the first men of his age. The story of his captivity by the Indians — his trial, condemnation and preparation for death — his timely rescue by the beautiful Indian girl Pochabontas, who threw herself upon his person, and averted the blow of the savage — one of the most remarkable instances of true philanthropy upon record — is too familiar to all readers of American history, to be given here. Suffice it, that Smith was the master spirit of the colony; and to his discriminating judgment, keen sense of right and wrong, and his enlightened policy towards the Indians, may be ascribed the fact, that the little band of adventurers did not share a fate similar to that of the unfortunate colonists of Roanoke.

# CHAPTER III. EARLY FRENCH DISCOVERIES.

France, with her characteristic spirit of enterprise, could not long remain inactive when other maritime nations were extending their dominion, and explorations throughout the vast field laid open by Columbus. At a very early day she discovered the importance of the Northern fisheries. In 1524 John Verrazzani a Florentine mariner, while sailing under a commission from Francis the First, ranged the coast of North America from Wilmington, North Carolina, to the 50th degree of North latitude. He landed at several points, and called the country New France, and this constituted the claim of France to her American possessions. In 1534 a new expedition was fitted out, commanded by James Cartler, who was the first European to penetrate the river Lawrence, and give an intelligent description of the country. After sailing up that river until he could "see land on both sides," which he claimed and declared French territory, Cartier returned to France, and gave such a glowing description of the newly discovered regions, as to induce Francis I. to take immediate steps for farther exploration and colonization. Accordingly, three ships, well manned and provided, summit of a rugged mountain, which his guide had informed him commanded a view of the adjacent country. With much difficulty he reached the top, and emerging from a dense forest upon a bluff, rocky point, a prospect burst upon the astonished and delighted Frenchman, which it would be vain to attempt to describe. Hundreds of feet beneath, and stretching around for miles, lay the sylvan landscape in all its wild luxuriance of summer clothing, slightly variegated by the first tinge of early autumn. The clear, sparkling waters of the St. Lawrence wound along in the distance like cords of silver, presenting a scene such as he had never before witnessed. Enraptured with the prospect before him, and filled with anticipations of its future glory, he named it Montreal. Erecting a cross bearing the arms of France, and an inscription declaring Francis I. to be the sovereign of the territory, he returned to his fleet, and soon after sailed for home.

Intestinal feuds, with a variety of other causes, prevented anything farther being done for more than half a century. In 1608, one year after the founding of Jamestown, Admiral Champlain was sent out at the head of another expedition. In the same year he founded Quebec, and associating with him a party of Hurons and Algonquins, traversed the wilds of that Northern region, penetrating to the beautiful lake which now bears his name, where he spent the winter.

He subsequently erected the castle of St. Louis at Quebec, thus establishing the authority of France in the New World. French emigrants continued to arrive, and the dominion of France to increase, until her influence was felt and extended from the St. Lawrence to the Gulf of Mexico.

Many of those who thus forsook their pleasant homes on the banks of the Seine, were missionaries of the Cross; who not content to settle down with their friends on the shores of the St. Lawrence, pushed forward into the wilderness, in the sacred discharge of their religious trusts. With the Bible in one hand and a cross in the other, they threaded the sombre shade of those dark old woods; and often with a bowlder of granite for a footstool, and the eternal cataracts thundering amid the everlasting solitudes, for an organ, those devout men, preached to the unlettered children of the forest, of "Christ crucified" that they might live.

Among those who thus went abroad in the sacred character of missionary, was Father Marquette, a recollect Monk. He had heard from the simple-minded natives of an "endless river" in the far West, which came from, — they knew not where; and went, — they knew not whither. Strongly impressed with a belief, common at that day, that a passage could be effected by water, to the Pacific, he determined to undertake an expedition to the West. Accordingly, in company with an Indian trader named Joliet, in the year 1668, he proceeded to St. Mary's, and was there joined by Allouez, a Jesuit Missionary, of many years intercourse with the natives. These three, with an Indian for a guide, paddled their light pirouge over the restless waters of Lake Michigan, and effected a landing upon its western shore. Marquette was perfectly fascinated with the great beauty of the country, — the fertility of its soil, and grandeur of its scenery. Pushing on into the wilderness, the devout Missionary, lit up at the council fires of wondering natives, the sacred torch of the Christian's faith. Reaching at last, the waters of a considerable stream, (Wisconsin) they descended it, and on the morning of the 17th of June, 1673, discovered the great Father of Waters, which afforded them "joy," says Marquette, "that I cannot express." Kneeling down on the banks of that ancient river, they returned thanks; and thus went up the first white man's prayer, that ever broke the silence of those solitary wilds. Descending the Mississippi to the mouth of the Arkansas, and satisfying themselves that it emptied into the Gulf of Mexico, they retraced their steps to the Illinois, thence up that river and across to where Chicago now stands. Here Marquette concluded to remain and preach to the Indians, while Joliet proceeded to Green Bay and gave information of the discovery. Continuing for a time to preach to the simple-minded natives, Marquette finally sailed for Mackinaw, but putting into a small river in Michigan, which still bears his name, went ashore, and desired that he might not be disturbed for half an hour. Erecting a rude altar on that lonely beach, he "knelt down by its side, and sank to sleep, to wake no more." Becoming uneasy at his long absence, search was made, and he was found as described. His companions buried him on the spot where he had breathed his last; a "light breeze from the Lake sighed his requiem, and the Algonquin nation became his mourners."

Thus died the discoverer of the Upper Mississippi. His was the first white man's grave ever dug in the magnificent solitudes of the Great West; which were yet to repose in the slumber of ages ere they should be trodden by the footsteps of civilization.

The discoveries of Marquette, although permitted to slumber for a season, were the means of inducing M. de la Salle, commandant at Fort Frontenac, now Kingston, to undertake, in 1679, a second expedition to the West. In company with Father Hennepin, a Monk of the Order of Franciscan, and thirty-four men, he set sail in a small vessel of forty tons, named the "Griffin," — the first of its class that ever ploughed the waves of our great Northern Lakes. What a world of thought is called up by the recital of this simple fact! The birchen canoe of the simple-hearted native, and the miniature ship of La Salle, have been multiplied by the magic wand of commerce, until those vast inland seas have become literally white with sails, and their waters murmur with the rush of keels. Prosperous cities, like sea sybils with their 'tiara of proud towers,' now occupy the shores of those then desolate lakes; while a population of millions, blessed with all the arts and refinements of civilized life, throng their borders of many thousand miles.

La Salle having reached the mouth of Chicago river, disembarked, and crossing the country, descended the Illinois river to near where Peoria now stands. He there erected a fort which in the bitterness of his heart he called Creve Coeur, (broken heart) chiefly on account of the hopeless difficulties which beset him. Having completed his fort, and despatched Hennepin to explore the country north, La Salle returned to Frontenac for additional men and means. Hennepin struck across the country to the Mississippi, and ascended above the falls, to which he gave the name St. Anthony. Hennepin afterwards claimed to have discovered the source of the Mississippi.

La Salle rejoined his companions (1682) and building a small vessel, sailed down the Mississippi "to the sea." He called the country Louisiana, in honor of his sovereign, Louis XIV.

On returning, a portion of the company were left at Cahokia, Kaskaskia, &c., where, for a time, flourished luxuriantly, the snow-white lily, opening its fragrant beauties to the enraptured gaze of tawny savages.

La Salle made his way back to Canada, thence sailed for France; and on a subsequent visit to the mouth of the Mississippi, was assassinated by one of his own company.

We have thus endeavored to present, in a succinct form, some of the principal events connected with the early movements and discoveries of the French, on the continent of North America. This has been deemed necessary, in order the more fully to elucidate some of the points of history upon which we shall have occasion to touch in the progress of our inquiry.

# PART II. EARLY SETTLEMENT OF WESTERN VIRGINIA. 1700-1754.

# CHAPTER I. INDIAN TOWNS ON THE OHIO.

When the whites first penetrated the beautiful valley of the Upper Ohio, they found it occupied by numerous and powerful tribes of hostile savages, who held it more as a common hunting ground than a place of permanent abode.

With the exception of Logstown, eighteen miles below the forks of the Monongahela and Alleghany; a Mingo village at the mouth of Beaver; a Shawanee town near the Great Kanawha, and another near the Scioto, but few native settlements were to be found on the banks of the "River of Blood:" the fearfully significant name given by some of the tribes of Indians to the beautiful stream which sweeps along our Western border.

Tradition tells of many a bloody battle along the shores of this grand old river, over whose sylvan banks has so often rushed the crimson tide of Indian massacre. Many, indeed, are said to have been the warlike feats here enacted, between bands of fierce and savage warriors. Here it was that the stern Iriquois met the equally determined and relentless Massawomee, and maintained those long and bloody strifes which ultimately imparted to the whole region the very appropriate title of "dark and bloody ground."

The most powerful confederacy of native tribes, found here by the French and English, was the Massawomees, so called by the Indians of Eastern Virginia, to whom they were a constant source of dread and alarm.

The Massawomees occupied, to the exclusion of almost every other tribe, the entire region stretching from the Blue Ridge to the Ohio river. The encroachments of the whites compelled them gradually to retire, until at last they were forced over the Alleghanies, leaving the "Valley" unoccupied, save by occasional predatory bands of Southern tribes.

But the march of the Anglo-Saxon westward was slow in the extreme. It was not until more than one hundred years had elapsed from the settlement of Jamestown, that a project was conceived for crossing the great rocky barrier, whose frowning heights seemed to shut out all communication between the primitive settler and the region west.

In 1710, Lieutenant Governor Spottswood, whose military genius, as displayed in the campaigns of Marlborough, had won the esteem of his sovereign, and secured him the appointment of Colonial Governor in

Virginia, determined to explore the trans-montane region. He had heard of the great beauty and extent of the country lying between the parallel mountains, but of the region beyond the Alleghany nothing definite could be ascertained, as the most daring adventurer had rarely tried to surmount its rugged height, and scan the outspread landscape which opened its charms to the setting sun.

Equipping a company of horsemen, Gov. Spottswood headed it in person, and commenced his march from Williamsburg in great pomp. Nothing occurred to mar the interest of the occasion, and in due time the expedition reached the Valley.

The governor was enraptured with the view. Bright flowers, rendered doubly beautiful by the transparent purity of the atmosphere and the deep serenity of the azure heavens, covered the ground in almost every direction. Amid forests of fragrant trees, or deep hid in perfumed alcoves, — spots more enchantingly beautiful than were ever graced by Calypso and her nymphs; they found those mysterious Hygeian fountains whose health-preserving properties now enjoy a world-wide fame. Pushing on, the expedition at length reached the base of the Alleghanies, and struggling upward through rugged defile, and over frowning precipice, the intrepid governor, with his little party, at length gained the summit of that great mountain barrier. Never, perhaps, before had the voice of civilized man broken the solitude which reigned around. The point attained, commanded a magnificent view of the outspread country beyond. It was one of the highest peaks of the great Appalachian range; and gazing down into the illimitable wilderness, they there resolved that the whole extent should be peopled, and the forest be made to blossom as the rose. How well the spirit which prompted that resolution has been carried out by the descendants of the Virginia colonists, let the eight or ten millions of happy and prosperous people who now throng the great Valley of the West answer.

After the return of Governor Spottswood and his party, he established the "Transmontane Order, or Knights of the Golden Horse-Shoe," giving to each of those who accompanied him a miniature golden horse-shoe, bearing the inscription, "Sic jurat transcendere Montes."

# CHAPTER II. FIRST SETTLEMENT OF THE VALLEY.

In 1732, the first permanent settlement by whites west of the Blue Ridge, was made near where Winchester now stands. Sixteen families from Pennsylvania, headed by Joist Hite, composed this little colony, and to them is due the credit of having first planted the standard of civilization in Virginia, west of the mountains.

In 1734, Benjamin Allen, with three others, settled on the North Branch of the Shenandoah, about twelve miles south of the present town of Woodstock. Other adventurers pushed on, and settlements gradually extended west, crossing Capon River, North Mountain and the Alleghany range, until finally they reached the tributaries of the Monongahela.

The majority of those who settled the eastern part of the Valley were Pennsylvania Germans; a class of people distinguished for their untiring industry, and love of rich lands.

Many of these emigrants had no sooner heard of the fertility of the soil in the Shenandoah valley, than they began to spread themselves along that stream and its tributaries. "So completely did they occupy the country along the north and south branches of that river, that the few stray English, Irish or Scotch settlers among them did not sensibly affect the homogeneousness of the population. They long retained, and for the most part do still retain, their German language, and the German simplicity of their manners."

Tradition informs us that the Indians did not object to the Pennsylvanians settling the country. From the exalted character for benevolence and virtue enjoyed by the first founder of that State, (William Penn,) the simple-minded children of the woods believed that all those who had lived under the shadow of his name, partook alike of his justice and humanity. But fatal experience soon taught them a very different lesson. Towards Virginians, the Indians had a most implacable hatred. They called them, by way of distinction, "Long Knives," and "warmly opposed their settling in the Valley."

For twenty years after the settlement about Winchester, the natives, inhabiting the mountains and intervening vales, remained in comparative quietude.

Shortly after the first settlement at Winchester, a circumstance occurred which speedily led to settlements along the upper part of the Valley, and opened to the public mind the fine regions lying west of the Alleghanies. Two resolute spirits, Thomas Morlen and John Sailing, full of adventure, determined to explore the "Upper Country," about which so much had been said, but so little was known. Setting out from Winchester, they made their way up the valley of the Shenandoah, crossed the waters of James river, not far from the Natural Bridge, and had progressed as far as the Roanoke, when a party of Cherokees surprised them, and took Sailing prisoner. Morlen made his escape, and returned in safety to his friends. Sailing was carried captive into Tennessee, and finally habituating himself to the Indians, remained with them several years. While on a hunting excursion with some of his tribe, some years afterwards, they were attacked by a party of Illinois Indians, with whom the Cherokees were at bitter variance, and Sailing a second time borne off a prisoner.

These transactions took place in Kentucky, whither the Southern, Western, and Northern tribes resorted to hunt. By his new captors, Sailing was carried to Kaskaskia; afterwards sold to a party of Spaniards on the lower Mississippi; subsequently returned to Kaskaskia; and finally, after six years' captivity, was ransomed by the Governor of Canada, and transferred to the Dutch authorities at Manhattan. Thence he succeeded in making his way to Williamsburg, in Virginia.

His captivity became the subject of general conversation. The accounts which he gave of the extent and resources of the great West, embracing almost every variety of soil, climate, and production, and extending into remote parts, where human foot had probably never penetrated; where majestic rivers, issuing from unknown sources in the far North, rolled their volumed waters in solemn grandeur to the South; where vegetation was most luxuriant, and game of every description inexhaustible, — were enough, as they proved, to excite a deep interest in all who heard his glowing accounts.

Shortly before the return of Sailing, a considerable addition had been made to the population of Virginia by recent arrivals at Jamestown. Of this number were John Lewis and John Mackey, both of whom, desirous of securing suitable locations, were much interested in the statements of Sailing. Pleased with his description of the Valley, they determined to visit it, first having induced Sailing to accompany them as guide. The three penetrated the fastness of the mountain, descended into the luxuriant valley, and pleased with the physical appearance of the country, determined to fix there their abode. Lewis selected the place of his future residence on a stream still bearing his name; Mackey chose a spot on the Shenandoah; and Sailing, having concluded to remain, made choice of a beautiful tract of land on the waters of James river, and built his cabin.

Early in the Spring of 1736, an agent for Lord Fairfax, who held, under a patent from James II., all that part of Virginia known as the Northern Neck, came over, and after remaining a short time at Williamsburg, accepted an invitation to visit John Lewis. During his sojourn at the house of Lewis, he captured, while hunting with Samuel and Andrew, (the latter afterwards the distinguished General,) sons of the former, a fine buffalo calf. Returning shortly after to Williamsburg, he presented the mountain pet to Governor Gooch, which so much gratified that functionary, that he forthwith directed a warrant to be made out, authorizing Burden (the agent) to locate 500,000 acres of land on the Shenandoah, or James rivers, west of the Blue Ridge. The grant required that Burden should settle one hundred families upon said land within ten years. The grantee lost no time in returning to England, and in the following year came out with the required number, embracing among his little colony many who became the founders of some of the most distinguished families in our state. Of these were the McDowells, Crawfords, McClures, Alexanders, Wallaces, Pattons, Prestons, Moores, Matthews, &c.

The spirit of adventure now slumbered for a season, and but few additional improvements were made beyond the limits of the Burden grant, until 1751, at which time an influx of population took place; and then it was, the prophetic line of Bishop Berkeley began to be realized, —

"Westward, the star of empire takes its way."

Many of the new settlers in the Valley had come in with Governor Dinwiddie, and were men of undoubted worth, and great probity of character. They embraced the Stuarts, Paulls, McDowells, etc., names distinguished in the annals of Virginia. Most of those who thus forsook the pleasures, refinements and enjoyments of comfortable homes in the old world, to find a dwelling-place in the untrodden wilds of the new, were Scotch Covenanters; those stern, inflexible sectarians, who preferred religious freedom abroad, to ease and oppression at home. How different was this class of people from the Spanish adventurers who subdued Mexico and South America; those bloody conquerors, whose remorseless cruelty to the simple-minded natives, cast so much obloquy upon Spain, and darken her history with some of the foulest stains that ever disgraced a civilized nation! Who can wonder, that the smiles of Heaven attended the one, while the avenging hand of an outraged God smote the other!

# CHAPTER III. FIRST SETTLERS WEST OF THE ALLEGHANIES.

Previous to 1749, Western Virginia was untrodden by the foot of white man, if we except an occasional trader, who may have ventured upon the heads of some of the tributary streams which take their rise in the Alleghany Mountains.

Some time during this year, a man laboring under aberration of intellect, wandered from Frederick county into the wilderness of the Greenbriar country. Although a supposed lunatic, there seemed yet enough of "method in his madness," to tell his friends, on returning home, that he had discovered rivers flowing in a contrary direction to those of the Valley. His description of the country soon induced some to visit it, among whom were Jacob Martin and Stephen Sewell. These men settled on the Greenbriar river, where they built a cabin; but soon disagreeing about some trivial matter, Sewell left his companion, and took up his abode in a hollow tree. In the Spring of 1751, when Andrew Lewis visited the country as agent for the Greenbriar Company, he discovered the lonely pioneers in the deep seclusion of their mountain home. Upon inquiry as to the cause of their estrangement, the gallant .Lewis soon reconciled matters, but only for a brief time, as Sewell shortly afterwards removed farther into the wilderness, where he fell a victim to Indian barbarity.

Further attempts to colonize the Greenbriar country were not made for many years. John Lewis, and his son Andrew, proceeded with their explorations, until interrupted by the breaking out of the French war. In 1762, a few families began to penetrate the region on Muddy creek, and the Big Levels; but a royal proclamation of the next year, commanded that all who had settled, or held improvements on the Western waters, should at once remove, as the claim of the Indians had not been extinguished; and it was most important to preserve their friendship, in order to prevent them coalescing with the French. Those families already in the enjoyment of their improvements, refused to comply with the King's mandate, and most of them were cut off by the savages in 1763-4. From the date of these occurrences, up to 1769, the Greenbriar country contained not a single white settlement. In that year, Captain John Stuart, with a number of others, made improvements, which they continued to hold despite every effort of the Indians to dispossess them. Seven years later, (1776) settlements were made on New river. The lands taken up in this region, being held by what were known as "corn rights" — whoever planted an acre of corn, acquired a title to one hundred acres of land.

# CHAPTER IV. LAND OPERATORS IN THE WEST.

Time had scarcely been allowed to dry the ink on the signatures to the treaty of Aix-la-Chapelle, ere the British government proceeded to carry out one of its well matured plans for forestalling the movements of the French, and taking immediate possession of the country lying west of the Mountains, and east of the Ohio. This scheme was the formation by an act of Parliament, of a great landed corporation, which was designed to check the encroachments of France, despoil the Indians of their inheritance, and secure permanent possession of the valley of the Ohio.

We will quote from Sparks, the nature, &c., of this corporation. In 1749, Thomas Lee, one of His Majesty's Council in Virginia, formed the design of effecting settlements on the wild lands west of the Alleghany Mountains. * * * With the view of carrying his plan into operation, Mr. Lee associated himself with twelve other persons in Virginia and Maryland, and with Mr. Hanbury, a merchant in London, who formed what they called "The Ohio Company." Five hundred thousand acres of land were granted almost in the terms requested by the company, to be "taken on the south side of the Ohio river, between the Monongahela and Kanawha rivers. Two hundred thousand acres were to be located at once, and held for ten years free of quit-rent, provided one hundred families were settled on it within seven years, and a fort erected of suitable strength to protect the inhabitants." This may be considered the first decisive step on the part of the English, to take possession of the country bordering the Ohio river. Other companies were organized about the same time by the colonial authorities of Virginia, under direct instruction from the mother country. Of these, were the Greenbriar Company, with a grant of 100,000 acres; and the Loyal Company, incorporated on the 12th June, 1749, with a grant for 800,000 acres, from the "line of Canada, North and West." The British Ministry had evidently become alarmed at what they were pleased to term the encroachments of the French; and it was to forestall their movements by throwing into the disputed territory an "armed neutrality," in the shape of several hundred American families, that made the English Government and its Virginia agents, so solicitous to colonize the regions of the West. We will revert to this subject in another chapter, and now resume the thread of our narrative.

Early in 1750, the Ohio Company sent out Christopher Gist on an exploring expedition. He is represented to have crossed from the south branch of the Potomac, to the headwaters of the Juniata; thence to the Alleghany, crossing that river a few miles above where Pittsburgh now stands. Descending the Ohio to the mouth of Beaver, he went up that stream, thence across to the Muskingum, and down to the Miami. After an absence of several months, he returned to the Kanawha, and made a thorough examination of the country lying east of that river and south of the Ohio.

In 1751, as already stated, Andrew Lewis, afterwards so distinguished in the military annals of our State, commenced a survey of the Greenbriar tract. The movements of both these agents, however, had been closely watched, and information conveyed to the French, who by this time had fairly got their eyes open as to the policy and designs of the English. Determined to maintain their rights, and to assert their claim to the country bordering the Ohio, the French crossed Lake Champlain, built Crown Point, and without delay proceeded to fortify certain other positions on the waters of the upper Ohio. With this view, they erected a fort at Presque He, on Lake Erie; another about fifteen miles distant, which they called Le Boeuf; and a third, at the mouth of French Creek, now Venango. But lest, while these little fortresses were quietly rising in the wilderness, the English might attempt corresponding means for defence, a company of soldiers was despatched by the French Commandant, with positive orders to keep intruders out of the valley of the Ohio; but to use no violence, "except in case of obstinate continuance, and then to seize their goods."

This party doubtless heard of the movements of Gist, and the presence of English traders on the Miami. Thither they directed their steps and demanded that the intruders should leave, or be given up as trespassers upon French soil.

The traders refusing to depart, and the Indians being unwilling to give them up, a fight ensued, in which fourteen of the Twigtees or Miamas were killed, and the traders, four in number, taken prisoners.

This occurred early in 1752, as the Indians referred to the fact at the treaty of Logstown, in June. It may justly be regarded as the prologue to that long and bloody drama, the catastrophe of which, was the expulsion of the French from the Ohio valley, and the consequent loss to France of all her territory east of the Mississippi.

Thus stood matters in the spring of 1752. The English thwarted in their attempt to locate lands on the Ohio, deemed it expedient to invite the chiefs of the neighboring tribes to a convention at Logstown, when they hoped to have the claims of Great Britain recognized, as they were clearly determined to possess themselves of the lands in question, by fair means or foul. Accordingly, in June 1752, Joshua Fry, Lunsford Loamax, and James Patton, commissioners on the part of Virginia, met the Sachems and chiefs of the Six Nations, and desired to know to what they objected in the treaty of Lancaster, and of what else they complained. They produced the Lancaster treaty, insisted upon its ratification, and the sale of the Western lands; but the chiefs said "No; they had heard of no sale of lands west of the warriors' road which ran at the foot of the Alleghany ridge." The Commissioners finding the Indians inflexible, and well aware of the rapid advance of the French, decided to offer great inducements in goods, &c., for the ratification of the treaty, and the relinquishment of the Indian title to lands lying south of the Ohio and east of the Kanawha.

The offers and importunities of the Virginians at length prevailed, and on the 13th June, the Indians consented to confirm the Lancaster deed in as "full and ample a manner as if the same was here recited," and guaranteeing that the settlements south-east of the Ohio should not be disturbed by them. The Virginia Commissioners, both at Logstown and Lancaster, were men of the highest character, "but treated with the Indians according to the ideas of their day."

The French in the meantime had not been idle observers; and no sooner did they ascertain the result of the conference at Logstown, than it was resolved to check the English the moment they should set foot upon the banks of the Ohio. Vigorous measures were taken to complete their line of fortifications on the head-waters of the Ohio, and to supply each post with an abundance of ammunition. In the spring of 1753, the Ohio Company directed Gist to lay out a town and erect a fort at the mouth of Chartier's Creek, two and a half miles below the forks of the Monongahela and Alleghany. This order, however, was not carried into effect, as Washington, in his journal, uses the following language: — "About two miles from this place, (the forks,) on the southeast side of the river, at the place where the Ohio Company intended to lay off their fort, lives Shingiss, king of the Delawares."

Well do we remember, how often, in the joyous days of ripening youth, we have roamed over the beautiful grounds celebrated as the once residence of the noble and generous Shingiss. The spot is a short distance from the river, and a little south by west from McKee's rocks; — a rugged promontory just below the mouth of Chartier's Creek. Associated with this locality are many wild and startling Indian legends.

# CHAPTER V. FRENCH AND ENGLISH CLAIMS TO THE OHIO.

The claim of France to all the country watered by the Ohio and its tributaries, was based upon that recognized law of nations that the discovery of the mouth of a river entitled the nation so discovering to the whole country drained by that river and its tributaries. This claim set up by France and resisted by the colonies, is precisely the same upon which we have recently based our title to the "whole of Oregon."

On the part of Great Britain, it was claimed, that independent of her title by purchase, she held, under the discovery of Cabot, the entire region lying between the 38th and 67th degree of north latitude, and stretching from the Atlantic to the Pacific — a zone athwart the continent. She also set up another claim, — priority of discovery, — to the Ohio Valley: a claim utterly absurd and entirely untenable.

Such were the grounds upon which two of the greatest European nations claimed supremacy in the beautiful and luxuriant Valley of the Ohio. Without stopping to discuss the merits of either, we will proceed in the continuation of our history.

France, convinced of the justness of her claim, and determined not to be overawed by the threatening attitude of her great rival, adopted at a very early day, the most efficient means for maintaining her position in the great valley of the West. In 1720, she erected Fort Chartres, in Illinois, one of the strongest posts in its day on the Continent of North America. It was constructed by a military engineer of the Vauban school, and was designed to be one of a cordon of posts reaching from the St. Lawrence to the Gulf of Mexico. That at Vincennes was established in 1735, at which time the valley of the Wabash, or Ouabache, was strongly defended.

Viewing the restless energy of that people, can it be doubted that they penetrated far up the valley of the Ohio, and made themselves familiar with the country bordering "La Belle Riviere," long previous to any account now upon record? We have now in our possession, a singular and interesting relic, taken from an ancient mound, near the mouth of Fishing creek, Wetzel county,

Va., which may aid some little in establishing the era of French visitation to the Ohio. The relic is a crucifix, and its appearance plainly indicates great antiquity. The cross is of iron and much corroded, but the image of the Saviour, being of more enduring metal than the cross, is as perfect as when it came from the hand of the artist. (See Wetzel Co. for further notice.) The mound in which this remarkable relic was found, was one of the most ancient in appearance along the river. The depth at which it had been placed, with many other attending circumstances, leaves but little doubt that it must have lain in that aboriginal tomb for at least two centuries. The presumption is, by all who have examined it, that the relic belonged to some Jesuit missionary who visited the Ohio Valley at a very early period.

Immediately following the treaty of Aix-la-Chapelle, (1748,) "the Court of London formed the plan of several new settlements, in which they consulted rather the interest of their own commerce, than the articles of those treaties which were renewed by that of Aix-la-Chapelle." Among the projected movements was the formation of the Ohio Company, the settlement of the upper Ohio valley, &c. These steps naturally alarmed the French, who, believing that the spirit of the compact had been violated, determined to resist, at all hazards, the encroachments upon their soil.

As a preliminary step in taking formal possession of the Ohio and its tributaries, the Marquis de la Galissoniere, Governor-general of Canada, determined to place along the "Oyo" or La Belle Riviere, at the confluence of important tributaries, leaden plates, suitably inscribed, asserting the claim of France to the lands on both sides of the river, even. to the heads of the tributaries. One of these plates has recently been discovered at the mouth of Kanawha (Point Pleasant). It was found by a son of John Beale, Esqr., in April, 1846. (Mr. Beale now lives in Covington, Ky.) We have procured an exact drawing of the relic, and made a literal translation of the inscription; both of which are here given.

Two other plates, similar to the one found at Point Pleasant, have been recovered. The first at Venango, and the other at Marietta, a copy of which is given by Dr. Hildreth in his Pioneer History. Others were doubtless deposited at different points between French Creek and the mouth of the Ohio.

M. Celeron, commandant of the expedition depositing these plates, having ascertained from some of the traders, that they acted under commissions from the Governor of Pennsylvania, wrote to that officer, enjoining upon him the necessity of preventing his people from trading beyond the Apalachian mountains, as he had been authorized to seize the traders and confiscate their goods. Celeron having discharged the duty imposed upon him, to the satisfaction of his government, was shortly afterward appointed Commandant at Detroit.

"M. Celeron was no sooner gone from La Belle Riviere, than the English traders returned in crowds. They had orders from the Government, to excite the Indians to take up arms against France; nay, they even brought them arms and ammunition."

# CHAPTER VI. ENGLAND PREPARES TO ASSERT HER CLAIM.

Thus stood matters at the close of the year 1752. The two great powers beyond the Atlantic, glad of a respite after eight years successful and unsuccessful war, were resting under the truce secured by the treaty of Aix-la-Chapelle; while their commissioners were trying to outwit one another on the matter of the disputed lands in the West.

But the calm was that which precedes the storm. Although all seemed "peace" at home, a very different state of affairs existed in the backwoods of America. Sere, the clangor of arms, the stern word of command, the daily reveille — sounds so strange in the deep seclusion of an American forest — all told of the approaching conflict.

The unprejudiced reader cannot but deplore the short-sighted policy which induced England to bring on the unfortunate and protracted struggle of which we are about to speak. Had it not been for her rapacity — her insatiate craving — her horse-leech cry, — "Give! give!" none can doubt but that all the horrors and bloody wrongs attending her six years' war with France, would have been averted. The English principle of action, both at home and abroad, seems ever to have been,

"That they should take, who have the power,
And they should keep, who can."

The spring of 1753 opened with every prospect of matters coming to a crisis. The English traders had been driven off, and the warlike movements of the French indicated a determined resolution on their part. Information of these movements having been conveyed to the colonial authorities of Pennsylvania and Virginia, the former voted six hundred pounds for distribution among the Indians of the West, and two hundred additional to the Twigtees, who had lost some of their number in endeavoring to protect the Pennsylvania traders taken captive by the French. Conrad Wieser, an experienced provincial interpreter, was sent out to ascertain the number, condition, situation, and feeling of the tribes on the Ohio and tributaries, "so that he might regulate the distribution of the goods that were to be divided among them." In June a messenger was despatched to the French, cautioning them against invading his "Majesty's dominions." This commissioner only went to Logstown, — being afraid to go up the Alleghany as instructed.

In October instructions reached the colonies, from the Earl of Holdernesse, Secretary of State, to resist all encroachments on the part of the French; and as better security, to erect two forts at suitable points in the disputed territory. Accompanying these instructions to Virginia, came thirty pieces of cannon and eighty barrels of powder. This looked like bringing matters to an issue, and so thought all who heard of it.

Disposed to adjust the difficulty by mild means, Governor Dinwiddie determined to send a messenger to the French commandant on the head waters of the Ohio, threatening him that unless the French forces were immediately withdrawn, war would be the consequence.

In looking around for one whose zeal, energy, valor and sagacity, might be equal to the herculean task of making his way hundreds of miles through an unbroken wilderness, and countless hordes of savages, his eye fell upon a young Virginia surveyor; scarcely twenty-one years of age, but whose courage and manly bearing as an officer in the provincial ranks, had won for him the esteem and admiration, not only of his companions in arms, but of the Governor himself. That young man was George Washington, afterwards the glory and the pride of his country. He was selected above all others, and the choice proved the wisdom and judgment of Governor Dinwiddie.

Receiving his instructions, and a passport, he left Williamsburg on the 31st day of October, 1753. In two weeks, he had reached Wills creek, where Cumberland now stands. With Gist as his guide, and accompanied by six other men, he commenced, on the 15th of November (1753) the arduous ascent of the rugged and winter-bound Alleghanies. Who can realize the untold perils of that mountain march! All around was terribly wild, — the howling of the storm, — the roar of the winter's blast, — the fierce sweep of the snow, — and the hoarse voice of distracted waters, with the awful solitude and strength which reigned around, were enough to make the very souls of men shrink back in unwonted awe. But undismayed amid all this terrible war of the elements, the young Virginian struggled on, reaching the Monongahela on the 23d, near the spot where two years afterwards, he took part in one of the most sanguinary conflicts of the six years' war. He reached the forks (Pittsburgh) on the 23d, and his keen eye at once saw the great advantage presented by the place for a fortified post.

Inviting Shingiss, king of the Delawares, to meet in council at Logstown, they proceeded thither, "where we arrived between sun-setting and dark, on the twenty-fifth day after leaving Williamsburg."

At this place, Washington met Tanacharison, Half King of the Six Nations f but finding little could be done with the natives on account of their fear of the French, he set out, accompanied by the Half King and three other Indians, for the French post at the head of French creek.

Through incessant rains and interminable swamps, they travelled on to Venango, (seventy miles) where, meeting Captain Joncaire, who had command of the station, Washington was informed that they (the French) had taken possession of the Ohio, (meaning the entire region from the Lakes to the river Ohio) and, "by — they would hold it." Joncaire advised Washington to proceed to the quarters of St. Pierre (Le Boeuf) who was a higher officer in command. Four days more of severe fatigue, brought the little party to St. Pierre. Delivering Gov. Dinwiddie's message, the commandant replied that he could do nothing more than send it on to the Marquis Du Quesne, Governor-general of Canada. As to withdrawing from his present position, he could not. This was all done in the most polite and respectful manner. During his stay, Washington was handsomely cared for; every attention and kindness being shown him.

Returning, they reached Venango, after a "tedious and fatiguing passage down the creek. Several times, we had like to have been staved against rocks, and many times, were obliged to get out and remain in the water half an hour or more, getting over the shoals. At one place, the ice had lodged and made it impassable by water: we had therefore, to carry our canoes across a neck of land, a quarter of a mile."

From Venango, Washington and Gist set out on foot, "with gun in hand, and pack on back" for the Ohio. Of the hardships which they underwent during this perilous march, we will quote a few passages from the journal of the illustrious chief. Reaching a place in the Alleghany river, where they desired to cross, but the ice driving in such vast quantities, it was found impossible to effect a passage except on a raft, "which we set to work with our poor hatchets, and finished just after sun-setting. This, was a whole day's work; we next got it launched, then went on board of it, and set off; but before we were half-way over, we were jammed in ice in such a manner, that we expected every moment our raft to sink, and ourselves to perish. I put out my setting pole, to try to stop the raft that the ice might pass by, when the rapidity of the stream threw it with so much violence against the pole, that it jerked me out into ten feet water; but I fortunately saved myself, by catching one of the raft logs. — Notwithstanding all our efforts, we could not get to either shore, but were obliged, as we were near an island, to quit our raft and make to it.

"The cold was so extremely severe, that Mr. Gist had all his fingers and some of his toes frozen, and the water was shut up so hard, that we found no difficulty in getting off the island, on the ice, in the morning." Who can read this plain, simple and touching narrative, and not shudder at the imminent danger of a life so valuable? At one time, a treacherous Indian, at the distance of fifteen paces, fired upon them; but, escaping all, they reached the house of a friend at the mouth of Turtle creek, and thence Washington returned in safety to Williamsburg, reaching that place on the 16th of January, 1754.

# CHAPTER VII. VIRGINIA ASSUMING THE QUARREL.

The answer of St. Pierre, left no other course for the provincial authorities to pursue, than prepare for war. Washington's journal was published by order of the Council, to arouse the people of the provinces. It was re-published in England, exciting not only respect for its author, but a determination to meet and resist the encroachments of France.

Governor Dinwiddie sent messengers to the provinces of North Carolina, Pennsylvania and New York, advising them of the crisis, and calling upon them for assistance. Two companies were ordered to be immediately raised in Virginia, — one East, the other in the West, to proceed at once to the erection of a fort at the point where Pittsburg now stands. Washington was given the command of the force thus to be raised. One company was to be enlisted by himself, and the other by Captain Trent, an experienced frontierman. — Five thousand acres of land were to be divided among those who should enlist; one thousand acres of which were to be laid off contiguous to the fort, for the use of the soldiers doing duty there, which were to be called the 'garrison lands.'

The company raised by Trent, was ordered on, and directed to put up, at the forks, with the least practicable delay, a fort of suitable strength to resist any ordinary attack, and with orders to destroy or capture any hostile or resisting force.

On the 17th of February, 1754, Capt. Trent, with his company, reached the forks, and immediately commenced the erection of a fort. Early in April, Capt. Trent, left his command to visit Wills creek, and soon after, Lieutenant Frazier absented himself on a visit to his family at the mouth of Turtle creek. Thus the command devolved upon Ensign Ward, an officer of courage, but not much experience, who with his little company of forty-one men, vigorously pushed forward the fort. On the morning of the 16th of April, when all seemed security, and none dreamed of danger, Ensign Ward, with what terror may well be imagined, beheld approaching the point, a French fleet of such magnitude as to startle the rustic backwoodsman out of all notions of war, and war-like defences. The French fleet numbered several hundred vessels. They descended the

Alleghany, and sweeping round in front of the "garrison," Monsieur Contrecoeur, sent on shore the following imperious summons to surrender.

"A SUMMONS,

"By Order of Monsieur Contrecoeur, Captain of one of the Companies of THE Detachment op the French Marine, Commander-in-Chief of his most Christian Majesty's Troops, now on the Beautiful River, to the Commander of those of the King of Great Britain, at the mouth of the River Monongahela.

"Sir, — Nothing can surprise me more than to see you attempt a settlement upon the lands of the king, my master, which obliges me now, sir, to send you this gentleman, Chevalier Le Mercier, captain of the artillery of Canada, to know of you, sir, by virtue of what authority you are come to fortify yourself within the dominions of the king, my master. This action seems so contrary to the last treaty of peace, at Aix La Chapelle, between his most Christian Majesty and the King of Great Britain, that I do not know to whom to impute such an usurpation, as it is incontestable that the lands situated along the Beautiful River belong to his most Christian majesty.

"I am informed, sir, that your undertaking has been concerted by none else than by a Company, who have more in view the advantage of a trade than to endeavor to keep the union and harmony which subsists between the two crowns of France and Great Britain, although it is as much the interest, sir, of your nation as ours to preserve it.

"Let it be as it will, sir, if you come out into this place, charged with orders, I summon you in the name of the king, my master, by virtue of orders which I got from my general, to retreat peaceably with your troops from off the lands of the king, and not to return, or else I will find myself obliged to fulfil my duty, and compel you to it. I hope, sir, you will not defer an instant, and that you will not force me to the last extremity. In that case, sir, you may be persuaded that I will give orders that there shall be no damage done by my detachment.

"I prevent you, sir, from asking me one hour of delay, nor to wait for my consent to receive orders from your governor. He can give none within the dominions of the king, my master. Those I have received of my general are my laws, so that I cannot depart from them.

"On the contrary, sir, if you have not got orders, and only come to trade, I am sorry to tell you, that I can't avoid seizing you, and to confiscate your effects to the use of the Indians, our children, allies and friends, as you are not allowed to carry on a contraband trade. It is for this reason, sir, that we stopped two Englishmen, last year, who were trading upon our lands: moreover, the king, my master, asks nothing but his right; he has not the least intention to trouble the good harmony and friendship which reigns between his Majesty and the King of Great Britain.

"The Governor of Canada can give proof of his having done his utmost endeavors to maintain the perfect union which reigns between two friendly princes. As he had learned that the Iroquois and the Nipissingues of the Lake of the Two Mountains had struck and destroyed an English family, towards Carolina, he has barred up the road, and forced them to give him a little boy belonging to that family, and which Mr. Ulerich, a merchant of Montreal, has carried to Boston; and what is more, he has forbid the savages from exercising their accustomed cruelty upon the English, our friends.

"I could complain bitterly, sir, of the means taken all last winter to instigate the Indians to accept the hatchet and to strike us, while we were striving to maintain the peace. I am well persuaded, sir, of the polite manner in which you will receive M. Le Mercier, as well out of regard to his business as his distinction and personal merit. I expect you will send him back with one of your officers, who will bring me a precise answer. As you have got some Indians with you, sir, I join with M. Le Mercier, an interpreter, that he may inform them of my intentions upon that subject.

" I am, with great regard, sir,

"Your most humble and most obedient servant,

"CONTRECOEUR.

"Done at our Camp, April 16, 1754."

With this summons Ensign Ward could do no less than comply, and accordingly delivered up to the French entire possession of the post; himself and men retiring up the Monongahela as far as Redstone. Contrecoeur took immediate possession, and finishing the fort, called it Du Quesne, after the Governor-general of Canada.

In the meantime, it having been determined by the Council of Virginia to appropriate ten thousand pounds toward carrying on the war, the two companies ordered to be raised were increased to six, and Joshua Fry appointed colonel, with Washington for lieutenant-colonel. The latter having organized two companies at Alexandria, marched to Wills creek, (Cumberland), where he received intelligence of the surrender of Ward. Startled at this information, he was at a loss how to act, as Colonel Fry had not arrived. But resolved on checking the encroachments of the French, he determined to erect a fort at the mouth of Redstone, (Brownsville,) and pushing on boldly into the wilderness, had, by the 9th of May, reached the Little Meadows, at the head of the Youghiogheny river.

Halting here his little command, Washington descended the Youghiogheny to ascertain the chances of transporting his men and artillery by water, and also to gather information as to the movements of the French.

Finding the route by water impracticable, he returned, and soon after a messenger from his old friend, the Half King, came into camp to apprize him of the rapid advance of a small party of Frenchmen. On the same day, his former guide. Gist, called and confirmed the statement of the Indian. But this information did not in the least dishearten the gallant young commander. With the least possible delay he hurried on to the "Great Meadows," an open and level piece of ground, and well adapted for a place of defence. Here a hurried entrenchment was formed, and every preparation made for meeting and resisting an attack. Some time during the night a second express from Tanacharison brought intelligence that the French were encamped in a deep vale about six miles from his own position, and to strike an effective blow it would be necessary to move at once. Although the night was intensely dark, and the rain falling in torrents, Washington, with the Indian guide, led his little army forward, determined to anticipate the attack of the French. Who can conceive the terrors of that midnight mountain march over cragged rocks, through deep ravines, amid the thunder of the elements and the darkness visible which reigned around! With undaunted nerve the youthful officer pressed on in the track of his Indian guide, while his men followed in silence, for the sullen sound of the thunder and fierce sweeping of the tempest smothered alike the heavy tread of the one, and the stern command of the other.

At gray dawn, the united force of provincials and Indians surrounded the camp of the French, who, little dreading an attack at that time and place, were reposing in conscious security. The guard, discovering the presence of their foe, sounded the alarm, when an almost simultaneous discharge took place.

M. De Jumonville, commander of the French, with ten of his men, fell at the first fire; the balance surrendered without further resistance.

Thus was shed the first blood in a war which Smollett has ignorantly termed a "Native of America," and which, speedily involved England and her colonies in a long and bloody conflict.

It deserves to be commemorated as Washington's first battle. It marked the man as one born to no ordinary destiny; it served to prepare him for the great and splendid achievements which so gloriously crowned his after life.

In this affair Washington had one man killed and two wounded. The prisoners were marched to the "Meadow," and thence sent to Virginia. During the action, a Canadian made his escape, and conveyed information of the defeat to the commandant at Fort Du Quesne.

Washington, anticipating renewed efforts on the part of the French, enlarged and strengthened his position, which he very appropriately called "Fort Necessity." He was soon joined by Captain Mackey's independent company from South Carolina, and a number of friendly Indians. Captain Mackey, holding a commission from the English Crown, claimed precedence over a colonial officer of equal grade, and attempted to take command of the little army. But this idea he was very soon compelled to abandon, as the disaffection became so manifest, that he knew it would be dangerous to insist upon his conceived rights. Very reluctantly, he was forced to yield to the superior genius of our incomparable Washington.

On the 31st of May, Colonel Fry died at Wills creek, and thus the whole command devolved upon Washington. On the 10th of June, Indian runners notified him that the Shawanese and Delawares had leagued with the French against the English. On the following day, Colonel Washington marched with his entire force, except Captain Mackey's company, left in command of Fort Necessity. His object was to reach the Monongahela, and erect a fort at the mouth of Red-stone. He had time only to reach Gist's place, at the foot of Laurel hill, when he was apprized of the advance of the French, and cautioned against proceeding, as they "were as numerous as the pigeons in the woods." Convinced, by the various accounts, that the French force was very great, a retreat was ordered. Washington set the noble example of lending his horse for the transportation of public stores, &c. The army reached its entrenchments on the 1st day of July. It was the intention of Washington to have proceeded to Wills creek, but the men, greatly fatigued by their mountain march, were unwilling to go further.

Every effort was made to prepare to give a vigorous resistance. But what could four or five hundred men, without bread, and shut up in a half-finished fortress on the top of a mountain, hope to accomplish against a well-fed and well-disciplined force of three times their own number?

Early on the 3d of July, the French and Indians came in view of the fort. In a short time, and while at the distance of six hundred yards, they commenced firing.

"Colonel Washington had drawn up his men on the level ground outside of the trench, waiting for an attack, which he presumed would be made as soon as the enemy's forces emerged from the woods." He suspected the distant firing a mere ruse to draw his men into the forest; but finding they would not approach, he stationed his men within the trenches, and ordered them to fire at discretion.

The French and their allies kept at a respectable distance during most of the day, but maintained a brisk fire from about 11 o'clock A.M. to 8 P.M. It rained heavily during the whole day, and most of Washington's army stood in water above their knees.

At 8 o'clock in the evening, the French commander ordered a parley, as he saw it would be useless to continue the siege any longer. A large number of his men had fallen before the unerring aim of colonial riflemen, and a truce of any kind was highly acceptable.

Washington's position was no better, and he was glad of a respite on any honorable terms. He well knew that the enemy's forces were vastly superior to his own, and could not but apprehend the result of a second day's siege. Darkness too, lay upon the earth; his men were in mud and water above their knees; many had their guns wet and out of order; they were without provisions, and no hope of a supply; what else then, could he do, but agree to terms?

But, when the truce flag was sent him, apprehending treachery, he refused to receive it. On a second application, however, accompanied by a request that an officer might be sent out, De Villier pledging his honor that no violence should be done him. Colonel Washington despatched Captain Van Braam, who was the only person under his command who pretended to understand the French language. In a short time the Captain returned, bearing with him articles of capitulation. These he read, and pretended to interpret to his commander; but from gross ignorance of the French language, he was the means of inflicting a great wrong upon the fame and character of Washington. The terms of capitulation were alike honorable to both parties. Washington, with his men, were to leave Fort Necessity with everything but their artillery; to march out with drums and fife, displaying colors, &c. The prisoners taken at the defeat of Jumonville, were to be returned; and for the observance of this condition, Captains Van Braam and Stobo were to be retained by the French as hostages. It was further agreed, that the party yielding, should not attempt to "build any more entrenchments west of the mountains," for one year.

Washington and his men marched out early on the following morning, July 4, and proceeded at once to Wills creek, but were greatly harassed during most of the way, by bands of savages, who hung upon their trail. Colonel Washington lost no time in repairing to Williamsburg, and communicating to the colonial authorities the events of the campaign. So well satisfied were the members of the Assembly, that a vote of thanks was passed to the gallant commander and all who had served under him. This acknowledgment of the bravery, skill, and energy of the little army, was well merited. It had surmounted formidable difficulties, kept a superior foe at bay, and even in defeat, had secured a most honorable capitulation.

The conduct of Washington throughout this expedition, gave a glorious presage of the illustrious career which an All-wise Providence had marked out before him.

As a copy of the capitulation signed on this occasion may not be uninteresting to many of our readers, we give it below in full. In connection with this matter, we will state that a very old copy (supposed to have been made at the time,) has recently been found in possession of an aged Frenchman at Detroit. The paper had been in the family for many years, without their appearing to know its value or character. At length, Hon. W. Woodbridge, late United States Senator from Michigan, looking over the old man's papers, found the relic alluded to.

Art. 1. We permit the English commander to withdraw, with all his garrison, to go back peaceably to his country, and we engage on our part, to prevent that any insult should be committed upon him by our Frenchmen, and to hinder as much as will be in our power all the savages who are with us.

Art. 2. He will be permitted to withdraw and carry away all that belongs to them, with the exception of the artillery, which Ave reserve for ourselves.

Art. 3. That we accord them the honors of war; that they will go out, drum beating, with a small cannon, wishing by that to prove to them that we treat them as friends.

Art. 4. That as soon as the articles are signed on both sides, they will bring the English flag.

Art. 5. That to-morrow at the break of day a French detachment will go to cause the garrison to file off, and take possession of said fort.

Art. 6. That as the English have scarcely any horses or oxen left, they will be at liberty to hide or secrete their goods, so that they may carry them away when they have obtained horses; to this end they will be permitted to leave guards in such number as they think proper, upon condition that they will give parol of honor, that they will not labor at any settlement in this place, nor beyond the high grounds, for one year to commence from this day.

Art. 7. That as the English have in their power an officer and two cadets, and generally the prisoners which they have made at the time of the murder of Sir de Jumonville, and that they engage to send them with safe guard to Fort Du Quesne, situated upon the Beautiful River, (Ohio) therefore, for the security of this article, as well as of this treaty, Messrs. Jacob Vanbraam and Robert Stobo, both captains, will be given us as hostages, until the arrival of our Frenchmen and Canadians, as above mentioned. We oblige ourselves on our part to give escort, and return in safety the two officers who promised us our Frenchmen in two months and a half at the furthest.

Made duplicate upon one of the posts of our block house, the day and year as above stated.

Have signed, Messrs. James Mackey, George Washington, Coulon Villier.

As we have already stated, when the Virginia House of Burgesses met in August, they requested the Governor to lay before them a copy of the capitulation, and, upon a due consideration of the subject, passed a vote of thanks to Colonel Washington and his officers for their bravery and gallant defence of their country. The names of all the officers were enumerated, except those of the Major of the regiment, and of Captain Vanbraam, the former of whom was charged with cowardice, and the latter with having acted a treacherous part in his interpretation of the articles. The Burgesses, also, in an address to the Governor, expressed their approbation of the instructions he had given to the officers and forces sent on the Ohio expedition. In short, all the proceedings of the campaign were not only approved, but applauded, by the representatives of the people, and by the public generally. A pistole was granted to each of the soldiers, who had been in the engagement. To the vote of thanks Washington replied as follows:

TO THE SPEAKER OF THE HOUSE OF BURGESSES.

Williamsburg, October 23, 1754.

Sir — Nothing could give me, and the officers under my command, greater satisfaction, than to receive the thanks of the House of Burgesses, in so particular and public a manner, for our behaviour in the late unsuccessful engagement with the French; and we unanimously hope that our future proceedings in the service of our country will entitle us to a continuance of your approbation, I assure you, sir, I shall always look upon it as my indispensable duty to endeavor to deserve it.

I was desired by the officers of the Virginia regiment to make their suitable acknowledgments for the honor they have received in your thanks. I therefore hope the enclosed will be agreeable, and answer their, and the intended purpose of, sir, your most obedient and humble servant,

George Washington.

TO THE WORSHIPFUL THE SPEAKER, AND THE GENTLEMEN OF THE HOUSE OF BURGESSES.

We, the officers of the Virginia regiment, are highly sensible of the particular mark of distinction with which you have honored us, in returning your thanks for our behaviour in the late action, and cannot help testifying our grateful acknowledgments for your high sense of what we shall always esteem a duty to our country and the best of kings.

Favored with your regard, we shall zealously endeavor to deserve your applause, and by our future actions strive to convince the worshipful House of Burgesses, how much we esteem their approbation, and, as it ought to be, regard it as the voice of our country.

Signed for the whole corps,

George Washington.

NOTE A.

A number of recent writers on Western History, among whom we may mention Dr. Hildreth, in bis "Pioneer History," Col. Geo. W. Thompson, one of the Commissioners appointed to adjust the boundary question between Virginia and Ohio, and several others, speak of the destruction in 1753 of an English trading house at Logstown.

Col. Thompson, in support of his position, that Virginia authority extended west of the Ohio, alleges, "That the first acts of hostility on the part of the French, clearly indicate the possession and extensive establishment of Virginia, west of the Apalachian mountains — west of the Ohio river." And then quotes from Smollett and Burke, in reference to the destruction of the post at Logstown.

Without desiring to enter upon a discussion of this point, it may be alone necessary to say, that apart from the unreliable statements of Smollett and other British writers, we have no evidence of the existence of any trading post at Logstown, of the date referred to. Washington, who was there in 1753, makes no allusion to it in his journal. Important cotemporary papers, now among the archives of the Ohio Historical Society, make no mention of such a thing; and it is therefore most probable that the destruction of the post referred to by Smollett, Burke, Russell, and others, was on the Miami, and not at Logstown, on the Ohio.

NOTE B.

The treaty of Lancaster, made in 1744, presents a very correct idea of the manner in which the simple-hearted children of the forest were dealt with by their Christian brethren.

The necessity for this treaty grew out of the fact that settlements had been made on the Indian lands in Virginia, Pennsylvania, and Maryland. Passing over the first three days' proceedings as detailed by Marshe, one of the Secretaries, we commence with the operations of Monday, June 24th. "On this day, speaking began, to the satisfaction of all parties, and ended merrily with dancing and music, and a great supper. On Tuesday and Wednesday also, speeches were made, varied by dances, in which appeared some very disagreeable women, who danced wilder time than any Indian! On Thursday, the goods were opened, wherewith the Maryland people wished to buy the Indian claim to the lands on which settlements had been made. These goods were narrowly scanned by the red men, but at last taken for £220, Pennsylvania money, after which, they drank punch. Friday, the Six Nations agreed to the grant, and punch was drank again. On Saturday, a dinner was given the Indians, at which they drank heartily, fed heartily, and were very greasy before they finished! After this, came the Commissioners from Virginia, supported by a due quantity of wine and bumbo, and received 'a deed releasing their claim to a large quantity of land lying in that colony,' the Indians being persuaded to 'recognize the King's right to all lands that are, or by his Majesty's appointment shall be within the colony of Virginia.' For this, they received £200 in gold, and a like sum in goods, with a promise, that as settlements increased, more should be paid, which promise was signed and sealed."

Such was the treaty of Lancaster, upon which the British based their claim by purchase to the lands on the Ohio.

# PART III. EARLY SETTLEMENT OF NORTH-WESTERN VIRGINIA. 1754-1793.

# CHAPTER I. FIRST SETTLEMENT ON THE MONONGAHELA.

In North-western Virginia, the earliest attempts at settlement were made on the Monongahela and its tributaries. Early in the spring of 1754, David Tygart and a man named Files, established themselves and families on the east branch of that river; Tygart in the beautiful and highly productive valley which still bears his name, and Files at the mouth of a creek, where Beverly, the county-seat of Randolph, has since been located. These were the first settlements in Virginia west of Laurel Ridge, and the family of Files became the first of that long and terrible list of unfortunate victims to savage ferocity with which the early annals of the west are stained. The pioneers soon felt convinced that their removal had been premature. Their provisions were about to fail, and not having been able to raise any, they wisely determined to retrace their steps as speedily as possible. But, alas! before the family of Files could be got off, the savages discovered them, and every member, except the oldest son, massacred. Tygart with his family escaped, and returned to their friends, east of the mountains.

Two years previous to these occurrences, Christopher Gist, agent of the Ohio Company, settled on a tract of land in Fayette county, Pa., now well known as Mount Braddock. His was the first actual settlement west of the mountains on any of the tributaries of the upper Ohio. Being well known as an active and efficient backwoodsman, his presence in the west induced several other families to come out and settle around him. During the following year several adventurers visited that part of Pennsylvania, (supposed at the time to be in Virginia). Of these were Wendell Brown, his two sons, and Frederick Waltzer, who settled near where Brownsville now stands. Others visited different points on the Monongahela, above the mouth of Redstone, (Brownsville).

Among this number were Dr. Thomas Eckarly and his two brothers. They were Pennsylvanians, and belonged to that peculiar order called Dunkers. In the wild and solitary regions of the West, these followers of the founder of Euphrate, hoped to find seclusion from the world, and the undisturbed opportunity of carrying out the principles of their faith. After exploring the country for some distance, they finally settled on Cheat river, at the place now known as Dunker bottom. Here they lived in peace and plenty for some years (not, however, as a recent writer says, in "eating an abundance of meat, as delicious as the refined palate of a modern epicure could well wish," because, all animal food was expressly forbidden by their creed, except on special occasions). At length the despoiler came, and the single-hearted recluse fell before his ruthless hand.

In the year 1758, a settlement was effected near the mouth of Decker's Creek, by Thomas Decker and others. In the spring of 1759, a party of Mingoes and Delawares made a descent upon the inhabitants, and cut them off.

Although adventurers continued to penetrate the country lying between the Monongahela river and Laurel ridge, no regular emigration took place, nor were any permanent settlements effected until 1768. During this year a number of persons made improvements on Buchanan, an important tributary to Tygart valley river; other settlements were effected on the Monongahela. Tradition acquaints us with some circumstances attending the earlier settlements in this part of Virginia. In 1761, four men, (Childers, Linsey and two brothers, by the name of Pringle,) deserted from Fort Pitt. Ascending the Monongahela, eight or ten miles above Brownsville, the party made a short stay, then crossed to the Youghiogheny, where they wintered.

In one of their hunting rambles, Samuel Pringle came on a path which he supposed would lead to the inhabited parts of Virginia. On his return, he mentioned the discovery and his supposition, to his comrades, and they resolved on tracing it. This they accordingly did, and it conducted them to Loony's creek, then the most remote western settlement. While among the inhabitants on Loony's creek, they were recognized, and some of the party apprehended as deserters. John and Samuel Pringle succeeded in making an escape to their camp in the glades, where they remained till some time in the year 1764.

During this year, and while in the employ of John Simpson, (a trapper, who had come there in quest of furs,) they determined on removing further west. Simpson was induced to this by the prospect of enjoying the woods free from the intrusion of other hunters (the glades having begun to be a common hunting ground for the inhabitants of the south branch;) while a regard for their personal safety caused the Pringles to avoid a situation in which they might be exposed to the observation of other men.

In journeying through the wilderness, and after having crossed Cheat river, at the horse-shoe, a quarrel arose between Simpson and one of the Pringles; and notwithstanding that peace and harmony were so necessary to their mutual safety and comfort, yet each so far indulged the angry passions which had been excited as at length to produce a separation.

Simpson crossed over the Valley river, near the mouth of Pleasant creek, and passing on to the head of another water course, gave to it the name of Simpson's creek. Thence he went westward, and fell over on a stream which he called Elk: at the mouth of this he erected a camp, and continued to reside for more than twelve months. During this time he neither saw the Pringles nor any human being; and at the expiration of it went to the south branch, where he disposed of his furs and skins and then returned to, and continued at, his encampment, at the mouth of Elk, until permanent settlements were made in its vicinity.

The Pringles kept up the Valley river till they observed a large right hand fork, (now Buchanan,) which they ascended some miles; and at the mouth of a small branch, (afterwards called Turkey run,) they took up their abode in the cavity of a large sycamore tree. The stump of this is still (1831) to be seen, and is an object of no little veneration with the immediate descendants of the first settlers.

The situation of these men, during a residence here of several years, although rendered somewhat necessary by their previous conduct, could not have been very enviable. Deserters from the army, a constant fear of discovery filled them with apprehension. In the vicinity of a savage foe, the tomahawk and scalping knife were ever present to their imaginations. Remote from civilized man, their solitude was hourly interrupted by the frightful shrieks of the panther, or the hideous bowlings of the wolf. And though the herds of buffalo, elk and deer which sported around, enabled them easily to supply their larder, yet the want of salt, of bread, and of every species of vegetable, must have abated their relish for the otherwise delicious loin of the one and haunch of the others. The low state of their little magazine, too, while it limited their hunting, caused them, from a fear of discovery, to shrink at the idea of being driven to the settlements for a supply of ammunition. And not until they were actually reduced to two loads of powder, could they be induced to venture again into the vicinity of their fellow-men. In the latter part of the year 1767 John left his brother, and intending to make for a trading post on the Shenandoah, appointed the period of his return.

Samuel Pringle, in the absence of John, suffered a good deal. The stock of provisions left him became entirely exhausted — one of his loads of powder was expended in a fruitless attempt to shoot a buck — his brother had already delayed his return several days longer than was intended, and the other was apprehensive that he had been recognized, taken to Fort Pitt, and would probably never get back. With his remaining load of powder, however, he was fortunate enough to kill a fine buffalo; and John soon after returned with the news of peace, both with the Indians and French. The two brothers agreed to leave their retirement.

Their wilderness habitation was not left without some regret. Every object around had become more or less endeared to them. The tree, in whose hollow they had been so frequently sheltered from storm and tempest, was regarded with so great a reverence that they resolved, so soon as they could prevail on a few others to accompany them, again to return to this asylum of their exile.

In a population such as then composed the chief part of the south branch settlement, this was no difficult matter. All of them were used to the frontier manner of living; the most of them had gone thither to acquire land; many had failed entirely in this object, while others were obliged to occupy poor and broken situations off the river; the fertile bottoms having been previously located. Add to this the passion of hunting, (which was a ruling one with many,) with the comparative scarcity of game in their neighborhood, and it need not excite surprise that the proposition of the Pringles to form a settlement, in such a country as they represented that on Buchanan to be, was eagerly embraced by many.

In the fall of the ensuing year, (1768,) Samuel Pringle, and several others who wished first to examine for themselves, visited the country which had been so long occupied by the Pringles alone. Being pleased with it, they repaired thither, with a few others, in the following spring, with the view of cultivating as much corn as would serve their families the first year after emigrating. Having examined the country, some of them proceeded to improve the spots of their choice. John Jackson, (who was accompanied by his sons, George and Edward,) settled at the mouth of Turkey run, where his daughter, Mrs. Davis, now (1831) lives — John Hacker, higher up on Buchanan river, where Bush's fort was afterwards established — Alexander and Thomas Sleeth, near to Jackson's, on what is now known as the Forenash plantation.

The others of the party, (William Hacker, Thomas and Jesse Hughes, John and William Radcliff and John Brown,) appear to have employed their time exclusively in hunting, neither of them making any improvement of land for his own benefit. Yet were they of very considerable service to the new settlement. Those who had commenced clearing land, were supplied by them with abundance of meat, while in their hunting excursions through the country a better knowledge of it was obtained than could have been acquired had they been engaged in making improvements.

In one of these expeditions, they discovered and gave name to Stone-coal creek, which, flowing westwardly, induced the supposition that it discharged itself directly into the Ohio. Descending this creek, to ascertain the fact, they came to its confluence with a river, which they then called, and which has since been known as the West Fork. After having gone some distance down the river, they returned by a different route to the settlement, better pleased with the land on it and some of its tributaries than with that on Buchanan.

Soon after this, other emigrants arrived under the guidance of Samuel Pringle. Among them were John and Benjamin Outright, who settled on Buchanan, where John Outright, the younger, now lives, and Henry Rule, who improved just above the mouth of Fink's run. Before the arrival of Samuel Pringle, John Hacker had begun to improve the spot which Pringle had chosen for himself. To prevent any unpleasant result. Hacker agreed that if Pringle would clear as much land on a creek which had been recently discovered by the hunters, as he had on Buchanan, they could then exchange places. Complying with this condition, Pringle took possession of the farm on Buchanan, and Hacker of the land improved by Pringle on the creek, which was hence called Hacker's creek. John and William Radcliff then settled on this stream. These comprise all the improvements which were made on the upper branches of the Monongahela in the years 1769 and 1770.

At the close of the working season of 1769, some of these adventurers went to their families on the south branch; and when they returned to gather their crops in the fall, found them entirely destroyed. In their absence the buffaloes, no longer awed by the presence of man, had trespassed on their enclosures, and eaten their corn to the ground — this delayed the removal of their families till the winter of 1770.

In 1770, emigrants began to reach the Monongahela and Ohio rivers in considerable number. During this year, Capt. Cresap erected a cabin at the mouth of Nemocalling creek, (now Dunlap's,) which at that time was the initial point of the great trail over the Alleghanies, a route pursued by Braddock, and afterwards with but few changes, and those for the worse, adopted for the Cumberland or National road. This point continued for many years the principal place of embarkation for the whole western and southern country.

The horse-shoe bottom on Cheat river was settled about this time by Capt. Parsons, while other portions of that very productive region were located by a number of enterprising men, among whom we may mention Cuningham, Fink, Goff, Minear, Butler, &c. &c.

The spirit of emigration seemed now effectually aroused, and as the fertility of the soil, salubrity of the climate, and apparently inexhaustible supply of game became more generally known to those east of the mountains, the rush of emigrants up to the breaking out of the Indian war, in 1774, was very great. They spread over the fine alluvion of the upper Monongahela; along West Fork, Elk, and Simpson's creek. Of those who settled about this time in the neighborhood of Clarksburg, we find the names of Nutter, Cotrial, Beard, Patton, Davisson, etc.

# CHAPTER II. FIRST SETTLEMENTS AT AND NEAR WHEELING.

A NEW impulse to Western emigration seemed given with the commencement of the seventh decade of the eighteenth century.

A spirit of inquiry and enterprise was awakened in many parts of the East, and men of indomitable courage and great energy of character pushed out into the illimitable wilderness, to explore the country and find themselves homes in the outspread bosom of the great west.

It was in this year that the Zanes first settled at the mouth of Wheeling creek, and the elder Tomlinson broke the silence of the wilds at Grave creek by the shrill echo of his never-failing rifle.

The number, however, of those who ventured to the Ohio were few, indeed. It was considered extremely unsafe for the self-protecting hunter, but would have been deemed madness to expose a family to so much hazard. Along the upper branches of the Monongahela settlements were made at several points. Of those who thus early struck for a home in the beautiful and highly fertile vallies of Western Virginia, were James Booth and John Thomas. They settled on what is now known as Booth's creek.

Previous, however, to the actual settlement of the country, above the forks of the Monongahela, some few families (in 1767) had established themselves in the vicinity of Fort Redstone, now Brownsville, Pennsylvania. At the head of these were Abraham Tegard, James Crawford, John Province and John Harden. The latter of these gentlemen afterwards removed to Kentucky, and became distinguished in the early history of that State, as well for the many excellencies of his private and public life, as for the untimely and perfidious manner of his death.

In the succeeding year Jacob Vanmeter, John Swan, Thomas Hughes and some others, settled on the west side of the Monongahela, near the mouth of Muddy creek, where Carmichaeltown now stands.

In the same year, the place which had been occupied for a while by Thomas Decker and his unfortunate associates, near where Morgantown now stands, was settled by a party of emigrants; one of whom was David Morgan, who became so conspicuous for personal prowess, and for the daring yet deliberate courage displayed by him during the subsequent hostilities with the Indians.

It was in June, 1770, that Joseph Tomlinson, from near Fort Cumberland, first visited the flats of Grave creek. He was accompanied by his brother Samuel. Delighted with the beauty, extent and fertility of the bottom, he determined to fix here his abode. Building a cabin, he remained during the summer and fall, and then returned east of the mountains to remove with his family in the following spring. Increased apprehensions of Indian troubles induced him to delay the final removal until the spring of 1773.

About the same time that Mr. Tomlinson first visited Grave creek, came Ebenezer Zane to Wheeling. Soon after, he was followed by his brothers, Andrew and Jonathan, with several others, from the south branch of Potomac.

In 1772 came Bonnett, Wetzel, Messer, Silas Zane, and many other hardy pioneers from the same region; men whose means and influence contributed greatly towards breaking the power of the savage and subduing the country to the wants of civilized life.

The emigrants crossed from Redstone by way of Cat-fish, (Washington,) and Scotch ridge, to the head of little Wheeling valley, thence down over the same path, afterwards taken for the National road. When within a few hundred yards of the forks of Wheeling, an incident occurred, trivial in its character, but important in its results. Wetzel was riding in advance of his company, when suddenly the girth of his saddle broke, and he was compelled to get off to repair it. Meantime Silas Zane passed on, and soon came to the forks, and greatly admiring the locality, commenced "tomahawking" his "right." The land thus secured, (one thousand acres,) is now one of the most valuable and highly improved farms in Western Virginia. At this point the company separated, Wetzel, Bonnett and others, going up big Wheeling, while Zane, with one or two others, went down. Other emigrants soon followed, and the fine lands along Wheeling, Buffalo and Short creeks, were not long unclaimed by actual settlers.

Some of the earliest occupants of the fine creek and river bottoms above Wheeling, were George Leffler, Benjamin Biggs, Joshua Baker, Zachariah Sprigg, Andrew Swearengen, David Shepherd, the McGollogh's, Mitchells, Van Metres, Millers, Kellers, &c. &c. &c.

During this year (1772) many emigrants also pushed into the fine regions along the upper Monongahela. The spirit of adventure seemed aroused, and many of the sturdy settlers from the south branch found their way into the fertile vallies of Western Virginia.

It was in this year, says Withers, that the comparatively beautiful region lying on the east fork of the Monongahela, between the Alleghany mountains, on its south-eastern, and the Laurel hill, or as it is there called the Rich mountain, on its north-western side, and which had received the denomination of Tygart's valley, again attracted the attention of emigrants. — In the course of this year, the greater part of the valley was located, by persons said to have been enticed thither by the description given of it, by some hunters from Greenbriar who had previously explored it. Game, though a principal was not however their sole object. They possessed themselves at once of nearly all the level land lying between these mountains — a plain of 25 or 30 miles in length and varying from three-fourths to two miles in width, and of almost unsurpassed fertility. Of those who were first to occupy that section of country, we find the names of Hadden, Connely, Whiteman, Warwick, Nelson, Stalnaker, Riffle and Westfall: the latter of these found and interred the bones of Files' family, which had lain, bleaching in the sun, since the murder of these unfortunate settlers, by the Indians, in 1754.

Cheat river too, on which no attempt at settlement had been made, but by the unfortunate Eckarly's became an object of attention.

In this year (1772) settlements were made on Simpson's creek, West-fork river, and Elk creek. Those who made the former were John Power, James Anderson and Jonas Webb.

On Elk, and in the vicinity of Clarksburg, there settled Thomas Nutter, near to the Forge-mills; Samuel Cottrial, on the east side of the creek and nearly opposite to Clarksburg; Sotha Hickman, on the west side of the same creek, and above Cottrial; Samuel Beard at the mouth of Nanny's run; Andrew Cottrial above Beard, and at the farm now owned by John W. Patten; Daniel Davison, where Clarksburg is now situated; and Obadiah Davison and John Nutter on the West-fork; the former near to the old salt works, and the latter at the place now owned by Adam Hickman, Jr.

There was likewise at this time, a considerable accession to the settlements on Buchanan and Hacker's creeks. So great was the increase of population in this latter neigborhood, that the crops of the preceding season did not afford more than one-third of the breadstuff, which would be ordinarily consumed in the same time, by an equal number of persons.

Such indeed was the state of suffering among the inhabitants, consequent on this scarcity, that 1773 is traditionally known as the starving year.

These were the principal settlements made in North-Western Virginia, previous to 1774. No sooner, however, was it known that such outposts had been established on the confines of civilization, than hundreds eagerly pressed forward, impatient to join their more adventurous brethren, and all anxious to secure themselves homes in the expanseless domain stretched out before them. The same spirit actuated those hardy pioneers which has since so distinguished their descendants. That spirit, which spurning all restraints, subduing all to their will, breaking over every obstacle, has planted down the standard of liberty — that standard which their fathers first raised in the valley of the Ohio, in 1774 — on the shores of the distant Pacific. It was the true spirit of the old Anglo-Saxon, — bending purposes to his will; it is now the proud impulse of every American heart, and will go on to subdue other people, and conquer other territories, until the whole of the "boundless continent" of North America is ours.

The men who settled North-Western Virginia, knew, when they commenced it, that 'twas to "do or die." A fierce, implacable, and deadly foe met them on every hand. To succeed, required caution, energy, courage and hope. These, severally and unitedly, they exercised, and by them conquered the savage and reclaimed the land.

Many of the first settlers along the Ohio, differed somewhat from those who improved farther back.

They were the same restless, energetic and enterprising people, united together by the same bonds of fraternal union, but looking for support through different channels.

The fine facilities afforded by the Ohio for transporting their surplus produce to market rendered them more ambitious, and more anxious of promoting their pecuniary interests, than their brethren in the interior.

Others, again, looking forward to the time when the Indians would be divested of the country north-west of the Ohio river, and it should be open to location in the same manner as its south-eastern shores were, selected this as a situation, from which they might more readily obtain possession of the fertile land, with which its ample plains were known to abound. In anticipation of this period, there were some who embraced every opportunity, afforded by intervals of peace with the Indians, to explore that country and select in it what they deemed its most valuable parts. Around these they would generally mark trees, or otherwise define boundaries by which they could be afterwards identified. The cession by Virginia to the United States, of the north-western territory, and the manner in which its lands were subsequently brought into market, prevented the realization of those flattering, and apparently well founded expectations.

There were also, in every settlement, individuals who had been drawn to them solely by their love of hunting, and an attachment to the wild, unshackled scenes of a wilderness life. These were, perhaps, totally regardless of all the inconveniencies resulting from their new situation; except that of being occasionally pent up in forts; and thus debarred the enjoyment of their favorite pastimes.

Although hunting was not the object of most of the old settlers, yet it was for a good part of the year, the chief employment of their time. And of all those who thus made their abode in the dense forest, and tempted aggression from the neighboring Indians, none were so well qualified to resist this aggression, and to retaliate upon its authors, as those who were mostly engaged in this pursuit. Of all their avocations, this "mimickry of war" best fitted them to thwart the savages in their purpose, and to mitigate the horrors of their peculiar mode of warfare. Those arts which enabled them, unperceived, to approach the watchful deer in his lair, enabled them likewise to circumvent the Indian in his ambush; and if not always punish, yet frequently defeat him in his object. Add to this the perfect knowledge which they acquired of the woods, and the ease and certainty with which they consequently, when occasion required, could make their way to any point of the settlements and apprize the inhabitants of approaching danger; and it will be readily admitted that the more expert and successful the huntsman, the more skilful and effective the warrior.

But various as may have been their objects in emigrating, no sooner had they come together, than there existed in each settlement, a perfect unison of feeling. Similitude of situation and community of danger, operating as a magic charm, stifled in their birth those little bickerings, which are so apt to disturb the quiet of society. Ambition of preferment and the pride of place, too often hindrances to social intercourse, were unknown among them. Equality of condition rendered them strangers, alike to the baneful distinctions created by wealth and other adventitious circumstances. A sense of mutual dependence for their common security linked them in amity; and conducting their several purposes in harmonious concert, together they toiled and together suffered.

In their intercourse with others they were kind, beneficent and disinterested; extending to all the most generous hospitality which their circumstances could afford. That selfishness, which prompts to liberality for the sake of remuneration, and proffers the civilities of life with an eye to individual interest, was unknown to them. They were kind for kindness sake; and sought no other recompense, than the never failing concomitant of good deeds — the reward of an approving conscience.

Such were the pioneers of the West; and the greater part of mankind might now derive advantage from the contemplation of "their humble virtues, hospitable homes and spirits patient, noble, proud and free — their self-respect, grafted on innocent thoughts; their days of health and nights of sleep — their toils, by danger dignified, yet guiltless — their hopes of cheerful old age and a quiet grave, with cross and garland over its green turf, and their grandchildren's love for epitaph."

The above picture, couched in such truthful, simple, but eloquent language, we have thought not inappropriate, or unmerited. It represents the sturdy pioneer in his true character; and could only be drawn by one who was an eye-witness to the scenes he so aptly, tersely and touchingly describes.

Although a dark cloud hung upon the horizon, and fear trembled upon the heart of the pioneer as he looked tenderly, devotedly and affectionately at his little household, — scarcely knowing at what moment the shaft of the destroyer might fall upon him, yet all was joy and happiness within. Content smiled upon his humble home. Sunshine was all around him, on the earth, in the sky, and beaming from the faces of little innocents who looked into his own, smilingly, touchingly, affectionately.

Such was the Western Pioneer. How many are there not in the haunts of civilized life, who would gladly exchange their condition for that of the rude frontierman?

At the time of the formation of these settlements, all was comparative peace with the Indians. But the restless and reckless character of some who had come out, not for the purpose of opening up the country, but to deprecate upon the Indians, soon made it manifest that the reign of peace would be short, as the Indians had threatened retaliation, unless the wrongs which they daily received should cease.

Many little stockade forts had sprung up at different points on the Ohio and elsewhere, previous to 1774, which seemed to inspire confidence, and induce settlers to come on.

Up to the spring of 1774, the tide of emigration flowed very steadily into this part of Virginia. But the atrocious murders committed near the mouth of Yellow creek, and at Captina, stirred the Indians up to vengeance, and for a long time checked the advancing footsteps of civilization.

The great object with all who emigrated hither was land. It could then be obtained literally, "for taking up." Erecting a cabin and raising a crop, entitled any one to a settler's right of four hundred acres, with a pre-emption claim to one thousand m6re, to be secured by a land-office warrant. These certainly were great inducements, and the lands thus obtained became princely fortunes to the descendants of the primitive settler.

Most of the early settlers in this part of North-western Virginia were from the upper counties of Virginia and Maryland. Many of them were men who had seen service, and been inured to the hardships of frontier life. They brought with them but little, as their removal had to be effected entirely on horseback. They were generally persons of staid habits and sterling worth; possessed of great energy of character and incorruptible patriotism.

As a description of the habits, customs, mode of living, &c., of the primitive settler may not be uninteresting to their descendants as well as the general reader, we will give from Dr. Doddridge's unpretending little volume a short account of some of these interesting features of pioneer life. The writer having been an eye-witness as well as an actor in most of the scenes he so aptly and graphically portrays, we doubt not he has drawn a faithful picture, and one which every old pioneer will be able to recognize. Only one who had been an eye-witness to such scenes, or derived them directly from the pioneer fathers, could properly describe them.

# CHAPTER III. MANNERS AND CUSTOMS.

A CORRECT and detailed view of the origin of societies, and their progress from one condition or point of wealth, science and civilization, to another is interesting, even when received through the dusky medium of history, often times but poorly and partially written. But when this retrospect of things past and gone is drawn from the recollections of experience, the impression which it makes on the heart must be of the most vivid and lasting kind.

The following history of the state of society, manners and customs of our forefathers has been drawn from the latter source; and is given to the world with the knowledge that many of my cotemporaries are still living, who, as well as myself, have witnessed all the scenes and events herein described, and whose memories will speedily detect and expose any errors it may contain.

The municipal as well as ecclesiastical institutions of society, whether good or bad, in consequence of their continued use, give a corresponding cast to the public character of the society, whose conduct they direct, the more so, because, in the lapse of time, the observance of them becomes a matter of conscience.

This observation applies with full force to that influence of our early land laws which allowed four hundred acres, and no more, to a settlement right. Many of our first settlers seemed to regard this amount of the surface of the earth as the allotment of Divine Providence for one family, and believed that any attempt to get more would be sinful. Most of them, therefore, contented themselves with that amount; although they might have evaded the law, which allowed but one settlement right to any one individual, by taking out the title papers in the names of others, to be afterwards transferred to them as if by purchase. Some few, indeed, pursued this practice; but it was held in detestation.

Owing to the equal distribution of real property directed by our land laws, and the sterling integrity of our forefathers, in their observance of them, we have no districts of "sold land," as it is called, that is, large tracts of lands in the hands of individuals or companies, who neither sell nor improve them, as is the case in Lower Canada and the northwestern part of

Pennsylvania. These unsettled tracks make huge blanks in the population of the country where they exist.

The division lines between those whose lands adjoined, were generally made in an amicable manner, before any survey of them was made by the parties concerned. In doing this, they were guided mainly by the tops of ridges and water courses, but particularly the former. Hence, the greater number of farms in the western parts of Pennsylvania and Virginia bear a striking resemblance to an amphitheatre. The buildings occupy a low situation, and the tops of the surrounding hills are the boundaries of the tract to which the family mansion belongs.

Our forefathers were fond of farms of this description, because, as they said, they are attended with this convenience, "that everything comes to the house down hill." In the hilly parts of the State of Ohio, the land having been laid off in an arbitrary manner, by straight parallel lines, without regard to hill or dale, the farms present a different aspect from those on the east side of the river. There the buildings as frequently occupy the tops of the hills as any other situation.

Our people had become so accustomed to the mode of "getting land for taking it up," that for a long time it was generally believed that the land on the west side of the Ohio would ultimately be disposed of in that way. Hence, almost the whole tract of country between the Ohio and Muskingum was parcelled out in tomahawk improvements; but these were not satisfied with a single four hundred acre tract. Many of them owned a great number of tracts of the best land, and thus, in imagination, were as "wealthy as a South Sea dream." Some of these land jobbers did not content themselves with marking trees, at the usual height, with the initials of their names, but climbed up the large beech trees, and cut the letters in their bark from twenty to forty feet from the ground. To enable them to identify those trees at a future period, they made marks on other trees around as references.

The settlement of a new country, in the immediate neighborhood of an old one, is not attended with much difficulty, because supplies can be readily obtained from the latter; but the settlement of a country very remote from any cultivated region is quite a different thing, because at the outset, food, raiment, and the implements of husbandry are only obtained in small supplies, and with great difficulty. The task of making new establishments in a remote wilderness, in a time of profound peace, is sufficiently difficult; but when, in addition to all the unavoidable hardships attendant on this business, those resulting from an extensive and furious warfare with savages are superadded; toil, privations and sufferings are then carried to the full extent of the capacity of men to endure them.

Such was the wretched condition of our forefathers in making their settlements here. To all their difficulties and privations the Indian war was a weighty addition. This destructive warfare they were compelled to sustain almost single-handed, because the Revolutionary contest gave full employment for the military strength and resources on the east side of the mountains.

The following history of the poverty, labors, sufferings, manners and customs of our forefathers, will appear like a collection of "tales of olden times," without any garnish of language to spoil the original portraits, by giving them shades of coloring which they did not possess.

I shall follow the order of things as they occurred during the period of time embraced in these narratives, beginning with those rude accommodations with which our first adventurers into this country furnished themselves at the commencement of their establishments. It will be a homely narrative, yet valuable on the ground of its being real history.

In this chapter it is my design to give a brief account of the household furniture and articles of diet which were used by the first inhabitants of our country. A description of their cabins and half-faced camps, and their manner of building them, will be found elsewhere.

The furniture for the table, for several years after the settlement of this country, consisted of a few pewter dishes, plates and spoons; but mostly of wooden bowls, trenchers and noggins. If these last were scarce, gourds and hardshelled squashes made up the deficiency.

The iron pots, knives and forks were brought from the East, with the salt and iron, on pack-horses.

These articles of furniture corresponded very well with the articles of diet. "Hog and hominy" were proverbial for the dish of which they were the component parts. Jonny-cake and pone were, at the outset of the settlements of the country, the only forms of bread in use for breakfast and dinner. At supper, milk and mush was the standard dish. When milk was not plenty, which was often the case, owing to the scarcity of cattle, or the want of proper pasture for them, the substantial dish of hominy had to supply the place of them; mush was frequently eaten with sweetened water, molasses, bear's oil, or the gravy of fried meat.

In our whole display of furniture, the delft, china and silver were unknown. It did not then, as now, require contributions from the four quarters of the globe to furnish the breakfast table, viz: the silver from Mexico; the coffee from the West Indies; the tea from China; and the delft and porcelain from Europe or Asia. Yet our homely fare, and unsightly cabins and furniture produced a hardy race, who planted the first footsteps of civilization in the immense regions of the West. Inured to hardships, bravery and labor, from their early youth, they sustained with manly fortitude the fatigue of the chase, the campaign and scout, and with strong arms "turned the wilderness into fruitful fields," and have left to their descendants the rich inheritance of an immense empire blessed with peace, and wealth, and prosperity.

The introduction of delft ware was considered by many of the backwoods' people as a culpable innovation. It was too easily broken, and the plates of that ware dulled their scalping and clasp-knives; tea ware was too small for men — they might do for women and children. Tea and coffee were only slops, which, in the adage of the day, "did not stick by the ribs." The idea then prevalent was, that they were only designed for people of quality, who did not labor, or for the sick. A genuine backwoodsman would have thought himself disgraced by showing a fondness for such "slops." Indeed, many of them have, to this day, very little respect for them.

But passing from the furniture, diet, &c., of our forefathers, we now come to speak of their dress, which will be found singular and interesting enough to many of the present day and generation. Some of our fashionables would scarcely be able to recognize in the picture, so faithfully and graphically drawn by our venerable historian, the persons of their grandsires and dames.

On the frontier, and particularly among those who were much in the habit of hunting, and going on scouts and campaigns, the dress of the men was partly Indian and partly that of civilized nations.

The hunting shirt was universally worn. This was a kind of loose frock, reaching half-way down the thighs, with large sleeves, open before, and so wide as to lap over a foot or more when belted. The cape was large, and sometimes fringed with a ravelled piece of cloth, of a different color from that of the hunting shirt itself. The bosom of this dress served as a wallet to hold bread, cakes, jerk, tow for wiping the barrel of the rifle, or any other necessary for the hunter or warrior. The belt, which was always tied behind, answered several purposes, besides that of holding the dress together. In cold weather, the mittens, and sometimes the bullet-bag occupied the front part of it. To the right side was suspended the tomahawk, and to the left the scalping-knife, in its leathern sheath. The hunting shirt was generally made of linsey, sometimes of coarse linen, and a few of dressed deer-skins. These last were very cold and uncomfortable, in wet weather. The shirt and jacket were of the common fashion. A pair of drawers, or breeches and leggins were the dress of the thighs and legs, a pair of moccasins answered for their feet much better than shoes. These were made of dressed deerskin. They were mostly of a single piece, with a gathering seam along the top of the foot, and another from the bottom of the heel, without gathers, as high or a little higher than the ankle joint. Flaps were left on each side, to reach some distance up the legs. These were nicely adapted to the ankles and lower part of the leg by thongs of deer-skin, so that no dust, gravel, or snow could get within the moccasin.

In cold weather the moccasins were well stuffed with deers' hair or dry leaves, so as to keep the feet comfortably warm; but in wet weather it was usually said, that wearing them was "a decent way of going barefooted;" and such was the fact, owing to the spongy texture of the leather of which they were made.

Owing to this defective covering of the feet more than to any other circumstance, the greater number of our hunters and warriors were afflicted with rheumatism in their limbs. Of this disease they were all apprehensive in cold or wet weather, and therefore always slept with their feet to the fire, to prevent or cure it as well as they could. This practice unquestionably had a very salutary effect, and prevented many of them from becoming confirmed cripples in early life.

In the latter years of the Indian war, our young men became more enamored with the Indian dress. The drawers were laid aside and the leggins made longer, so as to reach the upper part of the thigh. The Indian breech-cloth was adopted. This was a piece of linen or cloth nearly a yard long, and eight or nine inches broad. This passed under the belt, before and behind, leaving the ends for flaps hanging before and behind over the belt. These flaps were sometimes ornamented with some coarse kind of embroidery work. To the same belt which secured the breech-cloth, strings, which supported the long leggins, were attached. When this belt, as was often the case, passed over the hunting shirt, the upper part of the thighs and part of the hips were naked.

The young warrior, instead of being abashed by this nudity, was proud of his Indian dress. In some few instances I have seen them go into places of public worship in this dress. Their appearance, however, did not add much to the devotion of the young ladies.

The linsey coats and bed-gowns, which were the universal dress of our women in early times, would make a strange figure at this day.

The writer would say to the ladies of the present day, your ancestors knew nothing of the ruffles, leghorns, curls, combs, rings, and other jewels with which their fair daughters now decorate themselves. Such things were not then to be had. Many of the younger part of them were pretty well grown before they ever saw the inside of a store-room, or even knew there was such a thing, unless by hearsay, and, indeed, scarcely that.

Instead of the toilet, they had to handle the distaff or shuttle, the sickle or weeding-hoe, contented if they could obtain their linsey clothing, and cover their heads with a sun-bonnet made of six or seven hundred linen.

Truly, this is a contrast to the condition and appearance of some of their fair descendants, who, with their $500 shawls and $50 handkerchiefs, would appear oddly enough by the side of their grand-dams of 1776.

The Fort. — My reader will understand, by this term, not only a place of defence, but the residence of a small number of families belonging to the same neighborhood. As the Indian mode of warfare was an indiscriminate slaughter of all ages and both sexes, it was as requisite to provide for the safety of the women and children as for that of the men.

The fort consisted of cabins, blockhouses and stockades. A range of cabins commonly formed one side at least of the fort. Divisions, or partitions of logs, separated the cabins from each other. The walls on the outside were ten or twelve feet high, the slope of the roof being turned wholly inward. Very few of these cabins had puncheon floors, the greater part were earthen.

The blockhouses were built at the angles of the fort. They projected about two feet beyond the outer walls of the cabins and stockades. Their upper stories were about eighteen inches every way larger in dimension than the under one, leaving an opening at the commencement of the second story, to prevent the enemy from making a lodgment under their walls. In some forts, instead of blockhouses the angles of the fort were furnished with bastions. A large folding gate, made of thick slabs, nearest the spring, closed the fort. The stockades, bastions, cabins and blockhouse walls were furnished with port-holes at proper heights and distances. The whole of the outside was made completely bullet proof.

It may be truly said that necessity is the mother of invention, for the whole of this work was made without the aid of a single nail or spike of iron; and for this reason, — such things were not to be had.

In some places, less exposed, a single blockhouse, with a cabin or two, constituted the whole fort.

Such places of refuge may appear very trifling to those who have been in the habit of seeing the formidable military garrisons of Europe and America; but they answered the purpose, as the Indians had no artillery. They seldom attacked and scarcely ever took one of them.

The families belonging to these forts were so attached to their own cabins on their farms, that they seldom moved into their fort in the spring until compelled by some alarm, as they called it; that is, when it was announced by some murder that the Indians were in the settlement.

[Dr. Doddridge, in the above, is not sufficiently clear in his distinction between the several places of defence to which people resorted on the frontier in times of Indian trouble.

The reader of this work would find himself very much confused by the several references which are made to forts, blockhouses and stations, for the varied use of the terms would imply different structures. The description of Dr. D. does not imply this difference, and we shall therefore now supply the omission.

Briefly, we will then state, that a fort was generally a stockade enclosure, embracing cabins, &c., for the accommodation of several families. Blockhouses often formed two or more of its corners.

A station was a parallelogram of cabins, united by palisades, so as to present a continued wall on the outer side, the cabin doors opening into a common square, on the inner side.

A blockhouse was a square double-storied structure, the upper story projecting over the lower about two feet, which space was left so that the inmates could shoot from above upon an enemy attempting to climb the walls. But one door opened into these rude and peculiar structures, and that was always very strong, so as to defy entrance by any ordinary means of assault.

The men generally remained above; and many are the tales of border war wherein a few determined spirits successfully withstood the combined attacks of hundreds of Indians.

A blockhouse was considered the most safe for a small number. Those within felt themselves as secure against the ordinary assaults of their native enemy, as though they had been in the famous fortress of the Mediterranean.]

Hunting. — This was an important part of the employment of the early settlers of this country. For some years the woods supplied them with the greater amount of their subsistence, and with regard to some families at certain times, the whole of it; for it was no uncommon thing for families to live several months without a mouthful of bread. It frequently happened that there was no breakfast until it was obtained from the woods. Fur constituted the people's money. They had nothing else to give in exchange for rifles, salt, and iron, on the other side of the mountains.

The fall and early part of the winter was the season for hunting the deer, and the whole of the winter, including part of the spring, for boars and fur skinned animals. It was a customary saying, that fur is good during every month in the name of which the letter R occurs.

As soon as the leaves were pretty well down, and the weather became rainy, accompanied with light snows, these men, after acting the part of husbandmen, so far as the state of warfare permitted them to do so, soon began to feel that they were hunters. They became uneasy at home. Every thing about them became disagreeable. The house was too warm. The feather bed too soft; and even the good wife was not thought, for the time being, a proper companion. The mind of the hunter was wholly occupied with the camp and chase.

Hunting was not a mere ramble in pursuit of game, in which there was nothing of skill and calculation; on the contrary, the hunter, before he set out in the morning, was informed by the state of the weather in what situation he might reasonably expect to meet with his game; whether on the bottoms, sides, or tops of the hills. In stormy weather, the deer always seek the most sheltered places, and the leeward sides of the hills. In rainy weather, when there is not much wind, they keep in the open woods, on the high ground.

In every situation it was requisite for the hunter to ascertain the course of the wind, so as to get the leeward of the game. This he effected by putting his finger in his mouth, and holding it there until it became warm, then holding it above his head, the side which first becomes cold shows which way the wind blows.

As it was requisite, too, for the hunter to know the cardinal points, he had only to observe the trees to ascertain them. The bark of an aged tree is thicker and much rougher on the north than on the south side. The same thing may be said of the moss, it is much thicker and stronger on the north than on the south sides of the trees.

The whole business of the hunter consisted of a succession of intrigues. From morning till night he was on the alert to gain the wind of his game, and approach them without being discovered. If he succeeded in killing a deer, he skinned it, and hung it up out of the reach of the wolves, and immediately resumed the chase till the close of the evening, when he bent his course towards his camp; when arrived there he kindled up his fire, and together with his fellow hunter, cooked his supper. The supper finished, the adventures of the day furnished the tales for the evening. The spike buck, the two and three pronged buck, the doe and barren doe, figured through their anecdotes with great advantage.

The Wedding. — For a long time after the first settlement of this country, the inhabitants in general married young. There was no distinction of rank, and very little of fortune. On these accounts, the first impression of love resulted in marriage; and a family establishment cost but a little labor, and nothing else.

A description of a wedding from the beginning to the end, will serve to show the manners of our forefathers, and mark the grade of civilization which has succeeded to their rude state of society in the course of a few years.

In the first years of the settlement of the country, a wedding engaged the attention of a whole neighborhood; and the frolic was anticipated by old and young with eager expectation. This is not to be wondered at, when it is told that a wedding was almost the only gathering which was not accompanied with the labor of reaping, log-rolling, building a cabin, or planning some scout or campaign.

On the morning of the wedding-day, the groom and his attendants assembled at the house of his father, for the purpose of reaching the home of his bride by noon, which was the usual time for celebrating the nuptials; and which for certain reasons must take place before dinner.

Let the reader imagine an assemblage of people, without a store, tailor, or mantuamaker within an hundred miles; and an assemblage of horses, without a blacksmith or saddler within an equal distance. The gentlemen dressed in shoe-packs, moccasins, leather breeches, leggins, linsey hunting shirts, and all home made. The ladies dressed in linsey petticoats and linsey or linen bed gowns, coarse shoes, stockings, handkerchiefs, and buckskin gloves, if any. If there were any buckles, rings, buttons, or ruffles, they were the relics of olden times; family pieces from parents or grand parents. The horses were caparisoned with old saddles, old bridles or halters, and pack-saddles, with a bag or blanket thrown over them: a rope or string as often constituted the girth as a piece of leather.

The march, in double-file, was often interrupted by the narrowness and obstructions of our horse-paths, as they were called, for we had no roads; and these difficulties were often increased, sometimes by the good, and sometimes by the ill will of neighbors, by falling trees, and tying grape vines across the way. Sometimes an ambuscade was formed by the way side, and an unexpected discharge of several guns took place, so as to cover the wedding company with smoke. Let the reader imagine the scene which followed this discharge; the sudden spring of the horses, the shrieks of the girls, and the chivalrous bustle of their partners to save them from falling. Sometimes, in spite of all that could be done to prevent it, some were thrown to the ground. If a wrist, elbow, or ankle happened to be sprained, it was tied with a handkerchief, and little more was thought or said about it.

The ceremony of the marriage preceded the dinner, which was a substantial back-woods feast of beef, pork, fowls, and sometimes venison and bear meat, roasted and boiled, with plenty of potatoes, cabbage, and other vegetables. During the dinner the greatest hilarity always prevailed; although the table might be a large slab of timber, hewed out with a broad axe, supported by four sticks set in auger holes; and the furniture, some old pewter dishes, and plates; the rest, wooden bowls and trenchers; a few pewter spoons, much battered about the edges, were to be seen at some tables. The rest were made of horns. If knives were scarce, the deficiency was made up by the scalping knives which were carried in sheaths suspended to the belt of the hunting shirt. Every man carried one of them.

After dinner the dancing commenced, and generally lasted till the next morning. The figures of the dances were three and four handed reels, or square setts, and jigs. The commencement was always a square four, which was followed by what was called jiging it off; that is, two of the four would single out for a jig, and were followed by the remaining couple. The jigs were often accompanied with what was called cutting out; that is, when either of the parties became tired of the dance, on intimation the place was supplied by some one of the company without any interruption to the dance. In this way a dance was often continued till the musician was heartily tired of his situation. Toward the latter part of the night, if any of the company, through weariness, attempted to conceal themselves, for the purpose of sleeping, they were hunted up, paraded on the floor, and the fiddler ordered to play "Hang out till to-morrow morning."

About nine or ten o'clock, a deputation of the young ladies stole off the bride, and put her to bed. In doing this, it frequently happened that they had to ascend a ladder instead of a pair of stairs, leading from the dining and ball room to the loft, the floor of which was made of clapboards lying loose. This ascent, one might think, would put the bride and her attendants to the blush; but as the foot of the ladder was commonly behind the door, which was purposely opened for the occasion, and its rounds at the inner ends were well hung with hunting shirts, dresses, and other articles of clothing, the candles being on the opposite side of the house, the exit of the bride was noticed but by few. This done, a deputation of young men in like manner stole off the groom, and placed him snugly by the side of his bride. The dance still continued; and if seats happened to be scarce, which was often the case, every young man, when not engaged in the dance, was obliged to offer his lap as a seat for one of the girls; and the offer was sure to be accepted. In the midst of this hilarity the bride and groom were not forgotten. Pretty late in the night, some one would remind the company that the new couple must stand in need of some refreshment: black Betty, which was the name of the bottle, was called for, and sent up the ladder; but sometimes black Betty did not go alone, I have many times seen as much bread, beef, pork and cabbage sent along, as would afford a good meal for half a dozen hungry men. The young couple were compelled to eat and drink, more or less, of whatever was offered.

But to return. It often happened that some neighbors or relations, not being asked to the wedding, took offence; and the mode of revenge adopted by them on such occasions, was that of cutting off" the manes, foretops, and tails of the horses of the wedding company.

On returning to the infare, the order of procession, and the race for black Betty was the same as before. The feasting and dancing often lasted several days, at the end of which the whole company were so exhausted with loss of sleep, that many days' rest were requisite to fit them to return to their ordinary labors.

Should I be asked why I have presented this unpleasant portrait of the rude manners of our forefathers, I, in turn, would ask my reader, why are you pleased with the histories of the blood and carnage of battles? Why are you delighted with the fictions of poetry, the novel and romance? I have related truth, and only truth, strange as it may seem. I have depicted a state of society, and manners, which are fast vanishing from the memory of man, with a view to give the youth of our country a knowledge of the advantages of civilization, and to give contentment to the aged, by preventing them from saying, "that former times were better than the present."

House Warming. — I will proceed to state the usual manner of settling a young couple in the world.

A spot was selected on a piece of land belonging to one of the parents, for their habitation. A day was appointed shortly after the marriage, for commencing the work of building their cabin.

The materials for the cabin were mostly prepared on the first day and sometimes the foundation laid in the evening. The second day was allotted for the raising.

The cabin being furnished, the ceremony of house warming took place, before the young couple were permitted to move into it.

The house warming was a dance of a whole night's continuance, made up of the relations of the bride and groom, and their neighbors. On the day following the young couple took possession of their new premises.

We desire now to say a few words about the sports of the pioneers. These were such as might be expected among a people, who, owing to their circumstances, as well as education, set an higher value on physical than mental endowments, and on skill in hunting, and bravery in war, than any polite accomplishment or the fine arts.

Many of the sports of the early settlers of this country, were imitative of the exercises and stratagems of hunting and war. Boys were taught the use of the bow and arrow at an early age; but although they acquired considerable adroitness in the use of them, so as to kill a bird or squirrel, yet it appears to me that in the hands of the white people, the bow and arrow could never be depended upon for warfare or hunting, unless made and managed in a different manner from any specimen which I have ever seen.

One important pastime of our boys, was that of imitating the noise of every bird and beast in the woods. This faculty was not merely a pastime;

but a very necessary part of education, on account of its utility under certain circumstances. Imitating the gobbling and other sounds of the wild turkey, often brought those keen-eyed and ever watchful tenants of the forest, within the reach of the rifle. The bleating of the fawn brought its dam to her death in the same way. The hunter often collected a company of mopish owls to the trees about his camp, and amused himself with their hoarse screaming. His howl would raise and obtain responses from a pack of wolves, so as to inform him of their whereabouts as well to guard him against their depredation.

This imitative faculty was sometimes requisite as a measure of precaution in war. The Indians, when scattered about in a neighborhood, often collected together by imitating turkeys by day and wolves or owls by night. In similar situations our people did the same. I have often witnessed the consternation of a whole neighborhood in consequence of the screeching of owls. An early and correct use of this imitative faculty, was considered as an indication that its possessor would become in due time a good hunter and a valiant warrior.

Throwing the tomahawk was another boyish sport, in which many acquired considerable skill. The tomahawk, with its handle of a certain length, will make a given number of turns within a certain distance; say in five steps, it will strike with the edge, the handle downwards; at the distance of seven and a half, it will strike with the edge, the handle upwards; and so on. A little experience enabled the boy to measure the distance with his eye, when walking through the woods, and strike a tree with his tomahawk in any way he chose.

The athletic sports of running, jumping, and wrestling, were the pastimes of boys in common with men.

A well grown boy, at the age of twelve or thirteen years, was furnished with a small rifle and shot pouch. He then became a fort soldier, and had his port hole assigned him. Hunting squirrels, turkeys and racoons soon made him expert in the use of his gun.

Dramatic narrations, chiefly concerning Jack and the Giant, furnished our young people with another source of amusement during their leisure hours. Many of those tales were lengthy, and embraced a considerable range of incident. — Jack, always the hero of the story, after encountering many difficulties, and performing many great achievements, came off conqueror of the Giant. — Many of these stories were tales of knight errantry, in which some captive virgin was released from captivity and restored to her lover.

These dramatic narrations concerning Jack and the Giant, bore a strong resemblance to the poems of Ossian, the story of the Cyclops and Ulysses in the Odyssy of Homer, and the tale of the Giant and Greatheart in the Pilgrim's Progress; they were so arranged, as to the different incidents of the narration, that they were easily committed to memory. They certainly have been handed down from generation to generation, from time immemorial.

Civilization has, indeed, banished the use of those ancient tales of romantic heroism; but what then? it has substituted in their place the novel and romance.

Singing was another but not very common amusement among our first settlers. Their tunes were rude enough to be sure. Robin Hood furnished a number of our songs; the balance were mostly tragical. These last were denominated "love songs about murder." As to cards, dice, backgammon and other games of chance, we knew nothing about them. These are amongst the blessed gifts of civilization.

We have drawn upon the abundant store of our earlier laborer in this interesting field, more fully than was first intended. As it is important, however, that the present generation should know exactly how their progenitors lived in the days that tried men's souls, and as the information given will constitute an interesting feature in the pages of our work, we therefore feel justified in extracting as freely as we have done. It would be in vain for a writer of the present day to attempt a description of the manners, customs, habits, &c., of the early settlers. None but one who had lived among them, shared with their wants and suffered with their privations, could accurately describe the varied and peculiar life of the old pioneer. We have every reason to believe that the account of Dr. Doddridge is in the main correct, and cannot doubt it will be highly interesting to most of our readers.

# PART IV. FRENCH AND INDIAN WAR. 1754-1763.

# CHAPTER I. EXPEDITION OF BRADDOCK.

In order to impart to the events of the next nine years something of a distinctive character, we have prefixed the name by which that fierce and sanguinary struggle (the war of 1754 — 63) was known at the time. We desire, however, in the premises, to protest against the association — French and Indian, as it is clearly a misnomer. That was emphatically a war between France and England, in which the Indians were employed as allies.

The success of the French at the forks, and their triumph on the mountains, greatly chagrined the governor of Virginia, and moved the British crown to renewed and increased efforts for establishing their claim to the region of the Ohio. The Virginia Assembly having refused to vote men and means for carrying on the Avar, it remained with the parent government to adopt such measures as might ensure success. With as little delay as practicable, it was determined to send to America a force sufficient to repell the "invaders." Two regiments of foot, commanded by Cols. Dunbar and Halket, were ordered to Virginia, and 10,000 pounds in specie sent to Governor Dinwiddie to defray the expenses of the war.

In addition to the force just named, orders were sent to Governor Shirley and Sir William Pepperell to raise two regiments in Massachusetts and other northern states.

On the 20th of February, 1755, Major-general Edward Braddock, to whom had been given the command, reached Alexandria with the two regiments of Dunbar and Halket.

With the instructions to Governor Dinwiddie, came orders to place the colonial militia on the footing of independent companies. The effect of this was to cut down the commission of Washington to a captaincy, which he indignantly refused to receive, and forthwith resigned. Braddock, however, had heard enough of the gallant Virginian to make his services an object worth securing, and so tendered him the place of an aid in his staff. This Washington accepted, and an order announcing the appointment, was made to the army at fort Cumberland, May 10th.

On the 20th of April, the whole force, embracing about twenty-five hundred men, moved from Alexandria, and in due time reached Wills creek, where a fort had been erected by Colonel Innes, and named Cumberland in honor of the distinguished duke. Here the army was unfortunately delayed for near a month, by the Virginia contractors failing to furnish the required number of horses and wagons. At length, through the efforts and personal influence of Franklin, then Postmaster-general of the colonies, they were supplied by some Pennsylvania farmers. But this was only the commencement of their difficulties. The mountain wilderness the first three days march, the army advanced but nine miles. In many places they were compelled to double their teams in front, and often, in climbing the mountain sides, their line was extended to four miles in length.

On the seventh day, they had reached the Little Meadows, where Washington advised that the heavy artillery should be left, together with the wagons, and that the baggage, &c., be taken on pack horses. To this suggestion Braddock at last reluctantly assented. Twelve hundred men, with twelve pieces of cannon, were chosen as the advanced corps. This was headed by Braddock in person, assisted by Sir Peter Halket as Brigadier-general, Cols. Gage and Burton, and Major Sparks. Washington, who was too ill to travel, was left with Colonel Dunbar and the balance of the army.

On the 8th of July, after a march of nineteen days, which could have been accomplished in nine, had it not been for the "fastidiousness and presumption of the commander-in-chief," who, instead of pushing on with vigor, "halted to level every mole-hill and bridge every rivulet," the division reached a point near the mouth of Crooked run and the Monongahela. On the morning of the 9th, Colonel Washington rejoined the division under Braddock, whom he found in high spirits, and firm in the conviction, that within a few hours "he would victoriously enter the walls of Fort Du Quesne."

The men were in fine discipline, and as the noontide sun of mid-summer fell upon their burnished arms, and brilliant uniform, there was displayed one of the finest spectacles, as Washington afterwards declared, he had ever beheld. Every man was neatly dressed, and marched with as much precision as though he had been on parade at Woolwich. The glitter of bayonets, and the "flash of warlike steel, contrasted strangely with the deep and peaceful verdure of the forest shade." On the right of the army, calmly flowed the Monongahela, imaging upon its bosom the doomed host; while, on the left, rose up the green old mountain, the sides of which had never before echoed to the tramp of soldiery or to the strains of martial music.

"How brilliant that morning, but how melancholy that evening."

Before proceeding farther, it may be necessary to describe the ground now so celebrated as Braddock's field. It is a small bottom, embracing but a few acres, bounded on the west by the river and on the east by a bluffy bank, through which runs a deep ravine, and over which at the time of the battle, and for many years afterwards, grew heavy trees, matted brambles, vines, grass, etc. Upon this bluff lay concealed the Indian and French forces. By one o'clock the entire division had crossed the river: Colonel Gates with three hundred regulars, followed by another body of two hundred, led the advance. The commander-in-chief, supported by the main column of the army, next crossed. The whole of the advance party remained on the bottom until the rest of the division crossed, and herein, we conceive, was the great error. Had the three hundred, or five hundred men under Colonel Gates, advanced and drawn the enemy's fire, thus giving the seven hundred men in reserve an opportunity to rout the foe with ball and bayonet, the result of that bloody conflict might have been very different.

The general having arranged his plans, ordered a movement of the division under Colonel Gage, while he would bring up in person, the residue of the army. The gallant colonel moved forward with his men, and whilst in the act of passing through the ravine already noticed, a deadly and terrible fire was opened upon them by an invisible foe.

To the brave grenadiers, who had stood firm on the plains of Europe, amid tempests of cannon balls, cutting down whole platoons of their comrades, this new species of warfare was perfectly appalling; and unable longer to breast the girdle of fire which enveloped them, they gave way in confusion, involving the whole army in distress, dismay and disorder.

In such a dilemma, with hundreds of his men falling at every discharge, — his ranks converted into a wild and reckless multitude; unable to rally and too proud to retreat; Braddock obstinately refused to allow the provincial troops to fight the Indians in their own way, but with a madness incomprehensible, did his utmost to form the men into platoons and wheel them into close columns. The result was horrible, and the sacrifice of life without a parallel at that time, in Indian warfare. The Virginia regiments, unable to keep together, spread through the surrounding wood, and by this means did all the execution that was effected. Every man fought for himself, and rushing to the trees from behind which gleamed the flash of the rifle, the brave Virginian often bayoneted the savage at his post. This perilous enterprise, however, was attended with a terrible sacrifice. . Out of three full companies, but thirty men were left. Truly has it been said, "they behaved like men and died like soldiers." Of Captain Poison's company one only escaped. In that of Captain Peyronny, every officer from the captain down, was sacrificed.

Of those engaged in this fearful conflict, and who were so fortunate as to escape, were many who afterwards became distinguished in the military and civil annals of Virginia. Of this number, were the Lewis, Matthews, Grant, Field, etc.

This appalling seen lasted three hours, during which the army stood exposed to the steady fire of a concealed but most deadly foe, and men fell on every hand like grass before the sweep of the sickle.

Finally, Braddock, after having five horses killed under him, fell mortally wounded, by the avenging hand of an outraged American. At his fall, all order gave way, and what remained of that so lately proud army, rushed heedlessly into the river, abandoning all to the fury of the savages and French. Artillery, ammunition, baggage, including the camp chest of Braddock, which contained, it is said, £75,000 in gold, all fell into the hands of the victorious enemy.

The retreating army rushed wildly forward, and did not stop until coming up to the rear division. So appalled were the latter at the terrible disaster, that the entire army retreated with disgraceful precipitancy to Fort Cumberland. This, according to Smollett, "was the most extraordinary victory ever obtained, and the farthest flight ever made."

It was the most disastrous defeat ever sustained by any European army in America. Sixty-three officers, and seven hundred and fourteen privates were killed or dangerously wounded. There is perhaps, no instance upon record, where so great a proportion of officers were killed. Out of the eighty-six composing the regiment, but twenty-three escaped unhurt. Their brilliant uniform seemed sure marks for the deadly aim of the savage.

On that disastrous day, the military genius of Washington shone forth with much of that splendor, which afterwards made him so illustrious. Two aids of Braddock had fallen, and therefore, upon Washington alone devolved the duty of distributing orders. "Men were falling thick and fast, yet regardless of danger, he spurred on his steed, galloping here and there through the field of blood. At length his horse sunk under him; a second was procured, and pressing amid the throng, sent his calm and resolute voice among the frightened ranks, but without avail, A second horse fell beneath him, and he leaped to the saddle of a third, while the bullets rained like hail stones about him." Four passed through his coat, without inflicting the slightest wound, showing clearly, that a stronger hand than that of man's protected the body at which they had been aimed. An eye-witness says, he expected every moment to see him fall, as his duty exposed him to the most imminent danger. An Indian warrior was often afterwards heard to say, that Washington was not born to be shot, as he had fired seventeen times at his person without success.

The courage, energy, bravery and skill displayed by Washington on this occasion marked him as possessed of the highest order of military talents. Just from a bed of sickness, yet forgetting his infirmities, he pushed through the panic-stricken crowd, and his bright sword could be seen pointing in every direction as he distributed the orders of his commander.

At last, when

"—— Hapless Braddock met his destined fall,"

the noble Virginia aid, with his provincial troops, who had been held in so much contempt by the haughty and presumptuous general, covered the retreat, and saved the remnant of the army from annihilation.

At the fall of Braddock, Washington, with Capt. Stuart of the Virginia Guards, hastened to his relief, and bore him from the field of his inglorious defeat, in the sash which had decorated his person.

Braddock was taken to Dunbar's camp, on the summit of Laurel Hill, where he breathed his last, on the evening of the fourth day after the battle. His body was interred in the center of the road, and the entire army marched over the spot in order that the remains of the unfortunate general might not be desecrated by savage hands.

Tradition still designates the place of his burial. It is about nine miles east of Uniontown, and one hundred yards north of the National road.

The only words General Braddock was heard to utter after his fall were, "Is it possible — all is over!" What a volume of agony did those simple words express. Alas, such is glorious war!

General Braddock was a man of undoubted bravery, but imprudent, arrogant, headstrong and austere. He was a rigid disciplinarian, and could manoeuvre twenty thousand men on the plains of Europe equal to any officer of his age; but was perhaps the worst man the British government could have selected for leading an army against the savages of America. The Walpole Letters, in speaking of him, say he had been Governor of Gibraltar; that he was poor and prodigal as well as brutal — "a very

Iroquois in disposition." Also, that he had been engaged in a duel with Mr. Gamley, and an amour with Mrs. Upton.

Before leaving England, the Duke of Cumberland warned him against surprise from the savages. Dr. Franklin also had a conversation with him in Virginia, and strongly advised him to guard against ambuscades, at the same time acquainting him with the mode of warfare peculiar to the Indians. Braddock treated it all as no obstacle, talked of making short work of it, swore he could take Fort Du Quesne in a day, then proceed up the Alleghany, and destroy all the French posts between the Ohio and Canada, &c. &c. It was this spirit of arrogance, hauteur and overweening confidence, that brought about his disastrous defeat on the Monongahela. Had he taken the advice of Washington, Franklin, or Sir Peter Halket, and guarded against surprise, his name might not have gone down to posterity connected with the most inglorious defeat in the annals of modern warfare, and his bones not have filled a mountain grave in the unbroken solitudes of America.

Thus ended the expedition of General Braddock, certainly one of the most unfortunate ever undertaken in the west.

After the retreat of the army, the savages, unwilling to follow the French in pursuit, fell upon the field, and preyed on the rich plunder which lay before them. The wounded and slain were robbed of everything, and the naked bodies left a prey to the fierce beasts of the wood. In 1758, after Gen. Forbes had taken Fort Du Quesne, it was resolved to search up the remains of Braddock's army, and bury the bones. This was partly carried out at the time, but many years afterwards, (June, 1781,) a second and more successful attempt was made. George Roush, John Barr and John Rhodenhamer, engaged as scouts, gathered and carted several loads of human bones, and deposited them in a hole dug for the purpose. Our informant, who was one of the party, says the place of sepulture was directly on the battle-field.

Although nearly one hundred years have elapsed since that memorable day, still the plough of the husbandman occasionally turns up some relic of melancholy interest. During the past summer, (1850,) the workmen engaged in grading the track for a railroad, threw up numerous bones, bullets, and other relics of that melancholy affair.

The number of French and Indians actually engaged has never been fully ascertained, but variously estimated at from four to eight hundred.

# CHAPTER II. NEW MINISTRY AND NEW EXPEDITIONS.

The disastrous termination of Braddock's campaign was the means of inflaming the passions of the savages, and exciting them to deeds of blood, the very contemplation of which cannot fail to thrill us with horror. They pushed across the mountains into the unprotected settlements of Virginia and Pennsylvania, spreading terror, dismay and death wherever they went. Men, women and children were tortured and murdered in the most barbarous and brutal manner, their property destroyed, and improvements laid waste. All who could, fled across the Blue ridge, but many of course, there were, who could not get away, and these were compelled to stay and endure the dread, and often the horrid reality of savage cruelty. Intense fear pervaded the whole frontier settlements, from the Susquehanna to the Holston. The very name of an Indian struck terror into the hearts of the defenceless settlers.

Washington, in April, 1756, wrote as follows from Winchester: "The Blue ridge is now our frontier, no men being left in this county (Frederick) except a few, who keep close with a number of women and children in forts. . . . The supplicating tears of the women, and moving petitions of the men melt me with such deadly sorrow that I solemnly declare, if I know my own mind, I could offer myself a willing sacrifice to the butchering enemy, provided that would contribute to the people's ease."

Washington recommended to the Assembly that an expedition be fitted out against Fort Du Quesne, as it would be utter folly to strike against the marauding bands of Indians, so long as the French were permitted to hold their position at the head of the Ohio.

Notwithstanding the terrible defeat sustained by the British arms in America, no open declaration of war was made until May, 1756. During the early part of that year, however, both nations had been busy in forming alliances — France with Austria, Russia and Sweden; and England with Frederick the Great. Now commenced that long and bloody struggle known as the Seven Years' War, wherein most of Europe, North America, the East and West Indies partook and suffered.

Notwithstanding the warlike attitude of England, nothing was done to annoy the French or to check the depredations of the savages, until a change of ministry; and the mastermind of William Pitt, Earl of Chatham, assumed control of the government. Endowed with a high order of intellect — eloquent, profound and patriotic — it seemed as though the "Heavens began to brighten and the storm to lose its power" the moment his mighty hand laid hold of the helm of state. He seemed to possess in an eminent degree the full confidence of the nation, and the command of all its resources.

His plans of operation were grand, his policy bold, liberal and enlightened, all which seemed greatly to animate the colonists and inspire them with renewed hopes. They resolved to make every effort and sacrifice which the occasion might require. A circular from the premier assured the colonial governments that he was determined to repair past losses, and would immediately send to America a force sufficient to accomplish the purpose. He called upon the different governments to raise as many men as possible, promising to send over all the necessary munitions of war, and pledging himself to pay liberally all soldiers who enlisted.

Virginia equipped sixteen hundred men and sent them into the field under Col. Washington. Massachusetts, Connecticut, New Hampshire, Pennsylvania, &c., also contributed large quotas. Three expeditions were determined upon, and the most active measures taken to bring them to the field. The first was to be against Louisbourg, the second against Ticonderoga and Crown Point, and the third against Fort Du Quesne.

The first of these, consisting of 14,000 men, twenty ships of the line, and eighteen frigates, succeeded; the second, embracing 16,000 men, utterly failed; and of the third, we will now speak more in detail.

The western expedition was placed under the command of General John Forbes, an officer of great skill, energy and resolution. His army consisted of nearly nine thousand men, embracing British regulars and provincials from Virginia, North Carolina, Maryland, Pennsylvania, and the lower counties of Delaware. The Virginia, North Carolina and Maryland troops were ordered to rendezvous at Winchester, Col. Bouquet with the Pennsylvanians assembled at Raystown, now Bedford, while the commander-in-chief, with the British regulars, marched from Philadelphia to effect a junction with the Pennsylvania troops at Raystown. In consequence, however, of severe indisposition. Gen. Forbes did not get farther than Carlisle, when he was compelled to stop. He marched to Bedford about the middle of September, (1758,) where he met the provincial troops under Col. Washington. A controversy here arose between Washington and his commander as to the route they had better pursue. Washington maintained that the road cut by Braddock was the proper one as opposing less obstacles, and passing through an abundance of forage. Bouquet and the Pennsylvania officers contended for a new road direct from Raystown, and with the latter agreed Gen. Forbes.

Without farther parley, the road was cut to Loyal-hanna, a distance of forty-five miles, where Col. Bouquet built a fort. From this point, Major Grant, with a select body of eight hundred men, was sent forward to ascertain the situation of affairs at the forks, and to gain information as to the best mode of attack. During the night of the 20th of September, he reached the hill near the junction of the two rivers, now known by his name, and at early dawn, on the 21st, marched toward the fort, breaking the stillness of that autumnal morning with the spirit-stirring reveille. At the first drum-tap the gates flew open, and outrushed the French and Indians in great numbers. The air was rent with the savage war-whoop, and ere the commander had time to press his men to the conflict, or even before they could bring their guns to bear, the foe were upon them, dealing death at every blow. The savages were perfectly furious, and but for the French, who interposed to save the prisoners, not one perhaps of that ill-fated party would have escaped.

Major Andrew Lewis, who had been detached with a rear guard, hearing the sound of battle, rushed to the relief of the sufferers, leaving a guard of fifty Virginians under Captain Bullitt to protect the baggage. But this accession of strength was insufficient to check the headlong rush of the enemy. Both Majors Lewis and Grant were taken prisoners. Capt. Bullitt, seeing the men flying before their bloody pursuers, and knowing all was lost, resorted to an expedient which, although condemned by some, was the means of saving the remnant of the party. Ordering his men to lower their .arms. Captain Bullitt waited until the savages, who believing the party about to surrender, approached within a few steps, when giving the signal, a galling and deadly fire was poured upon the foe, followed up by a rush with the bayonet, so suddenly and vigorously, that the enemy gave way, and retreated in the utmost dismay and confusion. This ruse, so happily conceived and so well executed, was much admired, and the Virginians publicly complimented by the commander-in-chief.

Collecting what remained of the party he retreated to the camp of Col. Bouquet.

On the 1st of November, Gen. Forbes reached Loyal-hanna, and with as little delay as possible pushed on toward Fort Du Quesne. When within a few miles of the fort, the General was chagrined to learn that the French, becoming alarmed at the augmented force of the English, and having lost most of their Indian allies, determined to abandon their position at the forks. Unwilling, however, to leave to their successors any thing to rejoice over, they fired all the buildings and placed a slow match to their magazine. The whole party then descended the Ohio by water. About midnight, as the army of Forbes' lay at Turtle creek, "a tremendous explosion was heard from the westward, upon which the old general swore that the French magazine was blown up, either by accident or design." On the 25th of November, the army took peaceable possession of the place: the blackened walls and charred outposts, alone remaining of that once proud fortress. On its ruins rose Fort Pitt; which has long since given way to the leveling hand of civilization. Often have we stood upon the few remaining stones of these two celebrated structures, and wondered at the mutability of man's boasted greatness, — the utter littleness of all that constitutes the "pride and pomp and circumstance of glorious war."

The beautiful Fleur-de-lis here once opened its folds to the admiring gaze of the simple-hearted native; then came the rampant Lion of old England to overawe and subdue; — himself in turn, to be subdued by the never-sleeping eye of the American Eagle!

With the fall of Fort Du Quesne, terminated the struggle between France and England, in the valley of the Ohio. The posts on French creek still remained; but it was deemed unnecessary to proceed against them, as the character of the war in the north left very little doubt that the contest would soon cease, by the complete overthrow of the French.

In 1759, Ticonderoga, Crown Point, Niagara and Quebec, yielded to the British arms, and on the 8th September of the following year, Montreal, Detroit, and all of Canada were surrendered by the French governor. The treaty of Fontainbleau, in November 1762, put an end to the war.

# CHAPTER III. BRITISH INFLUENCE THE WEST.

In succeeding to the power, it was unhappily discovered, at an early day, that the English had not succeeded to the influence of the French over the Indians. Many of the northern tribes, embracing the Ottaways, Wyandotts, Chippeways, etc., were strongly attached to the French, and greatly deplored their downfall. A celebrated Chippeway chief once said in council, in speaking of the French, "They came and kissed us, — they called us children and we found them fathers; we lived like children in the same lodge." With feelings like these, it may readily be imagined, how the Red men received the success of the English.

One month precisely, after the surrender of Canada, a British officer (Major Rodgers) reached Erie on his way to take possession of Detroit. Near the latter place, lived a distinguished Ottoway chief, Pontiac, who had resolved to resist the English, and when Rodgers demanded a surrender of that post, the native warrior came forward and demanded how he dared to enter the Indian country.

Rodgers evasively answered, that he had not come to take the country, but only to take the place of the French, and open up the channels of trade.

This reply, with some manifestations of friendship, conciliated the chieftain, and the officer was permitted to pass on.

Causes, whether real or imaginary, and not now necessary to particularize, soon disturbed the good feeling between the Ottoway chief and his English neighbors. He questioned their motives, doubted their friendship, and openly declared that they had "treated him with neglect." These, always sufficient to excite the ire of an Indian, were not long in showing their effect upon Pontiac. With him to resolve was to do; and in his heart he determined to exterminate the new incumbents. Having perfected his plans he broke it to his people, by declaring that the Great Spirit had appeared to him and said, "Why do you suffer these dogs in red coats to enter your country and take the lands I gave you? drive them from it, and when you are in distress I will help you." His hosts were accordingly, marshaled, his plans of operation laid open to them, and at a concerted signal every English post save three, in the great valley of the west, — the gain of many years hard fighting, and at a sacrifice of blood and treasure scarcely to be comprehended, fell before the skill and cunning of this distinguished warrior.

In the brief period of fifteen days from the time the first blow was struck, Pontiac was in full possession of nine out of the twelve posts so recently belonging the English. His fearful threat, too, of extermination, was almost literally carried out. Over two hundred traders with their servants fell beneath his remorseless power, and goods estimated at over half a million of dollars became the spoils of the confederated tribes.

The attack on Detroit was led by Pontiac in person, but failed through the treachery of a squaw. Forts Pitt and Niagara were the other two that escaped.

Although unsuccessful against Fort Pitt, many depredations were committed in its vicinity. Families were murdered, houses burned, crops destroyed, and many similar outrages perpetrated.

Gen. Amherst, hearing that the fort held out, despatched Col. Bouquet, at the head of a sufficient force, to its relief. At Fort Ligonier, he determined to leave the wagons, and proceed on pack-horses. But his progress had been closely watched and faithfully reported to the Indian army that lay in ambush waiting his approach. Bouquet, however, was a prudent and brave man, and with the terrible lesson of Braddock before him, moved with great caution, and only in the track of experienced scouts. His vigilant spies soon reported the presence of Indians, but the gallant colonel kept his men ready for any emergency. His position, however, was becoming critical; before him lay a long and dangerous defile, surrounded by high hills and covered with dense wood. Fearing an ambuscade at this point, the colonel moved slowly, and ordered every man to be ready for an attack. The army had nearly approached this defile, when, quick as thought, a most violent descent was made upon his advanced guard by a large body of Indians. The enemy were met by a steady and well-directed fire, and the main army, hurrying up to the support of the guard, the savages were beaten back, and even pursued into their retreats along the hill-sides. But they soon rallied, and again and again fell upon the little army, so as to prevent its progress, and of course greatly annoy it. Finally, the savages completely surrounded their intended victims, cutting them off from all supplies of water, &c., and causing their chances to look hopeless in the extreme. Now it was that Bouquet's fine military genius suggested a movement which saved them all, perhaps, from utter defeat, if not extermination.

He posted his troops on an eminence, forming a circle around their convoy. This arrangement had been effected during the night, and early on the following morning he ordered the two companies occupying the most advanced situations to fall within the circle. The troops on the right and left immediately opened their files and filled up the vacancy as though they were endeavoring to cover the retreat of the others. Another company of infantry and one of grenadiers were ordered to lie in ambuscade to support the two first mentioned companies, who moved on the feigned retreat, and who were directed to commence the attack. The stratagem was admirably arranged, and most successfully executed.

The Indians, thinking the whites were retreating, rushed from the woods in great numbers, making a most furious onslaught against their enemy. At the very moment they believed themselves victorious, the two companies made a sudden turn from the rear of a hill which had concealed them from the savages, and rushing fiercely upon the enemy's right flank, completely routed them, and drove them from the field with great slaughter. The Indians lost about sixty men, including many of their best warriors, besides many wounded. The English loss, in killed and wounded, was over one hundred.

Thwarted in their attempts to cut off this reinforcement, the savages retreated toward their own country, wholly abandoning their designs against Fort Pitt. Without further interruption the gallant colonel made his way to the forks.

Unable to pursue the enemy into their own country, and take advantage of the victory obtained over them, Colonel Bouquet had to content himself with supplying Fort Pitt and other points with provisions, ammunition, &c. &c.

Such was the campaign of 1763, and its happy termination.

NOTE A. — Braddock's Route.

The following is an extract of a letter from the distinguished historian, Jared Sparks, in reference to the march of Genl. Braddock to the west, in 1755. It bears date, Salem, Mass., Feb. 18, 1847. * * *

Having therefore examined with care the details of Braddock's expedition, I am persuaded that the following, as far as it goes, is a correct account of his march from Gist's plantation.

On the 30th of June the army forded the Youghiogheny, at Stewart's crossings, and then passed a rough road over a mountain. A few miles onward they came to a great swamp, which detained them part of a day in clearing a road. They next advanced to Salt Lick creek, now called Jacob's creek, where a council of war was held, on the 3d of July, to consider a suggestion of Sir John St. Clair, that Col. Dunbar's detachment should be ordered to join the main body. This proposal was rejected, on the ground that Dunbar could not join them in less than thirteen days; that this would cause such a consumption of provisions as to render it necessary to bring forward another convoy from Fort Cumberland; and that in the mean time the French might be strengthened by a reinforcement which was daily expected at Fort Du Quesne — and moreover, the two divisions could not move together after their junction.

On the 4th the army again marched, and advanced to Turtle creek, about twelve miles from its mouth, where they arrived on the 7th inst. I suppose this to have been the eastern branch, or what is now called Brush creek, and that the place at which they encamped was a short distance northerly from the present village of Stewartsville. It was Gen. Braddock's intention to cross Turtle creek, and approach Fort Du Quesne on the other side; but the banks were so precipitous, and presented such obstacles to crossing with his artillery and heavy baggage, that he hesitated, and Sir John St. Clair went out with a party to reconnoitre. On his return before night, he reported that he had found the ridge which led to Fort Du Quesne, but that considerable work would be necessary to prepare a road for crossing Turtle creek. This route was finally abandoned, and on the 8th the army marched eight miles, and encamped not far from the Monongahela, west of the Youghiogheny, and near what is called in an old map, "Sugar Run." When Braddock reached this place, it was his design to pass through the narrows, but he was informed by the guides, who had been sent out to explore, that the passage was very difficult, about two miles in length, with a river on the left, and a high mountain on the right, and that much work must be done to make it passable for carriages. At the same time he was told that there were two good fords across the Monougahela, where the water was shallow, and the banks not steep. With these views of the case, he determined to cross the fords the next morning. The order of march was given out, and all the arrangements were made for an early movement.

About eight o'clock, on the morning of the 9th, the advanced division under Colonel Gage, crossed the ford and pushed forward. After the whole army had crossed and marched about a mile, Braddock received a note from Col. Gage, giving notice that he had passed the second ford without difficulty. A little before two o'clock, the whole army had crossed this ford, and was arranged in the order of march, on the plain near Frazier's house. Gage with the advanced party was then ordered to march, and while the main body was yet standing on the plain, the action began near the river. Not a single man of the enemy had before been seen.

The distance, by the line of march, from Stewart's crossing to Turtle creek, or Brush creek, was about thirty miles. At this point the route was changed almost to a right angle in marching to the Monongahela. The encampment was probably two or three miles from the bank of the river, for Col. Gage marched at the break of day, and did not cross the ford till eight o'clock. During the whole march from the Great Meadows, the pickets and sentinels were frequently assailed by scouting parties of French and Indians, and several men were killed. Mr. Gist acted as the general's guide. On the 4th of July two Indians went out to reconnoitre the country towards Fort Du Quesne; and Mr. Gist also, on the same day, in a different direction. They were gone two days, and all came in sight of the fort, but brought back no important intelligence. The Indians contrived to kill and scalp a French officer, whom they found shooting within half a mile of the fort.

The army seldom marched more than six miles a day, and commonly not so much. From Stewart's crossing to Turtle creek, there were six encampments. During one day the army halted. * * *

I am, Sir, respectfully yours,

Jared Sparks.

In addition to the foregoing, we will give a few extracts from the account of Mr. Atkinson, the engineer who surveyed the route. Mr. A. deserves much credit for the zeal he has manifested in this matter, and the faithful manner he has traced the route trodden by the unfortunate army.

On the 8th of June, Braddock left Fort Cumberland. Scaroodaya, successor to the Half-King of the Senecas, and Monacateotha, whose acquaintance Washington had made on the Ohio, on his mission to Le Boeuf, with about 150 Indians, Senecas and Delawares, accompanied him. George Croghan, the Indian agent of Pennsylvania, and a friendly Indian of great value, called Susquehanna Jack, were also with him.

The first brigade under Sir Peter Halket, led the way, and on the 9th, the main body followed. They spent the third night only five miles from the first. The place of encampment is marked by a copious spring bearing Braddock's name.

The route continued up Braddock's run to the forks of the stream, where Clary's tavern now stands, nine miles from Cumberland, when it turned to the left, in order to reach a point on the ridge favorable to an easy descent into the valley of George's creek. It is surprising that having reached this high ground, the favorable spur by which the National road accomplishes the ascent of the Great Savage mountain, did not strike the attention of the engineers, as the labor necessary to surmount the barrier from the deep valley of George's creek, must have contributed greatly to those bitter complaints which Braddock made against the Colonial governments for their failure to assist him more effectively in the transportation department.

Passing a mile to the south of Frostburg, the road approaches the east foot of Savage mountain, which it crosses about one mile south of the National road, and thence by very favorable ground, through the dense forests of white pine peculiar to this region, it got to the north of the National road, near the gloomy tract called the Shades of Death. This was the 15th of June, when the gloom of the summer woods, and the favorable shelter which these enormous pines would give an Indian enemy, must have made a most sensible impression on the minds of all, of the insecurity of their mode of advance.

This, doubtless, had its share in causing the council of war held at the Little Meadows' the next day. To this place, distant only about twenty miles from Cumberland, Sir John St. Clair and Major Chapman had been dispatched on the 27th of May to build a fort.

The conclusion of the council was to push on with a picked force of 1200 men, and 12 pieces of canon, and the line of march, now more compact, was resumed on the 19th. Passing over ground to the south of the Little Crossings, and of the village of Grantsville, which it skirted, the army spent the night of the 21st at the Bear Camp, a locality I have not been able to identify, but suppose it to be about midway to the Great crossings, which it reached on the 23d. The route thence to the Great Meadows or Fort Necessity, was well chosen, though over a mountainous tract, conforming very nearly to the ground now occupied by the National road, and keeping on the dividing ridge between the waters flowing into the Youghiogheny on the one hand, and the Cheat river on the other. Having crossed the Youghiogheny, we are now on the classic ground of Washington's early career, where the skirmish with Jumonville, and Fort Necessity, indicate the country laid open for them in the previous year. About one mile west of the Great Meadows, and near the spot now marked as Braddock's grave, the road struck off more to the north-west, in order to reach a pass through Laurel Hill, that would enable them to strike the Youghiogheny, at a point afterwards known as Stewart's crossings, and about half a mile below the present town of Connolsville. This part of the route is marked by the farm known as Mount Braddock. This second crossing of the Youghiogheny was effected on the 30th of June. The high grounds intervening between the river and Jacob's creek, though trivial in comparison with what they had already passed, it may be supposed, presented serious obstacles to the troops, worn out with previous exertions. From the crossing of Jacob's creek, which was at the point where Welchhanse's mill now stands, about a mile and a half below Mount Pleasant, the route stretched off to the north, crossing the Mount Pleasant turnpike near the village of that name, and thence, by a more westerly course, passing the great Sewickley near Painter's Salt Works, thence south and west of the post office of Madison and Jacksonville, it reached the brush fork of Turtle creek.

The approach to the river was now down the valley of Crooked run, to its mouth, where the point of fording is still manifest, from a deep notch in the west bank, though rendered somewhat obscure by the improved navigation of the river. The advance, under Col. Gage, crossed about eight o'clock, and continued by the foot of the hill bordering the river bottom to the second fording, which he had effected nearly as soon as the rear had got through the first.

The second and last fording, near the mouth of Turtle creek, was in full view of the enemy's position, and about one mile distant. By one o'clock the whole army had gained the right bank, and was drawn up on the bottom land, near Frazier's house, and about three-fourths of a mile from the ambuscade.

NOTE B.

In the ranks of Braddock were two brothers, Joseph and Thomas Fausett, or Fawcett; the first a commissioned, and the latter a non-commissioned officer. One of them, ("Tom Fausett,") the Hon. Andrew Stewart of Uniontown, says he knew very well, and often conversed with him about early times. "He did not hesitate to own, in the presence of his friends, that he shot Braddock." The circumstances, perhaps, were briefly these. Regardless of Genl. Braddock's positive and foolish orders that the troops should not protect themselves behind trees, Joseph Fausett had so posted himself, which Braddock discovering, rode up, and struck him down with his sword. Tom Fausett, who stood but a short distance from his brother, saw the whole transaction, and immediately drew up his rifle, and shot him through the body. This, as he afterwards said, was partly out of revenge for B.'s assault upon his brother, and partly to get the general out of the way, and thus save the remnant of the army.

In addition to the above, we may give the statement of a correspondent of the National Intelligencer, who seems to have been familiar with the facts. "When my father was removing with his family to the West, one of the Fausett's kept a public-house to the eastward from, and near where Uniontown now stands. This man's house we lodged in about the 10th of October, 1781, — twenty-six years, and a few months after Braddock's defeat; and then it was made anything but a secret, that one of the family dealt the death-blow to the British general. Thirteen years afterwards, I met Thomas Fausett, then, as he told me, in his 70th year. To him I put the plain question, and received the plain reply, 'I did shoot him.' I never heard the fact doubted or blamed, that Fausett killed Braddock."

Mr. Watson (Annals of the Olden Time, vol. i. pp. 141-2,) says, that in 1833, he met William Butler, a private in the Pennsylvania Greens at the defeat of Braddock. "I asked him particularly, who killed Braddock? and he answered promptly, one Fausett, brother of one whom Braddock had killed in a passion." In 1830, Butler saw Fausett near Carlisle, where he had gone on a visit to his daughter. The Millerstown (Perry county, Pa.,) Gazette, of 1830, speaks of Butler being there, and in company with an aged soldier in that town, "who had been in Braddock's defeat, and that both concurred in saying, that Braddock had been shot by Fausett,"

A Minister of the M. E. Church, writing to the Christian Advocate, says, "The old man died at the age of one hundred and fourteen years, in 1828, who killed Braddock." The Newburyport Herald of 1842, declares its acquaintance with Daniel Adams, an old soldier of that place, aged 82, who confirmed the shooting of Braddock by one of his own men.

"Braddock wore a coat of mail in front, which turned balls fired in front, but he was shot in the back, and the ball was found stopped in front by the coat of mail." The venerable William Darby of Washington City, has recently stated to the author, that during his early days, he never heard it doubted, that Fausett had killed Braddock. It seems a generally conceded fact, and most of the settlers were disposed to applaud the act.

NOTE C.

The identical sash worn by Braddock at the time of his defeat, and in which he was borne from the field bleeding and dying, recently passed into the hands of one of America's greatest and most successful generals.

It appears that the sash referred to, some years since became the property of a gentleman at New Orleans.

After the brilliant achievement on the Rio Grande in 1846, the owner of the relic forwarded it to Genl. Gaines, with a request that it might be presented to the officer who most distinguished himself on that occasion. The old general promptly sent it by special messenger, to the Commander-in-Chief.

The person who bore it, thus speaks of the presentation and interview. "General Taylor took the sash and examined it attentively. It was of unusual size, being quite as large, when extended, as a common hammock. In the meshes of the splendid red silk that composed it, was the date of its manufacture, '1707,' and although it was one hundred and forty years old, save where the dark spots, that were stained with the blood of the hero who wore it, it glistened as brightly as if it had just come from the loom.

Upon the unusual size of the sash being noticed. Gen. Worth, who had joined the party in the tent, mentioned that such was the old-fashioned style; and that the soldier's sash was intended to carry, if necessary, the wearer from off the field of battle. It was mentioned in the conversation, that after Gen. Ripley was wounded at Lundy's Lane, his sash, similar in form, was used as a hammock to bear him from the field, and that in it he was carried several miles, his body swaying to and fro between the horses, to which the ends "of the sash were securely fastened. To a wounded soldier, no conveyance could be more grateful, or more appropriate.

Gen. Taylor broke the silent admiration, by saying he would not receive the sash. Upon our expressing surprise, he continued, that he did not think he should receive presents until the campaign, so far as he was concerned, was finished. He elaborated on the impropriety of naming children after living men, fearing lest the thus honored might disgrace their namesakes. We urged his acceptance of the present; and he said, finally, that he would put it carefully away in his military chest, and if he thought he deserved so great a compliment, at the end of the campaign, he would acknowledge the receipt."

The stirring events that have transpired since he made that remark, have added the laurels of Monterey to those he then wore; and the would, as well as the donors of that sash, will insist upon his acceptance of it.

Since writing the above, the old chieftain himself has passed from the living to the dead. He died — a singular coincidence, on the anniversary of that terrible event — the defeat of Braddock. But a few weeks previous to his death, the author, then on a visit to Washington, freely conversed with the distinguished chieftain upon the very subject about which we have been writing. He said, that the sash referred to, was still in his possession, and at any time we desired it, would have it shown. Knowing that matters of state pressed heavily upon him, we did not ask it at that time; and thus, perhaps, the opportunity has been lost forever; — certainly deprived of one of its most interesting features — to be seen in the hands of General Taylor. During the interview referred to, he spoke much and frequently of Washington's early operations in the west, and inquired whether any of the remains of Fort Necessity could be seen.

# PART V. CIVIL AND MILITARY EXPEDITIONS IN THE WEST. 1764-1774.

# CHAPTER I. PEACE MOVEMENTS.

The British Government, anxious to secure amicable relationship with the Indians, resorted to various modes for effecting so desirable an object. Hoping to conciliate by fair words and fine promises, one of the first movements was to issue, through Col. Bouquet, the following proclamation:

"PROCLAMATION,

BY HENRY BOUQUET, ESQUIRE, COLONEL OF FOOT, ANB COMMANDING AT FORT PITT AND DEPENDENCIES.

"Whereas, by a treaty at Easton, in the year 1758, and afterwards ratified by his Majesty's ministers, the country to the west of the Alleghany mountain is allowed to the Indians for their hunting ground. And as it is of the highest importance to his Majesty's service, and the preservation of the peace, and a good understanding with the Indians, to avoid giving them any just cause of complaint: This is therefore to forbid any of his Majesty's subjects to settle or hunt to the west of the Alleghany mountains, on any pretence whatever, unless such have obtained leave in writing from the general, or the governors of their respective provinces, and produce the same to the commanding officer at Fort Pitt. And all the officers and non-commissioned officers, commanding; at the several posts erected in that part of the country, for the protection of the trade, are hereby ordered to seize, or cause to be seized, any of his Majesty's subjects, who, without the above authority, should pretend, after the publication hereof, to settle or hunt upon the said lands, and send them, with their horses and effects, to Fort Pitt, there to be tried and punished according to the nature of their offence, by the sentence of a court martial.

(Signed,) Henry Bouquet."

In October another and similar proclamation was issued by the government; and in the following spring, to aid the object in view, it was determined to make two movements into the Indian country. General Bradstreet was ordered to Lake Erie, and Col. Bouquet in direction of the Muskingum. The former moved to Niagara early in the summer in company with Sir William Johnson; and in the month of June held a grand council with twenty or more tribes, who had sued for peace. On the eighth of August they reached Detroit, and about the 20th of the same month a definite treaty was made with the Indians. Among the provisions of this treaty were the following:

1. All prisoners in the hands of the Indians were to be given up.

2. All claims to the posts and forts of the English in the west were to be abandoned; and leave given to erect Such other forts as might be needed to protect the traders, &c. Around each fort as much land was ceded as a "cannon-shot" would fly over.

3. If any Indian killed an Englishman he was to be tried by English law: the jury one-half Indians.

4. Six hostages were given by the Indians for the true fulfillment of the conditions of the treaty.

In the meantime, Col. Bouquet collected troops at Fort Pitt, and in the fall proceeded with his expedition to the Muskingum at the point where White Woman's river enters that stream. There, on the 9th of November (1764), he concluded a peace with the Delawares and Shawanese, and received from them two hundred and six prisoners. He also received from the Shawanese hostages for the delivery of some captives who could not be brought in at that time. These hostages made their escape, but the Shawanese, in good faith, restored the prisoners to a proper agent. The attachment, to which we have elsewhere alluded, as being often formed between the white captives and their new associates, was singularly illustrated in this instance.

West's pencil was made to show the curious fact to which we have alluded.

A number of very distinguished chiefs were present on this occasion. Of these were Kyashuta, Red Hawk, Custaloga, Captain John, etc.

In order to ascertain the true condition and feeling of the Western Indians, George Croghan, sub-commissioner to Sir William Johnson, went home with the returning deputies of the Delawares and Shawanese. His journal presents a very interesting account of the state of affairs in the "far West" at that day, particularly of the French settlements on the Wabash and in Illinois. Croghan left Fort Pitt on the 15th of May; by the 6th of June he was at the mouth of the Wabash; and on the 8th was taken prisoner by a party of Indians. Upon the 15th he reached Vincennes, which he describes as a "village of about eighty or ninety French families." We regret that our limits will not allow us to make some extracts from his journal. Croghan discharged the duties committed to his care with energy, and to the satisfaction of his principal. The information obtained was both valuable and important.

# CHAPTER II. TITLES TO WESTERN LANDS.

Thus stood matters in the west at the close of 1765. With the exception of a few military posts, and an occasional pioneer settler, all was an unbroken wilderness between the Alleghanies and the Wabash. The Red man, a few years since the undisputed owner of the broad prairies and fertile valleys, inherited from his father, now found himself the dependent of a foreign power; and it should therefore, not seem strange, if he felt and expressed both fear and hatred of the influence which surrounded and oppressed him.

The Indians had witnessed the silent encroachments of England; and despairing of holding or regaining their lands, the most bitter and abiding spirit of hatred and revenge was roused within them. They had seen the British coming to take their lands upon the strength of treaties they knew not of. They had been compelled to receive into their midst British agents and troops, who, although promising to protect them from settlers, the Indians very well knew would prove an empty bond if circumstances required a different line of policy.

Facts subsequently proved that the apprehensions of the Indians were not groundless, and that the pledge given them was not in good faith kept by either individuals or the government. As we have noticed elsewhere, settlements were made upon lands, to which the Indian title had not been extinguished, in the year following the treaty of German Flats; and although Sir William Johnson issued his orders for the removal of these settlers, his commands were defied, and the settlers remained where they were.

But not only were the sturdy pioneers passing the line tacitly agreed on, Sir William Johnson himself was clearly meditating a step which would have produced, had it been taken, a general Indian war.

This was the purchase and settlement of an immense tract south of the Ohio river, where an independent colony was to be formed. How early this plan was conceived we do not learn; but, from Franklin's letters, we find that it was in contemplation in the spring of 1766. At this time Franklin was in London, and was written to by his son, Governor Franklin, of New Jersey, with regard to the proposed colony. The plan seems to have been, to buy of the Six Nations the lands south of the Ohio, a purchase which it was not doubted Sir William might make, and then to procure from the King a grant of as much territory as the company, which it was intended to form, would require. Governor Franklin, accordingly, forwarded to his father an application for a grant, together with a letter from Sir William, recommending the plan to the ministry; all of which was duly communicated to the proper department. But at that time there were various interests bearing upon this plan of Franklin. The old Ohio company was still suing, through its agent Colonel George Mercer, for a perfection of the original grant. The soldiers claiming under Dinwiddie's proclamation had their tales of rights and grievances. Individuals, to whom grants had been made by Virginia, wished them completed. General Lyman, from Connecticut we believe, was soliciting a new grant similar to that now asked by Franklin; and the ministers themselves were divided as to the policy and propriety of establishing any settlements so far in the interior, Shelburne being in favor of the new colony, Hillsborough opposed to it.

The company was organized, however, and the nominally leading man therein being Mr. Thomas Walpole, a London banker of eminence, it was known as the Walpole Company. Franklin continued privately to make friends among the ministry, and to press upon them the policy of making large settlements in the west; and, as the old way of managing the Indians by superintendents was just then in bad odor in consequence of the expense attending it, the Cabinet Council so far approved the new plan as to present it for examination to the Board of Trade, with members of which Franklin had also been privately conversing.

This was in the autumn of 1767. But before any conclusion was come to, it was necessary to arrange definitely that boundary line, which had been vaguely talked of in 1765, and with respect to which Sir William Johnson had written to the ministry, who had mislaid his letters, and given him no instructions. The necessity of arranging this boundary was also kept in mind by the continued and growing irritation of the Indians, who found themselves invaded from every side. This irritation became so great during the autumn of 1767, that Gage wrote to the Governor of Pennsylvania on the subject. The Governor communicated his letter to the Assembly on the 5th of January, 1768, and representations were at once sent to England, expressing the necessity of having the Indian line fixed. Franklin, the father, all this time, was urging the same necessity upon the ministers in England; and about Christmas of 1767, Sir William's letters on the subject having been found, orders were sent him to complete the proposed purchase from the Six Nations, and settle all differences. But the project for a colony was for the time dropped, a new administration coming in which was not that way disposed.

Sir William Johnson having received, early in the spring, the orders from England relative to a new treaty with the Indians, at once took steps to secure a full attendance. Notice was given to the various colonial governments, to the Six Nations, the Delawares, and the Shawanese, and a congress was appointed to meet at Fort Stanwix during the following October (1768). It met upon the 24th of that month, and was attended by representatives from New Jersey, Virginia, and Pennsylvania; by Sir William and his deputies; by the agents of those traders who had suffered in the war of 1763; and by deputies from all the Six Nations, the Delawares and the Shawanese. The first point to be settled was the boundary line which was to determine the Indian lands of the west from that time forward; and this line the Indians, upon the 1st of November, stated should begin on the Ohio, at the mouth of the Cherokee (or Tennessee) river; thence go up the Ohio and Alleghany to Kittaning; thence across to the Susquehannah, &c.; whereby the whole country south of the Ohio and Alleghany, to which the Six Nations had any claim, was transferred to the British. One deed for a part of this land, was made on the 3d of November to William Trent, attorney for twenty-two traders, whose goods had been destroyed by the Indians in 1763. The tract conveyed by this was between the Kanawha and Monongahela, and was by the traders named Indiana. Two days afterwards, a deed for the remaining western lands was made to the King, and the price agreed on paid down.' These deeds were made upon the express agreement that no claim should ever be based upon previous treaties, those of Lancaster, Logstown, &c.; and they were signed by the chiefs of the Six Nations, for themselves, their allies and dependents, the Shawanese, Delawares, Mingoes of Ohio, and others; but the Shawanese and Delaware deputies present did not sign them.

Such was the treaty of Stanwix, whereon, in a great measure, rests the title by purchase to Western Virginia, Pennsylvania, and Kentucky. It was a better foundation, perhaps, than that given by previous treaties, but was essentially worthless; for the lands conveyed were not occupied or hunted on by those conveying them. In truth, we cannot doubt that this immense grant was obtained by the influence of Sir William Johnson, in order that the new colony, of which he was to be governor, might be founded there.

The fact that such a country was ceded voluntarily, — not after a war, not by hard persuasion, but at once and willingly, — satisfies us that the whole affair had been previously settled with the New York savages, and that the Ohio Indians had no voice in the matter.

But besides the claim of the Iroquois and the north-west Indians to Kentucky, it was also claimed by the Cherokees; and it is worthy of remembrance that after the treaty of Lochaber, made in October, 1770, two years after the Stanwix treaty recognized a title in the southern Indians to all the country west from a line drawn from a point six miles east of Big or Long Island, in Holsten river, to the mouth of the great Kanawha; although, as we have just stated, their right to all the lands north and east of the Kentucky river was purchased by Colonel Donaldson, either for the king, Virginia, or himself— it is impossible to say which.

But the grant of the great northern confederacy was made. The white man could now quiet his conscience when driving the native from his forest home, and feel sure that an army would back his pretensions, A new company was at once organized in Virginia, called the "Mississippi Company," and a petition sent to the King for two millions and a half of acres in the west. Among the signers of this were Francis Lightfoot Lee, Richard Henry Lee, George Washington, and Arthur Lee. The gentleman last named was the agent for the petitioners in England. This application was referred to the Board of Trade on the 9th of March, 1769, and after that we hear nothing of it.

The Board of Trade was, however, again called on to report upon the application of the Walpole Company, and Lord Hillsborough, the president, reported against it. This called out Franklin's celebrated "Ohio Settlement," a paper written with so much ability, that the King's council put by the official report, and granted the petition, a step which mortified the noble lord so much that he resigned his official station. The petition now needed only the royal sanction, which was not given until August 14th, 1772; but in 1770, the Ohio Company was merged in Walpole's, and the claims of the soldiers of 1756 being acknowledged both by the new company and by government, all claims were quieted. Nothing was ever done, however, under the grant to Walpole, the Revolution soon coming upon America. After the Revolution, Mr. Walpole and his associates petitioned Congress respecting their lands, called by them "Vandalia," but could get no help from that body. What was finally done by Virginia with the claims of this and other companies, we do not find written, but presume their lands were all looked on as forfeited.

During the ten years in which Franklin, Pownall, and their friends were trying to get the great western land company into operation, actual settlers were crossing the mountains all too rapidly; for the Ohio Indians "viewed the settlements with an uneasy and jealous eye," and "did not scruple to say, that they must be compensated for their right, if people settled thereon, notwithstanding the cession by the Six Nations." It has been said, also, that Lord Dunmore, then governor of Virginia, authorized surveys and settlements on the western lands, notwithstanding the proclamation of 1763; but Mr. Sparks gives us a letter from him, in which this is expressly denied. However, surveyors did go down even to the Falls of the Ohio, and the whole region south of the Ohio was filling with white men. The futility of the Fort Stanwix treaty, and the ignorance or contempt of it by the fierce Shawanese are well seen in the meeting between them and Bullitt, one of the early emigrants, in 1733. Bullitt, on his way down the Ohio, stopped, and singly sought the savages at one of their towns. He then told them of his proposed settlement, and his wish to live at peace with them; and said, that, as they had received nothing under the treaty of 1768, it was intended to make them presents the next year. The Indians considered the talk of the Long-knife, and the next day agreed to his proposed settlement, provided he did not disturb them in their hunting south of the Ohio; a provision wholly inconsistent with the Stanwix deed.

Among the earlier operators in western lands was Washington. He had always regarded the proclamation of 1763 as a mere temporary expedient to quiet the savages; and, being better acquainted with the value of western lands than most of those who could command means, he early began to buy beyond the mountains. His agent in selecting lands was the unfortunate Col. Crawford, afterwards burnt by the Indians. In September, 1767, we find Washington writing to Crawford on this subject, and looking forward to the occupation of the western territory; in 1770, he crossed the mountains, going down the Ohio to the mouth of the great Kanhawa; and in 1773 being entitled, under the king's proclamation of 1763, (which gave a bounty to officers and soldiers who had served in the French war,) to ten thousand acres of land, he became deeply interested in the country beyond the mountains, and had some correspondence respecting the importation of settlers from Europe. Indeed, had not the Revolutionary war been just then on the eve of breaking out, Washington would in all probability have become the leading settler of the West, and all our history, perhaps, have been changed.

But while in England and along the Atlantic, men were talking of peopling the west south of the river Ohio, a few obscure individuals, unknown to Walpole, to Franklin, and to Washington, were taking those steps which actually resulted in its settlement.

# CHAPTER III. THE WAR OF 1774 — ITS COMMENCEMENT.

The Mingoes, Shawanese and other powerful western tribes, feeling that they had been slighted in the Stanwix treaty — their rights disregarded, their homes invaded, and their hunting grounds wrested from them, — showed symptoms of great dissatisfaction, which the more observing of the settlers were not long in detecting. A deep and bitter feeling was evidently setting in against the whites: but still, the Indians remembered the war of 1763, and the terrible power of Britain. The older and wiser of the sufferers seemed rather disposed to submit to what seemed inevitable, than throw themselves away in a vain effort to withstand the power and influence which was exerted against them. Hopeless hatred, it will thus be perceived, filled the breasts of the natives at the period immediately preceding the war of 1774; a hatred needing only a few acts of violence to kindle it into rage and thirst for human blood. And such acts were not wanting; in addition to the murder of several single Indians by the frontier men, in 1772, five families of the natives on the Little Kanawha, were killed, in revenge for the death of a white family on Gauley river, although no evidence existed to prove who had committed the last-named outrage. And when 1774 came, a series of events, of which we can present but a faint outline, led to excessive exasperation on both sides. Pennsylvania and Virginia laid equal claim to Pittsburgh and the adjoining country. In the war of 1754, doubt had existed as to which colony the fork of the Ohio was situated in, and the Old Dominion having been forward in the defence of the contested territory, while her northern neighbor had been very backward in doing anything in its favor, the Virginians felt a certain claim upon the "Key of the West." This feeling showed itself before 1763, and by 1773 appears to have attained a very decided character. Early in 1774, Lord Dunmore, prompted very probably by Colonel Croghan, and his nephew, Dr. John Conolly, who had lived at Fort Pitt, and was an intriguing and ambitious man, determined, by strong measures, to assert the claims of Virginia upon Pittsburgh and its vicinity, and despatched Connolly, with a captain's commission, and with power to take possession of the country upon the Monongahela, in the name of the king. He issued his proclamation to the people, in the neighborhood of Redstone and Pittsburgh, calling upon them to meet upon the 24th and 25th of January, 1774, in order to be embodied as Virginia militia. Arthur St. Clair, who then represented the proprietors of Pennsylvania in the west, was at Pittsburgh at the time, and arrested Connolly before the meeting took place.

Connolly, soon after, was for a short time released by the sheriff, upon the promise to return to the law's custody, which promise he broke however; and having collected a band of followers, on the 28th of March came again to Pittsburgh, still asserting the claim of Virginia to the government. Then commenced a series of contests, outrages and complaints, which were too extensive and complicated to be described within our limited space. The upshot of the matter was this, that Connolly, in Lord Dunmore's name, and by his authority, took and kept possession of Fort Pitt; and as it had been dismantled and nearly destroyed by royal orders, rebuilt it, and named it Fort Dunmore.

At the time of issuing his proclamation, he wrote to the settlers along the Ohio, that the Shawanese were not to be trusted; that they had declared open hostility to the whites; and he (Connolly) desired all to be in readiness to redress any grievances that would occur. One of these circulars was addressed to Captain Michael Cresap, then at or near Wheeling.

A few days previous to the date of Connolly's letter (April 21,) a canoe loaded with goods for the Shawanese towns, the property of a Pittsburgh merchant named Butler, had been attacked by three Cherokee Indians, about sixty miles above, and one of the whites killed. This of course caused considerable sensation in the neighborhood of Wheeling. The people, too, aroused by the false cry of Connolly, became greatly excited; and when, a few days after, it was reported that a boat containing Indians was coming down the river, a resolution was at once taken to attack them.

Several men, one of whom it is alleged was Captain Cresap, started up the river, and firing upon the canoe, killed two Indians, whom they scalped. On the following day several canoes containing Indians were discovered a short distance above the island. Pursuit was immediately given; and that night, while the Indians were encamped near the mouth of Captina creek, twenty miles below Wheeling, the whites attacked them, killing one and wounding several of the company.

These were clearly the exciting causes to the war of 1774. It is true, however, as already stated, the magazine was charged, and needed but the match to produce instantaneous explosion. That match was fired by the murderer's torch at Captina and Yellow creek, (presently to be noticed,) and dreadful was the effect of that explosion.

A question of some importance now arises — one which we would fain avoid, but which our duty compels us to meet — and that is, what part did Captain Cresap take in the outset of this war? Most unfortunately for the memory of a brave and chivalrous soldier, his name has become so blended with the principal events of this dark page in our history, that it seems an almost hopeless task to controvert any of the points made by previous writers upon the subject.

So intimately associated has been Captain Cresap's name with these unfortunate and tragical occurrences, that this bloody record in our history — the war of 1774, has been, and by many still is, styled "Cresap's war."

Viewing the whole matter with a mind free from bias, or if prejudiced at all, confessedly in favor of the arraigned, we candidly acknowledge that the evidence before us bears strongly against him in the affairs at Wheeling and Captina; but wholly exculpates him from any participation in the diabolical transaction at Yellow creek. This we think the extent of his guilt, in the occurrences which led to the fierce and sanguinary conflict between the natives and whites on our western border, in the summer and fall of 1774.

Whilst upon this subject, we may take occasion to state, that in our opinion one unfortunate error has been committed by most, if not all, of Captain Cresap's friends, and that has been, in not stating exactly what he did. It cannot but have been known to Mr. Jacob and others, who have set up as the special defenders of Captain Cresap, that he did make one of the party who killed the two Indians near Wheeling, and also that he was engaged in the affair at Captina. Concealment of these facts has done irreparable injustice to the memory of a brave and gallant soldier. Had they conceded this much, but insisted upon his innocence of that other heinous charge, most of the calumny now afloat would have been saved, and the memory of Captain Cresap not been tarnished by that one foul stain, from the mere contemplation of which, civilized man turns with an involuntary shudder. This, we conceive, has been the fatal error. A uniform denial, for Captain Cresap, of all participation in the border outrages of 1774, left no alternative with those who knew differently, but to believe that he was connected with all.

Captain Cresap's known and avowed participation in the affairs at Wheeling and Captina, and the murder of Logan's family at Baker's bottom so soon thereafter, very reasonably caused many to believe that he did compose one of the latter party.

Logan thought so himself; and so asserted, not only in his celebrated speech at Camp Charlotte, but also in other oral and written declarations.

We come now to the last, and by far the most tragic part of this drama. George Rogers Clark, one of the most distinguished men of his day in the west, was at Wheeling at the time of these occurrences. It is not likely that such a man would be mistaken, and we therefore give his statement almost entire. It is from a letter written in June, 1798, to a friend of Mr. Jefferson, who sought information as to the affairs to which it refers.

This country was explored in 1773. A resolution was formed to make a settlement the spring following, and the mouth of the Little Kanawha appointed the place of general rendezvous, in order to descend the river from thence in a body. Early in the spring the Indians had done some mischief. Reports from their towns were alarming, which deterred many. About eighty or ninety men only arrived at the appointed rendezvous, where we lay some days.

A small party of hunters, that lay about ten miles below us, were fired upon by the Indians, whom the hunters beat back, and returned to camp. This and many other circumstances led us to believe that the Indians were determined on war. The whole party was enrolled and determined to execute their project of forming a settlement in Kentucky, as we had every necessary store that could be thought of. An Indian town called the Horsehead Bottom, on the Scioto and near its mouth, lay nearly in our way. The determination was to cross the country and surprise it. Who was to command? was the question. There were but few among us that had experience in Indian warfare, and they were such that we did not choose to be commanded by. We knew of Capt. Cresap being on the river about fifteen miles above us, with some hands, settling a plantation; and that he had concluded to follow us to. Kentucky as soon as he had fixed there his people. We also knew that he had been experienced in a former war. He was proposed; and it was unanimously agreed to send for him to command the party. Messengers were despatched, and in half an hour returned with Cresap. He had heard of our resolution by some of his hunters, that had fallen in with ours, and had set out to come to us.

We now thought our army, as we called it, complete, and the destruction of the Indians sure. A council was called, and, to our astonishment, our intended commander-in-chief was the person who dissuaded us from the enterprise. He said that appearances were very suspicious, hut there was no certainty of a war. That if we made the attempt proposed, he had no doubt of our success; but a war would, at any rate, be the result, and that we should be blamed for it, and perhaps justly. But if we were determined to proceed, he would lay aside all considerations, send to his camp for his people, and share our fortunes.

He was then asked what he would advise. His answer was, that we should return to Wheeling as a convenient post, to hear what was going forward. That a few weeks would determine. As it was early in the spring, if we found the Indians were not disposed for war, we should have full time to return and make our establishment in Kentucky. This was adopted; and in two hours the whole were under way. As we ascended the river, we met Kill-buck, an Indian chief, with a small party. We had a long conference with him, but received little satisfaction as to the disposition of the Indians. It was observed that Cresap did not come to this conference, but kept on the opposite side of the river. He said that he was afraid to trust himself with the Indians. That Kill-buck had frequently attempted to waylay his father, to kill him. That if he crossed the river, perhaps his fortitude might fail him, and that he might put Kill-buck to death. On our arrival at Wheeling, (the country being pretty well settled thereabouts,) the whole of the inhabitants appeared to be alarmed. They flocked to our camp from every direction; and all that we could say could not keep them from under our wings. We offered to cover their neighborhood with scouts, until further information, if they would return to their plantations; but nothing would prevail. By this time we had got to be a formidable party. All the hunters, men without families, etc., in that quarter, had joined our party.

Our arrival at Wheeling was soon known at Pittsburgh. The whole of that country, at that time, being under the jurisdiction of Virginia, Dr. Connolly had been appointed by Dunmore, Captain Commandant of the District, which was called Wagusta. He, learning of us, sent a message addressed to the party, letting us know that war was to be apprehended, and requesting that we would keep our position for a few days; as messages had been sent to the Indians, and a few days would determine the doubt. The answer he got, was, that we had no inclination to quit our quarters for some time. That during our stay we should be careful that the enemy did not harass the neighborhood that we lay in. But before this answer could reach Pittsburgh, he sent a second express, addressed to Capt. Cresap, as the most influential man amongst us, informing him that the messages had returned from the Indians, that war was inevitable, and begging him to use his influence with the party, to get them to cover the country by scouts until the inhabitants could fortify themselves. The reception of this letter was the epoch of open hostilities with the Indians. A new post was planted, a council was called, and the letter read by Cresap, all the Indian traders being summoned on so important an occasion. Action was had, and war declared in the most solemn manner; and the same evening two scalps were brought into camp.

The next day some canoes of Indians were discovered on the river, keeping the advantage of an island to cover themselves from our view. They were chased fifteen miles down the river, and driven ashore. A battle ensued; a few were wounded on both sides; one Indian only taken prisoner. On examining their canoes, we found a considerable quantity of ammunition and other warlike stores. On our return to camp, a resolution was adopted to march the next day, and attack Logan's camp on the Ohio about thirty miles above us. We did march about five miles, and then halted to take some refreshment. Here the impropriety of executing the projected enterprise was argued. The conversation was brought forward by Cresap himself. It was generally agreed that those Indians had no hostile intentions — as they were hunting, and their party were composed of men, women, and children, with all their stuff with them. This we knew; as I myself and others present had been in their camp about four weeks past, on our descending the river from Pittsburgh. In short, every person seemed to detest the resolution we had set out with. We returned in the evening, decamped, and took the road to Redstone.

It was two days after this that Logan's family were killed. And from the manner in which it was done, it was viewed as a horrid murder. From Logan's hearing of Cresap being at the head of this party on the river, it is no wonder that he supposed he had a hand in the destruction of his family.

# CHAPTER IV. WAPPATOMICA CAMPAIGN.

Well aware that a retaliatory blow would be given by the Indians, the settlers along the frontier of Virginia lost no time in erecting forts for their protection. An express was sent to Williamsburg, calling upon the governor for immediate aid; the House of Burgesses being in session, measures were at once adopted to protect the frontier and drive back the savages. Andrew Lewis, then a member from Bottetourt, proposed that an adequate force be raised and marched to the frontier with the least possible delay. His proposition was at once adopted and steps taken for carrying it into effect. In the meantime, the Indians were murdering the whites whenever an opportunity presented. Many of the traders who had penetrated the Indian country, could not retrace their steps in time, and thus fell before the merciless hand of the destroyer. One of these, near the town of White-eyes, the Peace Chief of the Delawares, was murdered, cut to pieces, and the fragments of his body hung upon the bushes, the kindly chief gathered them together and buried them. The hatred of the murderers, however, led them to disinter and disperse the remains of their victim anew; but the kindness of the Delaware was as persevering as the hatred of his brethren, and again he collected the scattered limbs and in a secret place hid them.

As considerable time must necessarily elapse before a large force could be collected and marched from the east, it was proposed, as the best means of diverting the Indians from the frontier, that an invading force should be sent against their towns. Accordingly, about the middle of June, (1774,) nearly four hundred men rendezvoused at Wheeling, embracing some of the most energetic and experienced on the frontier. Col. Angus McDonald, by whom this force was to be commanded, not having arrived, but being daily expected, the different companies under their respective commanders, went down the river in boats to the mouth of Captina creek, (twenty miles), at which place they were joined by Colonel McDonald, and thence proceeded to the Indian town, Wappatomica, which was ten or fifteen miles below the present Coshocton. In the command of Col. McDonald were some of the first and bravest men in the west. James Wood, afterwards Governor of Virginia, Daniel Morgan, the distinguished general of revolutionary memory, Michael Cresap, and others who became prominent, commanded companies. The expedition was piloted by Jonathan Zane, Thomas Nicholson and Tady Kelly, the first of whom had no superior as a woodcraftman.

The Indians having been notified by scouts of their approach, formed an ambush, and as the whites came up, opened upon them a brisk and stunning fire. But two of our men, however, were killed, although several were badly wounded. The Indians had one killed and a number wounded, but their exact loss was not ascertained, as both wounded and dead were borne from the field. A never failing characteristic of the dying savage is, a desire that his body may not fall into the hands of his pale-faced antagonist.

The army after this slight interruption, proceeded on its way to the Indian town, which was found evacuated. It was immediately discovered that the Indians were concealed on the opposite side of the river, waiting for the whites to cross. Col. McDonald determined to remain where he was, but took the precaution to despatch messengers up and down the river, to watch if the enemy should attempt to cross.

The Indians finding the whites would not follow in pursuit, sued for peace. This was offered on condition that they sent over their chiefs as hostages. Five accordingly crossed over. Early on the following morning these chiefs were marched in front of the army to the western bank of the river.

It was then ascertained that the Indians could not treat until the chiefs of the other tribes were present. To secure these, one of the hostage chiefs was sent off; but not returning in time, a second was despatched on the same errand, and he not returning, Col. McDonald, who now began to suspect treachery, marched his army rapidly against the upper towns (one and a half miles distant), when it was found that the inhabitants had also been removed. A slight skirmish with a concealed body of Indians here took place, in which one of the enemy was killed and one of our men wounded. Colonel McDonald now ordered the towns to be burned and the crops destroyed. The army returned to Wheeling and was disbanded. The three remaining hostages were sent to Williamsburg, where they were kept until after the treaty of Dunmore, in November following.

The army suffered much from want of provisions. Each man was put upon an allowance of one ear of corn per day.

This invasion did little in the way of intimidating the savages. They continued to collect their forces, and pushed forward at the same time, predatory bands, to the great annoyance of the settlers along the Ohio, Monongahela and their tributaries.

One of the first of these marauding parties was headed by Logan, who, burning with revenge for the murder of his family, had "raised the hatchet," and sworn vengeance against the guilty.

# CHAPTER V. DUNMORE'S CAMPAIGN.

In the east, the effort to organize a force sufficient to operate with effect against the savages, proved successful, and two bodies, numbering in all nearly twenty-five hundred, were collected, — one in the counties of Augusta, Bottetourt, &c., and the other in Frederick, Shenandoah, &c.

The first of these was placed under the command of General Andrew Lewis, who rendezvoused at Camp Union, now Lewisburg, while the governor in person commanded the second.

By the 1st of September, General Lewis only awaited the arrival of Col. Christian, and orders from Lord Dunmore, to march. In a few days a messenger reached him with orders from Dunmore to meet him on the 2d of October, at the mouth of Kanawha. On the 11th, he struck his tents and commenced the line of march through an unknown and trackless wilderness.

The division of General Lewis numbered between one thousand and twelve hundred men, composed of the very flower of the Virginia Valley.

Captain Arbuckle, an experienced and skilful frontier-man, conducted the division to the river, which they reached on the 30th, after a fatiguing march of nineteen days.

General Lewis was greatly disappointed in not meeting Dunmore, and still more in not hearing from him. It was not until the morning of the 9th, that a messenger reached him, bringing information that the plan of the campaign had been changed, and ordering him to march direct to the Indian towns on the Scioto, where the other division would join him. Arrangements were accordingly made preparatory to leaving, and on the following morning, (Monday, October 10th,) Gen. Lewis intended moving, as directed. Shortly after daybreak, on the morning referred to, two soldiers who had gone up the Ohio to hunt, discovered a large body of Indians just rising from their encampment. The men were fired upon and one killed, but the other escaping returned to camp, hallooing as he ran, that he had seen "a body of Indians covering four acres of ground."

All was, of course, surprise and confusion m the camp of the whites, but the commander-in-chief, "calm as a summer morning," lighted his pipe with the utmost sang froid, and ordered out the regiment under Col. Lewis, supposing that the discovery of the soldiers was merely that of a scouting party of Indians, similar to such as had watched the movements of the army since leaving Fort Savannah.

Colonel Lewis had barely passed the outer guard, when the enemy in great number appeared and commenced the attack. Col. Fleming was now ordered to reinforce Col. Lewis, and soon the battle raged with unparalleled fury. The sun had just risen, and was gilding with his bright autumnal tints the tops of the surrounding hills when the battle commenced, and not until it had sunk low in the heavens, did the sanguinary conflict materially abate.

Colonel Lewis was mortally wounded at an early hour in the engagement, but with a resolute devotion rarely equalled, concealed the character of his wound until the line of battle had been fairly formed. He then sunk exhausted from loss of blood, and was carried to his tent, where he died about twelve o'clock. A braver, truer or more gallant soldier the country has rarely produced; and it is a burning shame that his memory, as well as that of the brave men who fell with him, has not been perpetuated in some appropriate and enduring form on the scene of this memorable conflict.

On the fall of Col. Lewis, the line of his men stretching along the high ground skirting Crooked run, which was the first attacked and had sustained the heaviest fire, gave symptoms of irresolution, and momentarily did fall back; but Col. Fleming speedily rallying them, maintained the fortunes of the day until he, too, was struck down and borne bleeding from the field.

The troops now gave way, and in all probability would have been routed had not Gen. Lewis ordered up Col. Field with a fresh reinforcement. This command met the retreating troops and rallied them to the contest. The fight now became more desperate than ever, and was maintained by both parties with consummate skill, energy and valor. The Indians, sure of success when they beheld the ranks give way after the fall of Lewis and Fleming, became frantic with rage when they saw the reinforcement under Col. Field. With convulsive grasp they seized their weapons, and would have rushed headlong upon the whites had the latter not kept up a steady and most galling fire, which seemed to have the double effect of thinning their ranks and cooling their rage. The battle scene was now terribly grand. There stood the combatants; terror, rage, disappointment and despair riveted upon the painted faces of one, while calm resolution, and the unbending will to do, were strongly and unmistakably marked upon the other. Neither party, says an eye-witness, would retreat; neither could advance. The noise of the firing was tremendous. No single gun could be distinguished, but it was one constant roar. The rifle and tomahawk now did their work with dreadful certainty. The confusion and perturbation of the camp had now arrived at its greatest height. The confused noise and wild uproar of battle added greatly to the terror of the scene. The shouting of the whites, the continual roar of fire-arms, the war-whoop and dismal yelling of the Indians, sounds harsh and grating when heard separately, became by mixture and combination highly discordant and terrific. Add to this the constant succession of the dead and wounded, brought off from the battle-field, many of these with shattered limbs and lacerated flesh, pale, ghastly and disfigured, and besmeared with gore, their 'garments rolled in blood,' and uttering doleful cries of lamentation and distress; others faint, feeble and exhausted by loss of blood, scarcely able with quivering lips to tell their ail to passers-by. Sounds and sights and circumstances such as these were calculated to excite general solicitude for the issue of the battle, and alarm in each individual for his own personal safety. Early in the day General Lewis had ordered a breast-work to be constructed from the Ohio to the Kanawha, thus severing the camp from the neighboring forest. This breast-work was formed by felling trees and so disposing of their trunks and branches, as to form a barrier which was difficult to pass. It was designed that should the enemy gain an ascendancy in the field, this barrier might prevent their entrance into the camp, while at the same time it might serve as a protection to the garrison that was within."

About twelve o'clock the Indian fire began to slacken, and the enemy were seen slowly to retire. A desultory fire was kept up from behind trees; and often, as the Virginians pressed too hotly upon the retreating foe, were they fatally ambuscaded.

Gen. Lewis, noticing the manoeuvres of the enemy, detached three companies commanded respectively by Captains John Stuart, George Matthews and Isaac Shelby, with orders to move quietly beneath the banks of the Kanawha and Crooked run, so as to gain the enemy's rear.

This manoeuvre was so handsomely executed that the savages became alarmed, and fairly gave up the fight about 4 o'clock. The victory of the Virginians was complete. During the night the Indian army crossed the Ohio, and made off. The gradual retreat of the Indians was one of the most masterly things of the kind ever undertaken in the west. Cornstalk alternately led on his men, and then fell back in such a manner as to hold the whites in check and uncertainty. Between 11 o'clock A. M. and 4 p. M., the Indian army fell back more than three miles. This gave them an opportunity to bear offf their wounded and dead.

This battle scene, in an unbroken wilderness on the Ohio, is described as having been one of the most thrilling affairs that ever took place on our western frontier. The line of battle was at times nearly a mile long, and often throughout its entire length gleamed the blended flame from Indian and provincial rifles.

The Indians, under the lead of experienced and able chiefs, were confident of success, and fought with a desperation which no language can describe.

The exact losses sustained by the respective parties were never fully ascertained, as the Indians were known to have thrown many of their dead into the Ohio. Their loss has been estimated at about one hundred and fifty, while that of the provincials in killed and wounded was over two hundred; more than one-fourth of the whole number actually engaged. The annals of history do not show another instance where undisciplined troops held out so successfully and for so long a time against a foe vastly their numerical superior.

At least one hundred of Gen. Lewis' men were absent, hunting, and knew nothing of the battle until evening.

The Indian army was composed principally of Delawares, Mingos, Iroquois, Wyandotts and Shawanese. It was commanded by Cornstock, the celebrated and noble-minded Shawanese chief, whose melancholy end at the same place on a subsequent occasion, and under circumstances of the most revolting treachery, cannot be dwelt upon, even at this late day, without feelings of melancholy regret.

Logan assisted in the command, and burned to revenge the past wrongs which he had received at the hands of the "Long-knives."

In this prolonged and bloody battle the brave Virginians suffered terribly. Of the killed were Colonels Lewis, and Field,, Captains Morrow, Buford, Ward, Murray, Cundiff, Wilson and McClenachan; Lieutenants Allen, Goldsby and Dillon, with many gallant subalterns, whose names we have not been able to ascertain.

The Indian army is said to have comprised the pick of the northern confederated tribes. Cornstock's towering form was seen rapidly hurrying through their midst, and every now and anon, when he found the spirits of his men were flagging, was heard to exclaim in his native tongue, "Be strong! be strong!" One of his warriors showing signs of fear, the savage chieftain slew him at the moment with his tomahawk.

Gen. Lewis having buried his dead, and thrown up a rude fortress for the protection of the wounded, which he gave in charge of a sufficient force; crossed the Ohio to meet Dunmore at the point designated. He moved rapidly forward, and in an unprecedented short period reached the Pickawy plains. Here he was met by a message from Dunmore, ordering him to stop, as he (Dunmore) was about negotiating a treaty of peace with the Indians. Indignant at the manner he had been treated, and finding himself threatened by a superior force of Indians, who kept constantly in his rear, General Lewis disregarded the earl's orders, and pushed on.

A second flag was now sent, but treating it as he had done the first. Gen. Lewis continued to advance until he had reached within three miles of the governor's camp. Dunmore now became uneasy, and accompanied by White-Eyes, a noted Indian chief, visited Gen. Lewis, and peremptorily ordered him to halt. It is asserted by some, that at this juncture it was with much difficulty Gen. Lewis could restrain his men from killing Dunmore and his Indian companion.

Gen. Lewis' orders were to return forthwith to Point Pleasant; there to leave a force sufficient to protect the place, and a supply of provisions for the wounded, then to lead the balance of the division to the place of rendezvous, and disband them. Dunmore returned to camp Charlotte, and concluded a treaty with the Indians. The chief speaker on the part of the Indians was Cornstalk, who openly charged the whites with being the sole cause of the war, enumerating the many provocations which the Indians had received, and dwelling with great force and emphasis upon the diabolical murder of Logan's family. This great chief spoke in the most vehement and denunciatory style. His loud, clear voice was distinctly heard over the whole camp of twelve acres. Cornstalk had from the first, opposed a war with the whites, and when his scouts reported the advance of Gen. Lewis' division, the sagacious chief did all he could to restrain his men, and keep them from battle. But all his remonstrances were in vain, and it was then he told them, "As you are determined to fight, you shall fight." After their defeat, and return home, a council was convened to determine upon what was next to be done. The stern old chief rising, said, "What shall we do now? The Long-knives are coming upon us by two routes. Shall we turn out and fight them?" No response being made, he continued,

"Shall we kill all our squaws and children, and then fight until we are all killed ourselves?" Still the congregated warriors were silent, and after a moment's hesitation. Cornstalk struck his tomahawk into the war post, and with compressed lips and flashing eye, gazed around the assembled group, then with great emphasis spoke, "Since you are not inclined to fight, I will go and make peace."

This distinguished chief was one of the most remarkable men his race has ever produced. He possessed in an eminent degree all the elements of true greatness. Colonel Wilson, who was present at the interview between the chief and Lord Dunmore, thus speaks of the chieftain's bearing.

But there was one who would not attend the camp of Lord Dunmore, and that was Logan. The Mingoe chief felt the chill of despair at his heart; his very soul seemed frozen within him; and although he would not interpose obstacles to an amicable adjustment of existing difficulties, still he could not meet the Long-knives in council as if no terrible stain of blood rested upon their hands. He remained at a distance, brooding in melancholy silence over his accumulated wrongs during most of the time his friends were negotiating. But Dunmore felt the importance of at least securing his assent; and for that purpose sent a special messenger, Colonel John Gibson, who waited upon the chief at his wigwam.

The messenger in due time returned, bringing with him the celebrated speech which has given its author an immortality, almost as imperishable as that of the great Athenian orator.

It is due perhaps, in candor, to state that the authenticity of this celebrated speech has been questioned. To all, however, who have examined the testimony carefully, and with an unprejudiced eye, the conclusions in favor of its genuineness are overwhelming. A great deal of unnecessary bitterness has been shown by friends for and against this simple but touching appeal of the native chieftain. The friends of Cresap, feeling that he had been undeservedly reproached, were not willing to let his memory rest under the charges; while on the other hand, Mr. Jefferson and his friends, conceiving that his veracity had been attacked, exhibited much warmth and determination to establish the charge by confirming the speech.

But, the question of authenticity, we think should not depend upon the extent of Cresap's participation in the crime charged by Logan. As stated elsewhere, Logan was deceived as to the facts. Cresap, at that time, was one of the most prominent men on the frontier, and was known to have taken an active and energetic part in the defence of the settlements. He was known to have been engaged in the Captina affair, and is it therefore strange that he should have been charged with this third, or Yellow creek murder, occurring as it did only a few days after that at Captina? The circumstances certainly were strongly against him, and nothing but such a statement as that of Col. Clark, now submitted, could have availed to rescue his memory from the heavy reproach which was fast settling upon it. We therefore repeat, that it was not strange Logan should have been deceived. According to Doddridge, many of the settlers — those living in the neighborhood, and whose opportunities should have enabled them to know the facts, were mislead.

Mr. Jefferson, we think, at a very early day, had his confidence in the fullness of the charge against Cresap considerably shaken. The late John Caldwell of Wheeling creek, one of the earliest settlers in Ohio county, was one of the persons to whom Mr. Jefferson made application for facts concerning the unfortunate affair at Yellow creek. The affidavit which he gave, but which was never published, went far to exculpate Cresap from all immediate participation in that melancholy affair. But, we again repeat, whatever may have been Cresap's connection with the Yellow creek murder, it should not materially affect the genuineness of Logan's speech. He felt and believed that Cresap was the man, and so declared. If mistaken in the perpetrator, why should that one single error militate against the entire production?

But, to return from this digression. A treaty was concluded at Camp Charlotte, in the month of November, and the war known as Dunmore's, Cresap's, and Logan's terminated. By this, the Shawanese agreed not to molest travellers, or hunt south of the Ohio River. The termination of this war greatly dissatisfied the Virginians, who had marched many hundred miles through an unbroken wilderness to chastise the savages. Now that they were within their grasp, and about to strike an effective blow, to be thus compelled to return on the mere feint of a treaty, was, to them, entirely inexplicable.

The conduct of Dunmore could not be understood except by supposing him to act with reference to the expected contest between England and her colonies, a motive which the colonists regarded as little less than treasonable. And here we wish to notice a statement given as a curious instance of historical puzzles by Mr. Whittlesey, in his address before the Ohio Historical Society, delivered in 1841, at page 28.

In 1831, a steamboat was detained a few hours near the house of Mr. Curtis, on the Ohio, a short distance above the mouth of the Hockhocking, and General Clark came ashore. He inquired respecting the remains of a fort or encampment at the mouth of the Hockhocking river, as it is now called. He was told that there was evidence of a clearing of several acres in extent, and that pieces of guns and muskets had been found on the spot; and also, that a collection of several hundred bullets had been discovered on the bank of the Hockhocking, about twenty-five miles up the river. General Clark then stated, that the ground had been occupied as a camp by Lord Dunmore, who came down the Kanawha with 300 men in the spring of 1775, with the expectation of treating with the Indians here. The chiefs not making their appearance, the march was continued up the river twenty-five or thirty miles, where an express from Virginia overtook the party. That evening a council was held and lasted very late at night. In the morning the troops were disbanded, and immediately requested to enlist in the British service for a stated period. The contents of the despatches had not transpired when this proposition was made. A major of militia, by the name of McCarty, made an harangue to the men against enlisting, which seems to have been done in an eloquent and effectual manner. He referred to the condition of the public mind in the colonies, and the probability of a revolution, which must soon arrive. He represented the suspicious circumstances of the express, which was still a secret to the troops, and that appearances justified the conclusion, that they were required to enlist in a service against their own countrymen, their own kindred, their own homes. The consequence was, that but few of the men re-enlisted, and the majority, choosing the orator as a leader, made the best of their way to Wheeling. The news brought out by the courier proved to be an account of the opening combat of the Revolution at Lexington, Massachusetts, April 20, 1775. General Clark stated that himself (or his brother) was in the expedition.

Lord Dunmore is said to have returned to Virginia by way of the Kanawha river.

There are very few historical details sustained by better authority than the above relation. Desirous of reconciling this statement with history, I addressed a letter to General Clark, requesting an explanation, but his death, which happened soon after, prevented a reply.

This Ave know cannot be true in the form in which it is stated. The battle of Lexington was on April 19th; on April 21st, Lord Dunmore removed the powder from the public storehouse at Williamsburg on board a King's vessel, and was thenceforward at Williamsburg. June 5th he informs the Assembly that he had meant to go West and look after Indian matters, but had been too busy. It is one of many instances showing how sceptical we should be where a single person testifies, and especially from memory.

The charge of treasonable design so industriously made against Dunmore, although plausible in part, is not sustained by facts and circumstances. That his course was not disapproved at the time is clear from the fact, he was thanked for his conduct by the Virginia Convention, at the head of which stood Washington, Randolph, the Lees, &c. &c. He was also thanked by the House of Burgesses, and received an address praising his proceedings, from the people of Fincastle County. (American Archives, fourth series, ii. 301, 170.)

# CHAPTER VI. INDIANS EMPLOYED AS ALLIES.

The peace effected by Dunmore continued during most of the year 1775. Occasionally, however, there were symptoms of awakening hostility on the part of the Shawanese and other confederated tribes, instigated no doubt by agents of England, for by this time the contest between the two countries had fairly commenced.

The frontier people trembled at the anticipated danger of an alliance between Britain and the Indians; for they well knew that such an influence would be powerful and full of peril.

In the north Col. Guy Johnson, son-in-law of Sir William Johnson, who had died suddenly in May, 1774, was the King's agent, and using every endeavor to bring over the six nations. This fact was known in the west, and the people naturally felt uneasy lest a similar effort should be made upon the western tribes. Those apprehensions, unhappily, were soon to be realized. The keen eye of Washington too, was not long in discerning the fatal consequences of the western savages becoming united under the King's banner. Accordingly, on the 19th of April, 1776, the commander-in-chief wrote to Congress, saying, as the Indians would soon be engaged, either for or against, he would suggest that they be engaged for the colonies; upon the 3d of May, the report on this was considered; upon the 25th of May it was resolved to be highly expedient to engage the Indians for the American service; and, upon the 3d of June, the general was empowered to raise two thousand, to be employed in Canada. Upon the 17th of June, Washington was authorized to employ them where he pleased, and to offer them rewards for prisoners; and, upon the 8th of July, he was empowered to call out as many of the Nova Scotia and neighboring tribes as he saw fit.

Such was the course of proceeding, on the part of the colonies, with regard to the employment of the Indians. The steps, at the time, were secret, but now the whole story is before the world. Not so, however, with regard to the acts of England; as to them, we have but few of the records placed within our reach. One thing, however, is known, namely, that while the colonies offered their allies of the woods rewards for prisoners, some of the British agents gave them money for scalps — a proceeding that cannot find any justification.

In accordance with the course of policy thus pursued, the north-western tribes, already angered by the constant invasions of their territory by the hunters of Virginia and Carolina, and easily accessible by the lakes, were soon enlisted on the side of England; and had a Pontiac been alive to lead them, might have done much mischief. As it was, during the summer of 1776, their straggling parties so filled the woods of Virginia and Kentucky, that no one outside of a fort was safe.

# CHAPTER VII. MURDER OF CORNSTALK.

The entire frontiers of Virginia and Pennsylvania now became the theatre of renewed Indian depredations, and the scene of a most fierce and sanguinary war. The pioneer settlers shut themselves up in blockhouses, and never ventured out without the tomahawk and rifle. Still, notwithstanding this precaution, they were often shot down by the too vigilant savage. Britain had enlisted under her banner the tomahawk and scalping knife, and terror seized the almost defenceless frontierman, as he thought of the unequal chances against which he had to contend.

In consequence of these Indian murders along the frontier, it was determined to place an efficient force at Wheeling, Point Pleasant, &c., whose presence, it was supposed, would have the effect to overawe the savages, and keep them from penetrating to the interior. Most of the western tribes were allied with England, except the Shawanese, and they had only been restrained by the powerful influence of their great chief, Cornstalk. At length, they too, yielded to the potent arguments of British agents, and were preparing to espouse the cause of England against the colonies. Cornstalk, anxious to preserve peace, determined to visit the garrison at Point Pleasant, and use his influence to avert the threatened blow. In the Spring of 1777, he came to the fort on this friendly mission, accompanied by Red Hawk, a noted young Delaware chief, who had fought with distinction by the side of Cornstalk at the same place in 1774. A third chief also made one of the party. Captain Matthew Arbuckle commanded the fort at the time, and when he had heard Cornstalk's straight-forward statement, that the Shawanese were determined to join the other Western and Northern tribes, and that hostilities would commence immediately. Captain A. deemed it prudent to detain the old chief and his companions as hostages for the good behaviour of his tribe. Captain Arbuckle immediately communicated to the new State government of Virginia, the facts received from Cornstalk.

Upon the receipt of this intelligence, it was resolved, if volunteers could be had for the purpose, to march an army into the Indian country, and effectually accomplish the objects which had been proposed in the campaign of Dunmore. The volunteers in Augusta and Bottetourt, were to rendezvous as early as possible, at the mouth of the Big Kanawha, where they would be joined by other troops under General Hand, who would then assume the command of the whole expedition.

In pursuance of this resolve, three or four companies only, were raised in the counties of Bottetourt and Augusta; and these immediately commenced their march, to the place of general rendezvous, under the command of Colonel George Skillern. In the Greenbriar country, great exertions were made by the militia officers, to obtain volunteers, but with little effect. But one company was formed, of thirty men, and the officers, laying aside all distinctions of rank, placed themselves in the line as common soldiers, and proceeded to Point Pleasant with the troops of Colonel Skillern. Upon their arrival, nothing had been heard of General Hand, or of the forces which it was expected would accompany him from Fort Pitt; and the volunteers halted, to await some intelligence from him.

The provisions, for the support of the army in its projected invasion of the Indian country, were expected to be brought down the river from Fort Pitt; and the troops under Colonel Skillern had only taken with them what was deemed sufficient for their subsistence on their march to the place of rendezvous. This stock was nearly exhausted, and the garrison was too illy supplied, to admit of their drawing on its stores. — While thus situated, awaiting the arrival of General Hand with his army and provisions, the officers held frequent conversations with Cornstalk, who seemed to take pleasure in acquainting them with the geography of the country west of the Ohio river generally, and more particularly with that section of it lying between the Mississippi and Missouri rivers. One afternoon, while he was engaged in delineating on the floor a map of that territory, with the various water courses emptying into those two mighty streams, and describing the face of the country, its soil and climate, a voice was heard from the opposite side of the Ohio, which he immediately recognized as that of his son Ellinipsico, and who, coming over at the instance of Cornstalk, embraced him most affectionately. Uneasy at the long absence of his father, the son had made the visit to ascertain the cause of his delay.

On the day after the arrival of Ellinipsico, and while he was yet in the garrison, two men, from Captain Hall's company of Rockbridge volunteers, crossed the Kanawha river on a hunting excursion. As they were returning to the canoe for the purpose of recrossing to the fort, Gilmore was espied by two Indians, concealed near the bank, who fired at, killed and scalped him. A party of Captain Hall's men immediately sprang into a canoe and went over to relieve Hamilton, and to bring the body of Gilmore to the encampment. Before they re-landed with the bloody corpse of Gilmore, a cry arose, "Let us go and kill the Indians in the fort;" and pale with rage they ascended the bank, with Captain Hall at their head, to execute their horrid purpose. It was vain to remonstrate. To the interference of Captains Arbuckle and Stuart to prevent this bloody determination, they responded by cocking their guns, and threatening instant death to any one who should dare to oppose them.

The interpreter's wife, (who had lately returned from Indian captivity, and seemed to entertain a feeling of affection for Cornstalk and his companions,) seeing their danger, ran to their cabin to apprize them of it, and told them that Ellinipsico was charged with having brought with him the Indians who had killed Gilmore. This, however, he positively denied, averring that he came alone, and with the sole object of learning something of his father. In this time Captain Hall and his men had arrived within hearing, and Ellinipsico appeared much agitated. Cornstalk, however, encouraged him to meet his fate composedly, saying, "My son, the Great Spirit has seen fit that we should die together, and has sent you here to that end. It is his will and let us submit; — it is all for the best;" and turning to meet his murderers at the door, received seven bullets in his body and fell without a groan.

Thus perished the mighty Cornstalk, Sachem of the Shawanese, and king of the Northern confederacy. A chief remarkable for many great and good qualities. He was disposed to be at all times the friend of white men; as he ever was the advocate of honorable peace. But when his country's wrongs "called aloud to battle," he became the thunderbolt of war; and made her oppressors feel the weight of his uplifted arm. He sought not to pluck the scalp from the head of the innocent, nor to war against the unprotected and defenceless; choosing rather to encounter his enemies, girded for battle, and in open conflict. His noble bearing, — his generous and disinterested attachment to the colonies, when the thunder of British cannon was reverberating through the land — his anxiety to preserve the frontier of Virginia from desolation and death, (the object of his visit to Point Pleasant) — all conspired to win for him the esteem and respect of others; while the untimely and perfidious manner of his death, caused a deep and lasting regret to pervade the bosoms, even of those who were enemies to his nation; and excited the just indignation of all towards his inhuman and barbarous murderers.

Cornstalk is said to have had a presentiment of his approaching fate. On the day preceding his death, a council of officers was convoked, in consequence of the continued absence of General Hand, and their entire ignorance of his force or movements, to consult and determine on what would be the course for them to pursue under existing circumstances. Cornstalk was admitted to the council; and in the course of some remarks, with which he addressed it, said, "When I was young and went to war, I often thought each might be my last adventure, and I should return no more. I still lived. Now I am in the midst of you, and if you choose, may kill me. I can die but once. It is alike to me, whether now or hereafter."

General Hand reached Point Pleasant a few days after this diabolical outrage. He brought no provisions for the Virginia troops, and it was then resolved to abandon the expedition.

The Governor of Virginia offered a reward for the apprehension of the murderers, but without avail. Congress, too, made every suitable concession to the Shawanees, through Colonel Morgan, but the savages would not be appeased; and bitterly did the frontier suffer for this imprudent act of a few lawless men.

# CHAPTER VIII. RENEWAL OF INDIAN HOSTILITIES.

Convinced that the Indians would, on the breaking up of winter, make increased efforts to retrieve past losses, and also to avenge the death of their slaughtered chief, the whites lost no time in erecting new stockades, repairing old ones, and making such other preparations for repelling the enemy, as lay within their power.

But the settlers were not alone busy. Congress having witnessed the success of England in buying up the savages, determined to strike an effective blow against the allies, hoping thereby, to deter them from further acts of violence on the frontier. With this view, an expedition was ordered against the confederated tribes, of such force as would strike terror to their midst, and restrain them from further aggression. Three thousand troops were to be furnished by Virginia, — twenty-seven hundred from east of the mountains, and three hundred from the west. Fifteen hundred of these were to strike the Ohio by way of the Kanawha valley, while the others were to assemble at Fort Pitt, and thence proceed to effect a junction at Fort Randolph. From this point the united force was to march against the Indian towns. Col. Morgan was directed to make every suitable arrangement for provisioning this large number of men. Whilst these preparations were making, General Mcintosh, who had been appointed to the command of the western division, in place of General Hand, advanced across the mountains with five hundred men, and proceeding to the mouth of Beaver, twenty-eight miles below Pittsburg, erected Fort Mcintosh. This was considered a most favorable position for a body of troops to intercept parties of Indians on their way against the settlements of Virginia and Pennsylvania. The effect was very soon perceptible throughout the entire frontier.

Before proceeding with the projected invasion, it was thought prudent to convene the Delaware Indians, at Pittsburg, and obtain their consent to march through their territory. This was done the 17th of September, 1778, by Andrew Lewis and Thomas Lewis, commissioners on the part of the United States, and signed in presence of Lach. Mcintosh, Brigadier-general, commandant of the western department; Daniel Brodhead, Colonel of the 8th Pennsylvania regiment; William Crawford, Colonel; John Gibson, Colonel 13th Virginia regiment, and several others.

In the course of the following month. General Mcintosh assembled one thousand men at the newly erected fort, and marched into the enemy's country. The season was so far advanced that the troops only proceeded about seventy miles and halted on the west bank of the Tuscarawas river. Here, on an elevated plain, it was concluded to build a stockaded fort, which was named Fort Laurens, in honor of the President of Congress. It was garrisoned with one hundred and fifty men, and left under the command of Colonel Gibson, and the army returned to Fort Pitt. The other branch of the expedition, intended to be assembled at the mouth of the Kanawha, was never collected, the increasing demand for men in the east doubtless rendering it difficult to raise the number demanded. Although no opposition was made to the progress of the army under General Mcintosh, as the hostile Indians were hardly aware of his presence, before he had again retreated; yet in January following, the Shawanese and Wyandotts collected a large body of warriors and invested the fort, cutting off all intercourse with Fort Mcintosh, and suffering no one to go in or to come out; watching it so closely that it became very hazardous to procure either wood or water.

Colonel Stone having most faithfully described this siege in the wilderness, we will follow his account: —

"The first hostile demonstration of the forest warriors was executed with equal cunning and success. The horses of the garrison were allowed to forage for themselves upon the herbage, among the dried prairie-grass immediately in the vicinity of the fort, wearing bells, that they might be the more easily found, if straying too far. It happened, one morning in January, that the horses had all disappeared, but the bells were heard, seemingly at no great distance. They had, in truth, been stolen by the Indians, and conveyed away. The bells, however, were taken off, and used for another purpose. Availing themselves of the tall prairie-grass, the Indians formed an ambuscade, at the farthest extremity of which they caused the bells to jingle as a decoy. The artifice was successful. A party of sixteen men was sent in pursuit of the straggling steeds, who fell into the snare. Fourteen were killed upon the spot, and the remaining two taken prisoners, one of whom returned at the close of the war, and of the other nothing was ever heard.

Towards evening of the same day, the whole force of the Indians, painted, and in the full costume of war, presented themselves in full view of the garrison, by marching in single files, though at a respectful distance, across the prairie. Their number, according to a count from one of the bastions, was eight hundred and forty-seven; altogether too great to be encountered in the field by so small a garrison. After this display of their strength, the Indians took a position upon an elevated piece of ground at no great distance from the fort, though on the opposite side of the river. In this situation they remained several weeks, in a state rather of armed neutrality than of active hostility. Some of them would frequently approach the fort sufficiently near to hold conversations with those upon the walls. They uniformly professed a desire for peace, but protested against the encroachments of the white people upon their lands; more especially was the erection of a fort so far within the territory claimed by them as exclusively their own, a cause of complaint, nay, of admitted exasperation. There was with the Americans in the fort an aged friendly Indian, named John Thompson, who seemed to be in equal favor with both parties, visiting the Indian encampment at pleasure, and coming and going as he chose. They informed Thompson that they deplored the continuance of hostilities, and finally sent word by him to Colonel Gibson that they were desirous of peace, and if he would present them with a barrel of flour, they would send in their proposals the next day. The flour was sent, but the Indians, instead of fulfilling their part of the stipulation, withdrew, and entirely disappeared. They had, indeed, continued the siege as long as they could obtain subsistence, and raised it only because of the lack of supplies. Still, as the beleaguerment was begun in stratagem, so was it ended. Colonel Gibson's provisions were also running short, and, as he supposed the Indians had entirely gone off, he directed Colonel Clark, of the Pennsylvania line, with a detachment of fifteen men, to escort the invalids of the garrison, amounting to ten or a dozen men, back to Fort Mcintosh. But the Indians had left a strong party of observation lurking in the neighborhood of the fort, and the escort had proceeded only two miles before it was fallen upon, and the whole number killed with the exception of four, one of whom, a captain, escaped back to the fort. The bodies of the slain were interred by the garrison, on the same day, with the honors of war. A party was likewise sent out to collect the remains of the fourteen who had first fallen by the ambuscade, and bury them.

The situation of the garrison was now becoming deplorable. For two weeks the men had been reduced to half-a-pound of sour flour, and a like quantity of offensive meat, per diem; and for a week longer they were compelled to subsist only upon raw hides, and such roots as they could find in the circumjacent woods and prairies, when General Mcintosh most opportunely arrived to their relief."

The fort was evacuated and the position abandoned. Thus ended the disastrous occupancy of Fort Laurens, in which much fatigue and suffering were endured, and many lives lost, but with no material benefit to the country.

# CHAPTER IX. COLONEL BRODHEAD'S CAMPAIGN.

Colonel Daniel Brodhead having succeeded General Mcintosh, commanding the western division, determined to strike an effective blow against the Indian towns on the Muskingum. An expedition was accordingly fitted out in the spring of 1781, which rendezvoused at Wheeling, and proceeded thence to the scene of their intended operations. It embraced about eight hundred men, composed of some of the most experienced Indian hunters on the frontiers of Virginia and Pennsylvania. Colonel David Shepherd, of Wheeling creek, was one of the party.

With the least practicable delay, the expedition crossed the Ohio and moved rapidly towards the Indian towns, that they might strike a decisive blow before the enemy should discover their approach.

When the army had reached the river, a little below Salem, the lowest Moravian town. Col. Brodhead sent an express to the missionary of the place, the Rev. John Heckewelder, informing him of his arrival in the neighborhood with his army, requesting a small supply of provisions, and a visit from him in his camp. The Christian Indians sent the supply of provisions, and Mr. Heckewelder repaired to Col. Brodhead's camp. Col. Brodhead then said, "that being on an expedition against the hostile Indians, at or near the forks of the river, he was anxious to know before he proceeded any further, whether any of the Christian Indians were out hunting, or on business in the direction lie was going." Being answered in the negative, he declared, that "nothing would give him greater pain, than to hear that any one of the Moravian Indians had been molested by his troops: as these Indians had conducted themselves from the commencement of the war, in a manner that did them honor."

While, however, he was assuring Mr. Heckewelder that the Christian Indians had nothing to fear, an officer came with great speed from one quarter of the camp, and reported that a particular division of the militia were preparing to break off for the purpose of destroying the Moravian settlements up the river, and he feared they could not be restrained from so doing. Col. Brodhead and Col. Shepherd of Wheeling, immediately took such measures as prevented it.

The army then proceeded until within a few miles of Coshocton, when an Indian prisoner was taken. Soon after, two more Indians were discovered and fired upon, but notwithstanding one of them was wounded, both made their escape.

Col. Brodhead, knowing that these two Indians would endeavor to give immediate notice of the approach of the army, ordered a rapid march, in order to reach the town before them, and take it by surprise. This was done in the midst of a heavy fall of rain, and the plan succeeded. The army reached the place in three divisions, — the right and left wings approached the river a little above and below the town, while the centre marched directly upon it. The whole number of the Indians in the village, on the east side of the river, together with ten or twelve from a little village some distance above, were made prisoners, without firing a single shot. The river having risen to a great height, owing to the recent fall of rain, the army could not cross it. Thus, the villages on the west side of the river escaped destruction.

Among the prisoners, sixteen warriors were pointed out by Pekillon, a friendly Delaware chief, who was with the army of Col. Brodhead. A little after dark a council of war was held, to determine on the fate of the warriors. They were doomed to death. They were then bound, taken a little distance below the town, dispatched with tomahawks and spears, and scalped.

Early the next morning an Indian presented himself on the opposite bank of the river, and asked for the "Big Captain." Col. Brodhead presented himself, and asked the Indian what he wanted? The Indian replied, "I want peace." "Send over some of your chiefs," said Brodhead. "Maybe you kill?" He was answered, "They shall not be killed." One of the chiefs, a well looking man, came over the river and entered into conversation with Col. Brodhead in the street; but while engaged in conversation, a man belonging to the army, by the name of John Wetzel, came up behind him, with a tomahawk concealed in the bosom of his hunting shirt, and struck him a blow on the back of his head. He fell, and instantly expired.

About mid-day the army commenced its retreat from Coshocton. Col. Brodhead committed the care of the prisoners to the militia. They were about twenty in number. After marching about a mile, the men commenced killing them, and did not cease until the whole were murdered and scalped, except a few women and children who were spared and taken to Fort Pitt."

# CHAPTER X. WILLIAMSON'S CAMPAIGN.

This is a chapter in our history which we would fain drop, and draw over it the curtain of oblivion, did not our duty require us to speak in deference to a higher obligation. The murder of the Christian or Moravian Indians, was one of the most atrocious affairs in the settlement of the west. It is a reproach upon the character of the country, and a living stigma upon the memory of every man known to have been engage in the diabolical transaction. It is but justice, however, that those who protested against the enormity should be exonerated from blame.

The Moravian Indians consisted chiefly of Delawares, with a few Mohicans. These simple-minded children of the forest had become converted to Christianity through the zeal and influence of Moravian Missionaries. Their homes embraced the villages of Gnadenhutten, Schonbrunn, Salem and Lichtenau.

For ten years they had lived in peace and quietness. The harsh savage had been softened by the mild influences of Christianity; peace, content and happiness smiled upon him from year to year, and blessed him with their joys. But, alas, the destroyer came, and blotted this fair field of Christian labor utterly from existence.

The Moravian Indians early became objects of suspicion to both the whites and surrounding savages. The latter, because they had given up the customs of their race; and by the former, on account of their supposed protection to, or harboring of, hostile Indians. Their towns lay immediately on the track from Sandusky to the nearest point on the Ohio; and while passing to and fro, the hostile parties would compel their Christian brethren to furnish provisions. Thus situated, as it were, between two fires, it is not surprising that they should have fallen a sacrifice to one or the other. During the whole of our Revolutionary struggle, the Moravian Indians remained eutral, or if they took any part, it was in favor of the whites, advising them of the approach of hostile Indians, &c. Yet, notwithstanding all their former friendliness, they fell under the displeasure of the border settlers, who suspected them of aiding and abetting the savages, whose depredations upon the frontier had caused so much terror and misery throughout western Virginia and Pennsylvania. To add to this feeling, early in February, 1782, a party of Indians from Sandusky, penetrated the settlements, and committed numerous depredations. Of the families that fell beneath the murderous stroke of these savages was that of David Wallace, consisting of himself, wife and six children, and a man named Carpenter. Of these all were killed, except the latter, whom they took prisoner. The early date of this visitation, induced the people at once to believe that the depredators had wintered with the Moravians, and the excited settlers uttered vengeance against those who were supposed to have harbored them. An expedition was at once determined upon, and about the first of March a body of eighty or ninety men, chiefly from the Monongahela, rendezvoused at the old Mingo towns, on Mingo Bottom, now Jefferson county, Ohio. Each man furnished himself with his own arms, ammunition and provision. Many of them had horses. The second day's march brought them within one mile of the middle Moravian town, and they encamped for the night. In the morning the men were divided into two equal parties, one of which was to cross the river about a mile above the town, their videttes having reported that there were Indians on both sides of the river. The other party was divided into three divisions, one of which was to take a circuit in the woods, and reach the river, a little distance below the town, on the east side. Another division was to fall into the middle of the town, and the third at its upper end.

The victims received warning of their danger, but took no measures to escape, believing they had nothing to fear from the Americans, but supposed the only quarter from which they had grounds for apprehending injury, was from those Indians who were the enemies of the Americans.

When the party designed to make the attack on the west side, had reached the river, they found no craft to take them over; but something like a canoe was seen on the opposite bank. The river was high with some floating ice. A young man by the name of Slaughter swam the river, and brought over not a canoe, but a trough, designed for holding sugar water. This trough could carry but two men at a time. In order to expedite their passage, a number of men stripped off their clothes, put them into the trough, together with their guns, and swam by its sides, holding its edges with their hands. When about sixteen had crossed the river, their two sentinels, who had been posted in advance, discovered an Indian, whose name was Shabosh, whom they shot and scalped.

By this time, about sixteen men had got over the river, and supposing that the firing of the guns which killed Shabosh, would lead to an instant discovery, they sent word to the party designed to attack the town on the east side of the river, to move on instantly; which they did.

In the mean time, the small party which had crossed the river, marched with all speed, to the main town on the west side of the river. Here they found a large company of Indians gathering the corn, which they had left in their fields the preceding fall, when they removed to Sandusky. — On the arrival of the men at the town, they professed peace and goodwill to the Moravians, and informed them that they had come to take them to Fort Pitt, for their safety. The Indians surrendered, delivered up their arms, even their hatchets, on being promised that every thing should be restored to them on their arrival at Pittsburgh. The murderers then went to Salem, and persuaded the Indians there to go with them to Gnadcnhutten, the inhabitants of which, in the mean time, had been attacked and driven together, and bound without resistance; and when those from Salem were about entering the town, they were likewise deprived of their arms and bound.

The prisoners being thus secured, a council of war was held to decide on their fate. The officers, unwilling to take on themselves the whole responsibility of the awful decision, agreed to refer the question to the whole number of the men. The men were accordingly drawn up in a line. — The commandant of the party. Col. David Williamson, then put the question to them in form, "Whether the Moravian Indians should be taken prisoners to Pittsburgh, or put to death; and requested that all those who were in favor of saving their lives should step out of the line, and form a second rank?" On this sixteen, some say eighteen, stepped out of the rank, and formed themselves into a second line. But, alas! this line of mercy was far too short for that of vengeance.

Most of those opposed to this diabolical resolution protested in the name of high Heaven against the atrocious act, and called God to witness that they were innocent of the blood of those inoffensive people; yet the majority remained unmoved, and some of them were even in favor of burning them alive. But it was at length decided that they should be scalped in cold blood, and the Indians were told to prepare for their fate, that, as they were Christians, they might die in a Christian manner. After the first burst of horror was over, they patiently suffered themselves to be led into buildings, in one of which the men, and in the other, the women and children were confined, like sheep for slaughter. They passed the night in praying, exhorting each other to remain faithful, asking pardon from each other for any offences they had committed, and singing hymns of praise to God.

From the time they had been placed in the guard-house, the unfortunate prisoners foresaw their fate, and commenced singing, praying, and exhorting one another to place their faith in the Saviour of men.

The particulars of this catastrophe are too horrid to relate. When the morning arrived, the murderers selected two houses, which they named slaughter-houses — one for the women and children. The victims were then bound, two and two together, and led into the slaughter-houses, where they were scalped and murdered.

The number of the slain, as reported by the men on their return from the campaign, was eighty-seven or eighty-nine; but the Moravian account, which no doubt is correct, makes the number ninety-six. Of these, sixty-two were grown persons, one-third of whom were women, the remaining thirty-four were children. All these, with a few exceptions, were killed in the houses.

A few men, who were supposed to be warriors, were tied and taken some distance from the slaughter-houses, to be tomahawked.

Of the whole number of the Indians at Gnadenhutten and Salem, only two made their escape. These were two lads of fourteen or fifteen years of age. One of them escaped through a window on the night previous to the massacre, and concealed himself in the cellar of the house to which the women and children were brought next day to be murdered, whose blood he saw running in streams through the floor. On the following night he left the cellar, into which, fortunately, no one came, and got into the woods. The other youth received one blow upon his head, and was left for dead.

The Indians of the upper town, were apprized of their danger in due time to make their escape, two of them having found the mangled body of Shabosh. Providentially they all made their escape, although they might have been easily overtaken by the party, if they had undertaken their pursuit. A division of the men were ordered to go to Schonbrunn, but finding the place deserted, they took what plunder they could find, and returned to their companions without looking farther after the Indians.

After the work of death had been finished, and the plunder secured, all the buildings in the town were set on fire, including the slaughter-houses. A rapid retreat to the settlement concluded this deplorable campaign. It was, certainly, one of the most horrible affairs ever undertaken in this country, and is revolting to every feeling of the human heart. It must stand a record of infamy as long as time exists.

Doddridge, whose views, in part, we have embodied in a portion of this account, says:

"In justice to the memory of Col. Williamson, I have to say, that although at that time very young, I was personally acquainted with him, and from my recollection of his conversation, I say with confidence that he was a brave man, but not cruel. He would meet an enemy in battle, and fight like a soldier; but not murder a prisoner. Had he possessed the authority of a superior officer in a regular army, I do not believe that a single Moravian Indian would have lost his life; but he possessed no such authority. He was only a militia officer, who could advise, but not command. His only fault was that of too easy a compliance with popular opinion and popular prejudice. On this account his memory has been loaded with unmerited reproach.

Should it be asked what sort of people composed the band of murderers of these unfortunate people? I answer, — They were not miscreants or vagabonds; many of them were men of the first standing in the country. Many of them had recently lost relations by the hands of the savages, and were burning for revenge. They cared little upon whom they wreaked their vengeance, so they were Indians.

When attacked by our people, although they might have defended themselves, they did not. They never fired a single shot. They were prisoners and had been promised protection. Every dictate of justice and humanity required that their lives should be spared. The complaint of their villages being "Half-way houses for the warriors" was at an end, as they had been removed to Sandusky the fall before. It was therefore an atrocious and unqualified murder. But by whom committed? By a majority of the campaign? For the honor of my country, I hope I may safely answer this question in the negative. It was one of those convulsions of the moral state of society, in which the voice of the justice and humanity of a majority is silenced by the clamor and violence of a lawless minority. Very few of our men imbrued their hands in the blood of the Moravians. Even those who had not voted for saving their lives, retired from the scene of slaughter with horror and disgust. Why then did they not give their votes in their favor? The fear of public indignation restrained them from doing so. They thought well, but had not heroism enough to express their opinion. Those who did so, deserve honorable mention for their intrepidity. So far as it may hereafter be in my power, this honor shall be done them. While the names of the murderers shall not stain the pages of history, from my pen at least."

# CHAPTER XI. CRAWFORD'S CAMPAIGN.

The signal success attending the expedition against the Moravians induced many who had been engaged in that atrocious affair to get up a second one on a more grand and extensive plan against the Indian settlements at Sandusky. This was the ostensible motive, but some believed it was merely intended to finish the work of murder and plunder upon the Moravians. Such at least is said to have been the object with some who composed the expedition; with the majority, however, it was regarded as an expedition to punish the Wyandotts for their many and long-continued depredations upon the whites. Every inducement was held out to join the expedition. Placards were posted at Wheeling, Catfish, and other places, of a new State that was to be organized on the Muskingum, and no effort left untried that could excite either the cupidity or revenge of the frontier people. A force was soon raised in the western parts of Pennsylvania and Virginia of four hundred and eighty men, well mounted and armed; each man furnished his own horse and equipments, except a small supply of ammunition provided by the Lieutenant-colonel of Washington county, Pennsylvania. The place of rendezvous was Mingo Bottom, where, on the 2otli of May, 1782, nearly five hundred men mustered and proceeded to elect their commander. The choice fell upon Col. William Crawford, who will be remembered as Washington's old friend and agent. He was reluctant to go, but at length yielded to the entreaties of friends. (See biography of Col. C. in this volume.)

The army marched along "Williamson's trail," as it was then called, until they arrived at the ruins of the upper Moravian town, on the fourth day of their march, in the fields belonging to which, there was still an abundance of corn on the stalks, with which their horses were plentifully fed, during the night.

Shortly after the army halted at this place, two Indians were discovered, by some men who had walked out of the camp. Three shots were fired at one of them, but without hurting him. As soon as the news of the discovery of Indians reached the camp, more than one-half of the men rushed out, without command, and in the most tumultuous manner, to see what happened. From that time Colonel Crawford felt a presentiment of the defeat which followed.

The Indians were observing the motions of the troops. From the time the Christian Indians were murdered on the Muskingum, the savages had kept spies out, to guard against being again surprised. There was not a place of any importance on the Ohio, from Pittsburgh to Grave creek, left unobserved. Thus, when in May, two months after the destruction of the Moravian towns, the white settlers were seen in agitation, as if preparing for some enterprise, the news was brought to the Indians, and so from day to day, until Crawford's men had crossed the Ohio river, and even then their first encampment was reconnoitred. They knew the number of troops and their destination, visited every encampment immediately on their leaving it, when on their march, and saw from their writings on the trees, and scraps of paper, that "no quarter was to be given to any Indian, whether, man, woman or child."

Nothing of consequence happened during their march, until the 6th of June, when their guides conducted them to the site of the Moravian villages, on one of the upper branches of the Sandusky river. From this retreat, the Christian Indians had lately been driven away, by the Wyandotts, to the Scioto.

In this dilemma, what was to be done? The officers held a council, in which it was determined to march one day longer in the direction of Upper Sandusky, and if they should not reach the town in the course of the day, to make a retreat with all speed.

The march was commenced on the following morning through the plains of Sandusky, and continued until two o'clock, when the advance guard was attacked and driven in by the Indians, who were discovered in large numbers in the high grass with which the place was covered. The Indian army was at that moment about entering a piece of woods, almost entirely surrounded by plains; but in this they were partially prevented by a rapid movement of the whites. The battle then commenced by a heavy fire from both sides. From a partial possession of the woods, which they had gained at the outset of the battle, the Indians were soon dislodged. They then attempted to gain a small skirt of wood on the right flank of Colonel Crawford, but were prevented from so doing by the vigilance and bravery of Major Leet, who commanded the right wing at the time. The firing was heavy and incessant until dark, when it ceased, and both armies lay on their arms during the night. Both adopted the policy of kindling large fires along the line of battle, and then retiring some distance in the rear of them, to prevent being surprised by a night attack. During the conflict of the afternoon, three of Col. Crawford's men were killed and several wounded.

On the next morning, the army occupied the battle ground of the preceding day. The Indians made no attack during the day, until late in the evening, but were seen in large bodies traversing the plains in various directions. Some of them appeared to be carrying off their dead and wounded.

In the morning of this day, a council of officers was held, and a retreat was resolved on, as the only means of saving the army. The Indians appearing to increase every hour.

During this day, preparations were made for a retreat by burying the dead, burning fires over their graves to prevent discovery, and preparing means for carrying off the wounded. The retreat was to commence in the course of the night. The Indians, however, became apprized of this intended retreat, and about sundown attacked the army with great force and fury, in every direction, excepting that of Sandusky.

When the line of march was formed by the commander-in-chief, and the retreat commenced, the guides prudently took the direction of Sandusky, which afforded the only opening in the Indian lines, and the only chance of concealment. After marching about a mile in this direction, the army wheeled about to the left, and by a circuitous route gained, before day, the trail by which they came. They continued their march the whole of the next day, without annoyance, except the firing of a few distant shots, by the Indians at the rear guard, which slightly wounded two or three men. At night they built fires, took their suppers, secured the horses, and resigned themselves to repose, without placing a single sentinel or vidette for safety. In this careless situation, they might have been surprised and cut off by the Indians, who, however, did not disturb them during the night, nor afterwards, during the whole of their retreat. The number that retreated in the main body is supposed to be about three hundred.

At the commencement of the retreat. Colonel Crawford placed himself at the head of the army, and continued there until they had gone about a quarter of a mile, when missing his son John Crawford, his son-in-law Major Harrison, and his nephews Major Rose and William Crawford, he halted and called for them, as the line passed, but without finding them. After the army had passed him, he was unable to overtake it, owing to the weariness of his horse. Falling in company with Dr. Knight, and two others, they travelled all night, first north and then to the east to avoid the pursuit of the Indians. They directed their courses by the north star.

On the next day, they fell in with Capt. John Biggs and Lieut. Ashley, the latter of whom was wounded. Two others were in company with Biggs and Ashley. On the next day, Capt. Biggs and Dr. Knight insisted upon continuing their course through the woods, and avoiding all paths, but Crawford overruled, assuring them that the Indians would not urge the pursuit beyond the plains, which were already far behind, and abandoning their due eastern course, the party pursued the beaten tract, travelled over by the army a few days before. Crawford and Knight moved one hundred and fifty yards in front. Captain Biggs and his wounded friend, Lieut. Ashley, were in the centre, both on horseback, and the two men on foot brought up the rear.

Scarcely had they proceeded a mile, when several Indians sprang up before Crawford and Knight, and presenting their guns, ordered them, in good English, to stop. Knight sprang behind a tree and leveled his gun. Col. Crawford ordered him not to fire, Knight reluctantly obeyed, and the Indians ran up to Col. Crawford in a friendly manner, shook him by the hand cordially, and asked him how he did. Biggs and Ashley halted, while the two men in the rear prudently took to their heels and escaped. Colonel Crawford ordered Captain Biggs to come up and surrender, but the Captain took aim at one of the Indians, fired, and then he and Ashley put spurs to their horses and for the time escaped. They were both overtaken and killed the next day.

On the morning of the tenth of June, Col. Crawford and Dr. Knight, together with nine more prisoners, were conducted by seventeen Indians to the old Sandusky town, about thirty-three miles distant. The nine prisoners were marched ahead of Crawford and Knight, who were conducted by Pipe and Wingemund, two Delaware Chiefs. All the prisoners, including Col. Crawford and Dr. Knight, had been previously painted black by Pipe. Four of the prisoners were tomahawked and scalped on the way at different places; and when the other five arrived at the town, the boys and squaws fell upon them and tomahawked them in a moment. (For particulars of what followed, see sketch of Colonel Crawford.)

Thus ended this disastrous campaign. It was the last one which took place in this section of the country during the war of the Revolution. It was undertaken with the very worst views — those of murder and plunder. It was conducted without sufficient means to encounter, with any prospect of success, the large Indian forces upon the plains of Sandusky. There was not that subordination and discipline which is always necessary to success; and it ended in total discomfiture, and an awful sacrifice of life. Never did any enterprise more signally fail, and never was a deed of blood more terribly revenged, than the murder of the Christian Indians at the Moravian towns."

# CHAPTER XII. CLARK'S OPERATIONS IN THE WEST.

It has been seen that the army under Gen. Mcintosh, instead of checking or overawing the savages, did little more than stimulate them to further acts of hostility. Affairs now became alarming in the West. Bodies of fierce warriors prowled around the infant settlements of Virginia and Kentucky, and all saw the necessity of striking a vigorous blow against the savages and their white allies. Congress adhered to the policy of pushing an army against Detroit, but a master-mind in the West saw where a more effective blow could be given. George Rogers Clark, the "Hannibal of the West," had satisfied himself by personal observation, and through the agency of spies, that the British posts in Illinois could easily be taken, and at once laid open his whole scheme to Patrick Henry, then Governor of Virginia. His great mind readily comprehended all of Clark's proposed movements, and entering fully into the spirit, issued two sets of instructions, one open, authorizing him to enlist seven companies to go to Kentucky, subject to his orders, and the other private: the success of the enterprise depending entirely upon the secrecy of the movement. None but the Virginia authorities and a few personal friends knew the real destination of the troops.

Proceeding to Pittsburg without delay, Col. Clark attempted to enlist as many men as possible, while at the same time Major Smith was engaged for a like purpose in the southwestern part of Virginia. With three companies, a few private adventurers, and twelve hundred pounds in the depredated currency of the country, Col. Clarke descended the Ohio to the Falls, and fortified Corn Island opposite, where Louisville now stands. Concealing his boats, he marched directly out toward Kaskaskia, which, after a fatiguing journey of many days, part of the time subsisting upon roots, the intrepid leader and his little party reached in safety.

Arriving before Kaskaskia in the night, they entered it, unseen and unheard, and took possession of the town and fort, without opposition. Relying on the thick and wide extended forests which interposed between them and the American settlements, the inhabitants had been lulled to repose by fancied security, and were unconscious of danger until it had become too late to be avoided. Not a single individual escaped, to spread the alarm in the adjacent settlements.

But there still remained other towns, higher up the Mississippi, which, if unconquered, would afford shelter to the savages and furnish them the means of annoyance and of ravage. Against these Colonel Clarke immediately directed operations. Mounting a detachment of men, on horses found at Kaskaskia, and sending them forward, three other towns were reduced with equal success. The obnoxious governor at Kaskaskia was sent to Virginia, with the written instructions which he had received from Quebec, Detroit and Mackinaw for exciting the Indians to war, and remunerating them for the blood which they might shed.

Although the country within which Colonel Clark had so successfully carried on operations, was considered to be within the limits of Virginia; yet as it was occupied by savages and those who were but little, if any, less hostile than they; and being so remote from her settlements, Virginia had as yet exercised no act of jurisdiction over it. But as it now belonged to her, by conquest as well as charter, the General Assembly created it into a distinct county, to be called Illinois; a temporary government was likewise established in it, and a regiment of infantry and a troop of cavalry, ordered to be enlisted for its defence, and placed under the command of its intrepid and enterprising conqueror.

News of the success of Clark in capturing the British posts in Illinois having reached Governor Hamilton at Detroit, he determined to re-take them, also to conquer Kentucky, Western Virginia, &c., and repel the rebels from the west. With this view, at the head of a large body of well-disciplined troops, he made his appearance in front of the garrison at Vincennes, which had also surrendered to Clark's orders, and then under the command of Captain Helm. The fort being in a miserable condition for defence, surrendered to Hamilton, but upon such terms as were highly honorable to the Virginia commandant. Clark was, of course, immediately apprized of these movements, and in the midst of winter this remarkable man started for fort St. Vincent, determined, as he expressed it, "That he would have Hamilton, or Hamilton should have him." After great labor and exposure, marching often through ice and water waist-deep, the gallant little army appeared in front of the fort, and demanded an immediate and unconditional surrender. The British governor, unwilling to risk an attack, gave up possession, and allowed himself to become a prisoner of war in the hands of Clark. The capture of Hamilton, and the destruction of British power in the valley of the Wabash, and indeed in the whole west, south of Detroit, was one of the most important achievements during the war. As already intimated, great arrangements had been made by Hamilton for the successful prosecution of a campaign against all the white settlements in the west. The southern, western and northern Indians had joined him, and had Clark failed to defeat Hamilton, who can doubt but that the entire west, from the Alleghanies to the Mississippi, would have been swept over by the allied forces of British and Indians. But for this gallant body of imperfectly clothed and half starved Virginians, the project of Great Britain, so long one of the darling objects of her ambition, might have been carried out, and the whole current of our history changed.

# CHAPTER XIII. CLOSING MILITARY OPERATIONS IN THE WEST.

With this chapter we close the historical details, by bringing down the settlement of the country to 1795. Some of the chapters immediately preceding, would seem to come more appropriately under the head of Part VI., but constituting as they do, connecting links in the history and settlement of the west, it was deemed inexpedient to separate them; and thus they are given in regular historical and chronological order. That part of our work which we have distinctly classified as "Indian Wars," is designed alone to embrace the incidents of border life in Western Virginia, and the territory immediately adjacent.

By the treaty of Fort Stanwix, concluded October 22, 1784, between the United States and hostile tribes of the Iroquois, all the claim of the great Northern Confederacy to lands lying west of the western boundary of Pennsylvania became extinguished. It now remained to treat with the Western Indians, to secure the United States' title to the great expanse of country lying west of the Iroquois possessions.

The Commissioners for this purpose were Arthur Lee, Richard Butler, and George Rogers Clark. This Board organized at Fort Mcintosh, (Beaver,) January 21, 1785. The Indians represented were the Wyandots, Delawares, Chippeways, and Ottoways, and of the native Commissioners there assembled to treat, was the celebrated war chief of the Delawares, Buckongalielas. The third article of the treaty agreed upon defined the limits of the country ceded, as follows:

Art. 3. The boundary line between the United States and the Wyandot and Delaware nations, shall begin at the mouth of the river Cayahoga, and run thence, up the said river, to the portage between that and the Tuscarawas branch of the Muskingum; then, down the said branch, to the forks at the crossing place above Fort Lawrence, [Laurens;] then, westerly, to the portage of the Big Miami, which runs into the Ohio, at the mouth of which branch the fort stood which was taken by the French in one thousand seven hundred and fifty-two; then, along the said portage, to the Great Miami or Ome river, and down the south-east side of the same to its mouth; thence, along the south shore of Lake Erie, to the mouth of Cayahoga, where it began.

Such were the first steps taken for securing to the United States the Indian title to the vast realm lying beyond the Ohio.

Hostilities still continuing on the part of the Indians, and the west having suffered greatly, Congress authorized the President, September 29, 1789, to call out the militia to protect the frontier, and break the power of the savages. On the 6th of October, President Washington directed General St. Clair, then Governor of the North-West Territory, to draw fifteen hundred men from the western counties of Virginia and Pennsylvania, and proceed directly against the towns of the hostile tribes on the Maumee. In obedience to his instructions. Governor St. Clair called upon Virginia (July 15, 1790,) for her quota, which was furnished in due time; and his army, numbering nearly twenty-four hundred men, marched from Fort Washington (Cincinnati,) in the fall of 1791. On the morning of the 4th of November, the Indians attacked him in great force, totally routing the American army, with an immense loss of life and property. General Butler, and upward of six hundred men were killed.

This was a terrible blow to the west; and the savages, inflated with success, overspread the country, sending death into almost every settlement.

Washington, determined to subdue the savages, now urged forward the vigorous prosecution of the war; but various obstacles prevented a speedy organization of a force sufficient to strike an efficient blow. It was not until the spring of 1794, that an army, strong enough for the purpose, could be organized. This force, consisting of two thousand regular troops, and fifteen hundred mounted volunteers from Kentucky, assembled at Greenville, under the command of General Anthony Wayne, a bold, energetic and determined officer, in whom Washington reposed every confidence.

On the 20th of August, General Wayne encountered the enemy at the foot of the rapids on the Maumee, and after a short, but most deadly conflict, the Indians fled the field with great loss, and in utter confusion.

This brilliant victory brought the savages to terms, and soon after, a permanent treaty was negotiated at Greenville, between eleven of the most powerful north-western tribes, and the "thirteen fires," as these wild men called the United States. This treaty confirmed the boundary established at Fort Mcintosh, and extended westward from Loramie to Fort Recovery, and thence south-west to the mouth of Kentucky river. Now terminated the long and sanguinary struggle between the whites and Indians on the western frontier, a war which had raged with almost unabated fury for more than twenty years, involving a sacrifice of life, and consequent amount of misery, scarcely to be comprehended.

# PART VI. INDIAN WARS. 1775-1795.

# CHAPTER I. DEPREDATIONS EAST OF THE MOUNTAINS.

Although this part of our work is designed chiefly to embrace the operations, by and against, the western Indians during the twenty years immediately preceding the treaty of Greenville, still we cannot pass without some notice those which occurred prior to the peace of November, 1774. Premising this much, we will turn back the pages of history and briefly glance at some of the bolder acts in the bloody drama, performed on the then frontier of Virginia.

Allusion has already been made to the irruptions of savages in the Valley of Virginia, during the years following Braddock's defeat. One of their earliest acts was the captivity of a Mrs. Neff on the south-branch of the Wappatomaca. Having secured their prisoner and helped themselves to some plunder, the savages (fourteen in number) left for their homes, by way of Fort Pleasant. On the second night, they reached the vicinity of the fort, and leaving Mrs. Neff in the care of an old Indian, the warriors separated into two parties, that they might better watch the fort.

"At a late hour in the night, Mrs. Neff discovering that her guard was pretty soundly asleep, ran off. The old fellow very soon awoke, fired off his gun, and raised a yell. Mrs. N. ran between the two parties of Indians, got safe into Fort Pleasant, and gave notice where the enemy were encamped. A small party the same evening came from another fort a few miles above, and joined their friends in Fort Pleasant. After the escape of Mrs. N., the Indians collected into a deep glen, near the fort. Early the next morning, sixteen men, well mounted and armed, left the fort with a view to attack the Indians. They soon discovered their encampment by the smoke of their fire. The whites divided themselves into two parties, intending to enclose the Indians, but unfortunately, a small dog which followed them, starting a rabbit, alarmed the Indians, upon which they cautiously moved off, passed between the two parties of white men unobserved, took a position between them and their horses, and opened a most destructive fire. The whites returned the fire with great firmness and bravery, and a desperate and bloody conflict ensued. Seven of the whites fell dead, and four were wounded. The others retreated to the fort. Three Indians fell in this battle, and several were wounded. The victors secured the white men's horses, and took them off. This was called the battle of the Trough.

Just before the above action commenced, Mr. Vanmeter, an old man, mounted his horse, rode upon a high ridge, and witnessed the battle. He returned with all speed to the fort, and gave notice of the defeat."

These repeated depredations of the savages, induced Gov. Dinwiddie, early in 1756, to order an expedition against the Indian towns on the Ohio. Maj, Andrew Lewis was appointed to command this expedition, and directed to proceed against the Shawanese villages near the mouth of the Great Kanawha.

Major Lewis led his men through great peril and suffering within a few miles of the Ohio, when a message ordering a return of the expedition reached him. The whole party suffered intensely during this march, and once were reduced to the necessity of cutting their buffalo skins into tugs and eating them; hence the name of Tug river.

The Indians having noticed the advance and return of this expedition, naturally supposed that it was deemed unsafe to penetrate the Indian country with a force so inadequate to the duty before them; and thus elated, pushed their acts of depredation with increased fury. They struck across the mountains by way of the Kanawha, Monongahela, Cheat, &c., carrying death to many a helpless family, and spreading alarm throughout the entire valley.

In the summer of 1757, a body of Shawanese, led on by their celebrated chief Kill-buck, crossed the Alleghanies and committed various acts of depredation. Some thirty or forty of this party appeared in the neighborhood of Edward's fort and killed two men at a mill, whom they scalped, and then made off, taking with them a quantity of meal. Information having been conveyed to the fort, forty men, under Captain Mercer, started in pursuit of the murderers. The Indians, expecting this, concealed themselves beneath a bank and awaited the approach of the whites. As a decoy, they had strewn along the path some of the meal taken from the mill. Mercer's party discovering this, supposed the Indians were making a speedy retreat, and, not apprized of their strength, moved on at a brisk step, until the whole party were drawn immediately over the line of Indians beneath the bank, when the latter opened a most destructive fire upon them, sixteen falling dead at the first discharge. The others attempting to save themselves by flight, were pursued and slaughtered in every direction, until, out of the forty, but six escaped to the fort. One poor fellow, who ran up the side of the mountain, was fired at by an Indian; the ball penetrated just above his heel, ranged up his leg, shivering the bones, and lodged a little below his knee; he slipped under the lap of a fallen tree and there hid himself, and lay in that situation for two days and nights before he was discovered by his friends. It was that length of time before the people at the fort would venture out to collect and bury the dead. This wounded man recovered, and lived many years after.

Some time afterwards, the Indians, in much greater force, and aided, it was believed, by several whites, determined to carry this fort by storm. The garrison had been considerably reinforced; among others, by the late Gen. Daniel Morgan, then a young man. The Indians made the assault with great boldness; but on this occasion they met with a sad reverse of fortune. The garrison sallied out, and a desperate battle ensued. The assailants were defeated with great slaughter, while the whites lost comparatively but few men.

These constant inroads of the savages induced the people to erect suitable forts at convenient points. Many of these little stockades arose along the Valley, which greatly served to protect the inhabitants and restrain the savages. Of these were Ashby's, on Patterson creek, near the present town of Frankfort; Hedges, on the road from Martinsburg to Bath; Riddel's and Wardon's, on Lost river; George's, near Petersburg, &c.

During the following year, (1758,) the savages again reappeared east of the mountains, and spread desolation and terror wherever they went. These visitations, doubtless for better security, were generally made in large parties, and their presence could not but create alarm among the sparsely populated settlements. The following account of one of these marauding parties, we take from the interesting local history of that region. A party of about fifty Indians, penetrated the neighborhood of Mill creek, about nine miles south of Woodstock. This was pretty thickly settled; and among other houses, George Painter had erected a large log one, with a good sized cellar. On the alarm being given, the neighboring people took refuge in this house. Late in the afternoon they were attacked. Mr. Painter, attempting to fly, had three balls shot through his body, and fell dead, when the others surrendered. The Indians dragged the dead body back to the house, threw it in, plundered the house of what they chose, and then set fire to it. While the house was in flames, consuming the body of Mr. Painter, they forced from the arms of their mothers four infant children, hung them up in trees, shot them in savage sport, and left them hanging. They then set fire to a stable containing sheep and calves. After these atrocities they moved off with forty-eight prisoners; among whom were Mrs. Painter, five of her daughters, and one of her sons; a Mrs. Smith and several of her children; a Mr. Fisher and several of his children, among them a lad of twelve or thirteen years old, a fine well grown boy, and remarkably fleshy. This little fellow, it will presently be seen, was destined to be the victim of savage cruelty.

Two of Painter's sons, and a young man by the name of Jacob Myers, escaped. One of the Painters, with Myers, ran over that night to Powell's fort, a distance of at least fifteen miles, and to Keller's fort, for aid. A small party of men set out early the next morning, well mounted and armed. They reached Mr. Painter's early in the day; but on learning the strength of the Indians, they declined going in pursuit, as they were too weak to follow.

After six days' travel they reached their villages, and held a council, when it was determined to sacrifice their helpless prisoner, Jacob Fisher. They first ordered him to collect a quantity of dry wood. The poor little fellow shuddered, burst into tears, and told his father they intended to burn him. His father replied, "I hope not;" and advised him to obey. When he had collected a sufficient quantity of wood to answer their purpose, they cleared and smoothed a ring around a sapling, to which they tied him by one hand, then formed a trail of wood around the tree, and set it on fire. The poor boy was then compelled to run round in this ring of fire until his rope wound him up to the sapling, and then back until he came in contact with the flame, whilst his infernal tormentors were drinking, singing, and dancing around him, with "horrid joy." This was continued for several hours; during which time the wretches became beastly drunk, and as they fell to the ground, their squaws would keep up the fire. With long sharp poles, they pierced the body of their victim whenever he flagged, until the poor and helpless boy fell and expired with the most excruciating torments, whilst his father and brothers were compelled to be witnesses of the heart-rending tragedy.

After an absence of about three years, Mrs. Painter, with her son and two of her daughters; Mrs. Smith, who had the honor, if it could be so deemed, of presenting her husband with an Indian son, by a distinguished chief; Fisher, and his surviving sons, with several others, returned home. Three of Mrs. Painter's daughters remained with the Indians; one of whom, after many years captivity, returned. The others married and spent their lives with their swarthy companions.

In connection with this, we may state, that a most remarkable feature of the Indian life, was the peculiar power of fascination which it exercised over those subjected to its influence. Other instances are upon record which show that this attachment to the allurements of savage life, was often astonishing. The following will serve as an illustration.

About the year 1758, a man by the name of John Stone, near what is called the White House, in the Hawksbill settlement, was killed by Indians. Stone's wife, with her infant child and a son about seven or eight years old, and George Grandstaff, a youth of sixteen years old, were taken prisoners. On the south-branch Mountain, the Indians murdered Mrs. Stone and her infant, but took the boy and Grandstaff to their towns. Grandstaff remained about three years a prisoner. The boy Stone grew up with the Indians, came home, and after obtaining possession of his father's property, sold it, got the money, returned to the Indians and was never heard of again.

MASSACRE AT SEYBERT'S FORT.

There is no accomplishment which the Indian warrior more delights in than that of strategy. Studying from boyhood to excel in this particular, he often becomes so skilful as to outwit his more cautious, and frequently less sagacious antagonist. Where, in ancient or modern history, do we find schemes better matured and more successfully executed than those of Pontiac? The capture of Mackinaw never has been surpassed for ingenuity and skill; while the terrible catastrophe at fort Massac, stands without a precedent either among civilized or savage men. The famed wooden horse of old, from whose capacious body issued the armed foe against the astonished and bewildered Trojans, was but a dull idea compared with the admirable finesse of the American savage on the lower Ohio, or northern lake. We premise this much, to introduce a case of fatal subtlety in our own State, — the capture of a small frontier post known as Seybert's fort, which stood on the south-branch of the Potomac, about twelve miles west of the present town of Franklin, in Pendleton county. It was a rude enclosure, cut out of the heart of the forest, but sufficiently strong to have resisted any attack from the enemy had the inmates themselves but been strong. Our artist has given a very correct representation of this early and memorable fortress, the history of which fills such a dark page in the annals of Virginia.

Seybert's fort served as a place of resort for the people of all the adjoining settlements. Into this they gathered in times of threatening danger, and remained during the seasons when the Indians were most troublesome. In May, 1758, a party of Shawanese invested the fort, and demanded a surrender. Finding neither threatening words nor bullets of any avail, the cunning savages, after two days' trial, resorted to strategy, and, unhappily, with most fatal success. They made various propositions to the besieged to give up, and their lives should be spared; if not, the siege should be continued and every soul massacred.

The promise of safety lured the unfortunate victims from their line of duty, and they yielded quiet possession of the fort. There were thirty persons at the time within the enclosure, and these the savages proceeded to secure. Instantly the whites realized the horror of their situation, and saw the inevitable doom which awaited them. In a moment of false security, they trusted to the promise of savages, and now were about to pay the folly with their lives. Of the whole number, all were massacred but eleven. Various accounts of the mode of massacre have been given, but the following is doubtless most correct. Ten, whom they wished to save, were secured and removed from the fort, the others were tied hand and foot, and seated in a continuous line upon a log. Behind each of the unfortunates stood a stalwart savage, who, at a given signal, sunk his tomahawk through the skull of his quivering victim. The work was soon finished, and the fort destroyed. This horrible scene was witnessed by a youth named Dyer, who was spared, although not of the number removed from the limits of the fort. He was taken to Logstown, on the Ohio, and thence to the Shawanee towns on the Scioto. After nearly two years' captivity he escaped, and made his way home. Of the other ten borne off as prisoners, nothing satisfactory is known.

It was during this year (1758) that an incident occurred near the present village of Petersburg, in Hardy, which stands without a parallel in modern history. A man named Bingaman lived with his family in a cabin, remote from any neighbors. He had been cautioned against the Indians; but, a man of most determined resolution and herculean strength, he laughed at the idea of fear, and said, no cut-throat savages should ever drive him from his home. In the fall of this year, a party of eight Indians made a descent upon his cabin, late at night, while all the family were asleep. Before Bingaman was aware of his danger, the savages had forced the door, and were in the house. Mrs. Bingaman, the younger, was shot through the left breast, but not dangerously wounded. Bingaman got his parents, wife and child beneath the bed, and then prepared for battle. The hired man was called down, but refused to come. The room was dark, and having discharged his gun, he commenced beating about at random with his heavy rifle. In this manner he fought with the desperation of a giant, and terribly did his blows tell upon the enemy. One after another he beat down before him, until finally, of the eight, but one remained, and he, terror-stricken, made from the house, and escaped to tell his tribe, that he had met with a man who was a "perfect devil." The intrepid Virginian had actually killed seven of his foes, which certainly, is unexampled in the history of single-handed combat. During the fight, the Indians frequently grappled their powerful antagonist, but were unable to keep him down, as early in the engagement he had pulled off his shirt. In the morning, when he found that his wife was wounded, he became so exasperated at the cowardice of the hired man that he would have killed him, had not Mrs. Bingaman interposed to save his life.

Bingaman afterwards moved to Natchez, where his son Adam, who was a lad at the time of the fight, had previously moved, and there he (the elder) died. Most of these facts we have derived personally from the venerable William Darby, of Washington city, who knew both the Bingamans at Natchez, and heard from each of them a recital of the incidents of that terrible fight. Kercheval gives a somewhat different version, but we have every reason to believe that our account is in the main correct. We find in Kercheval another incident illustrative of the energy and courage of this man, which we give. A party of whites (of whom Bingaman was one) had started in pursuit of some retreating Indians. They were overtaken late at night, and the pursuing party dismounting, the captain ordered Bingaman to remain with the horses, whilst the rest made the attack. This he refused, and followed after the company. "To make the destruction of the enemy more certain, it was deemed advisable to wait until daylight before they began the attack; but a young man, whose zeal overcame his discretion, fired into the group, upon which the Indians sprung to their feet and fled. Bingaman singled out a fellow of giant-like size, whom he pursued, throwing aside his rifle that his speed might not be retarded, — passed several smaller Indians in the chase — came up with him — and with a single blow of his hatchet cleft his skull. When Bingaman returned to the battle-ground, the captain sternly observed, 'I ordered you to stay and guard the horses.' Bingaman as sternly replied, 'You are a rascal, sir; you intended to disgrace me; and one more insolent word, and you shall share the fate of that Indian,' pointing towards the one he had just slain. The captain quailed under the stern menace, and held his peace. The captain and Bingaman had, a few days before, had a falling out. Several Indians fell in this affair, while the whites lost none of their party."

The Indian depredations, during this and the following years, were particularly fatal on the frontier settlements of Virginia. Many families suffered severely and terribly. Of these we will give a few as we find them related by the Historian of the Valley. He gives many interesting incidents connected with the early settlement of that part of Virginia, which cannot but be interesting to the readers of the present day.

In this year (1764), a party of eighteen Delawares crossed the mountains. Furman's Fort was about one mile above hanging-rock, on the South Branch. William Furman and Nimrod Ashby had gone out from the fort to watch a deer lick in the Jersey mountains. The Indians discovered and killed them both, and passed on into the county of Frederick, where they divided into two parties. One party of eight moved on to Cedar creek settlement; the other of ten attacked the people in the neighborhood of the present residence of Maj. John White. On this place a stockade was erected. The people in the neighborhood had taken the alarm, and were on their way to this fort, when assaulted by these Indians. They killed David Jones and his wife. Also some of Mrs. Thomas' family, and carried off one of the daughters. An old man, named Lloyd, and his wife, and several of his children, were killed. Esther Lloyd, their daughter, about thirteen years old, received three tomahawk wounds in the head, was scalped, and left lying, supposed to be dead. Henry Clouser and two of his sons were killed, and his wife and four of his daughters taken. The youngest daughter was about two years old; and as she impeded the mother's travelling, they dashed her brains out against a tree, in the presence of the agonized parent. Mrs. Thomas was taken to the Wappatomaka; but the river being pretty full, and deep fording, they encamped near Furman's fort for the night. The next morning a party of white men fired off their guns at the fort, which alarmed the Indians, and they hurried across the river, assisting all their female prisoners, except Mrs. Thomas, who being quite stout and strong, was left to struggle for herself. The current, however, proved too strong for her, and she floated down the river — but lodged against a rock, upon which she crawled, and saved herself from drowning.

The other party of eight Indians committed several murders on Cedar creek. It is probable this party killed a Mr. Lyle, a Mr. Butler, and some others. Mr. Ellis Thomas, the husband of the woman whose story has just been given, was killed the preceding harvest. This party of eight Indians took off two female prisoners, but were pursued by some white men, overtaken in the South Branch mountain, fired upon, and one of the Indians killed. The others fled, leaving their guns, prisoners and plunder.

The same year, (1764,) a party of eight Indians, with a white man by the name of Abraham Mitchell, killed George Miller, his wife and two children, within two miles of Strasburg. They also the same day killed John Bellinger, and took his wife, with her infant child, prisoners. In crossing Sandy ridge, west of Capon river, this child had its brains beaten out against a tree. A party of white men pursued them, overtook them in the South Branch mountains, fired upon them, and killed one, when the others fled, leaving every thing behind.

In the latter part of this year, (1765,) the Indians made their appearance in the neighborhood of Woodstock. They killed an old man who, with some women and children, was making his way to the fort at Woodstock. His name was George Sigler.

Shortly before this, two Indians were discovered lurking in the neighborhood of Mill creek. Matthias Painter, John Painter, and William Moore, armed themselves, and went in pursuit. They had not proceeded far, before they approached a large fallen pine, with a very bushy top. As they neared it, Matthias Painter observed, "We had better look sharp; it is quite likely the Indians are concealed under the tops of this tree." He had scarcely uttered the words before one of them rose up and fired. The ball grazed the temple of John Painter. Moore and Painter fired at the same instant; one of their balls passed through the Indian's body, and he fell, as they supposed, dead enough. The other fellow fled. The white men pursued him some distance; but the fugitive was too fleet for them. Finding they could not overhaul him, they gave up the chase and returned to the pine tree: but to their astonishment, the supposed dead Indian had moved off with both guns and a large pack of skins. They pursued his trail, and when he found they were gaining upon him, he got into a sink hole, and as soon as they approached, commenced firing at them. He had poured out a quantity of powder on dry leaves, filled his mouth with bullets, and using a musket which was a self-primer, he was enabled to load and fire with astonishing quickness. He thus fired at least thirty times before they could get a chance to dispatch him. At last Mr. Moore got an opportunity, and shot him through the head. Moore and Painter had many disputes which gave the fellow the first wound. Painter, at length, yielded, and Moore got the premium allowed by law for Indian scalps.

The fugitive who made his escape, unfortunately met with a young woman on horseback, named Sethon, whom he tore from her horse, and forced off with him. This occurred near the present town of Newmarket, and after travelling about twenty miles, it is supposed the captive broke down from fatigue, and the savage monster beat her to death with a heavy pine knot. Her screams were heard by some people who lived upwards of a mile from this scene of horror, and who next day, on going to the place to ascertain the cause, found her stripped and weltering in her blood.

Allusion has been made in another part of this volume to the murder of the three Eckarlys, brothers, who, in 1755, settled on what is now known as Hunker's bottom, Cheat river. The circumstances were about these. Dr. Thomas Eckarly and his two brothers, all members of that peculiar Christian sect called Bunkers, visited the west, and erected a cabin, soon after the murder of the unfortunate Files family, to which reference has elsewhere been made. The three brothers continued to occupy undisturbed, for a number of years, their peaceful and quiet possessions. Growing short of ammunition, &c., the elder brother went on a trading expedition to the east. In returning, he stopped at Fort Pleasant, and there not being a very friendly feeling entertained by many of the hardy bordermen toward this singular sect, he was detained on a charge of being in alliance with the Indians. At length, however, it was determined to send a guard along with him, and if their suspicions were rightly founded, he was to be brought back and dealt with accordingly. In due time the escort reached the site of the humble cabin in the forest, but, alas! the destroyer had been there, and nothing remained but the half-consumed bodies of the unfortunate brothers.

A few years subsequent to this, several settlers on the Monongahela, near the mouth of Decker's creek, were cut off by a party of Delawares. Of these, were Thomas Decker, from whom the creek derives its name. But two or three of the settlers escaped, and one of these, making his way to Red-stone old fort, (Brownsville,) gave information of the catastrophe. The commandant. Captain Paull, despatched a message to Fort Pitt, conveying intelligence of the visitation, and notifying Colonel Gibson of the probable direction taken by the savages on their retreat. Colonel Gibson, leaving the garrison in command of a subordinate officer, passed rapidly down the river, hoping to intercept them. In this, however, he failed; but came accidentally upon a small party of Mingoes, encamped on Cross creek. Little Eagle, a distinguished chief of that tribe, commanded the party, and discovering the whites about the same time that Gibson saw them, he gave a fearful whoop, and at the same instant discharged his gun at the leader of the whites. The ball passed through Gibson's coat, but without injuring him. With the quickness of a tiger he sprang upon his foe, and with one sweep of his sword, severed the head of Little Eagle from his body. Two others were shot dead by the whites, but the remainder escaped, and reported that the white captain had cut off the head of their chief with a long knife. This was the origin of that celebrated and fearfully significant term, the "long-knives." It was applied throughout the war to the Virginians, and even to this day has not been forgotten by some of the western tribes. Captain Gibson, himself a Virginian, acquired the soubriquet of "Long-knife warrior," and was known by it always afterward.

In the Summer of 1761, there was an irruption of savages into the James river settlement, attended with most fatal results. The party embraced about fifty Shawanese warriors. On Purgatory creek, they killed Thomas Perry, Joseph Dennis, and a child; taking the wife of Dennis prisoner. Thence they proceeded to the house of Robert Renick, making prisoner of Mrs. Renick and her five children. Mr. Renick being absent at the time, escaped, but only to fall at another place. Proceeding to a near neighbor, where Mr. Renick happened to be, they there killed him, and a man named Thomas Smith, making captives of Smith's wife and a girl named Sally Jew. At the time these murderous proceedings were going on, three men (George Matthews, afterwards so distinguished in the battles of Point Pleasant and Germantown, with two brothers by the name of Maxwell,) rode up to the house, and discovering the dead bodies of Smith and Renick lying in the yard, made quick their retreat, but not before the Indians had noticed their movements, and fired after them. One of the Maxwells was slightly wounded in the arm. Mrs. Renick, on her return to her friends, after a captivity of five years, said the Indians saw the three men approach, and as they checked up their horses at the fence, four of the Indians detailed for that purpose, took aim, but the whites suddenly wheeling their horses, saved their lives.

A party of the savages, twenty in number, were despatched with their prisoners for the Ohio, whilst the remainder penetrated further into the country to renew their depredations. The alarm, however, had been sounded, and such of the inhabitants as lived convenient, collected at Paull's fort. Leaving five men to take care of the fort, a party of twenty-two, headed by Matthews, went in pursuit. They were soon overhauled, and after a severe fight, compelled to give way. In consequence of the intense darkness of the night, it was found impossible to pursue the enemy further, and the Indians rejoining their companions, made good their escape with prisoners and booty. Nine Indians and three whites were killed in the engagement, all of whom were decently buried.

Of the prisoners, Mrs. Renick and two of her sons were ransomed in 1766; one died in captivity; another intermarried with the Indians and became a chief; and a third settled on the Scioto, near Chillicothe, from whom has sprung an extensive and highly respectable family. Hannah Dennis made her escape after two years' captivity.

It was during this year (1763) that two of the Greenbriar settlements, (Muddy creek, and Big Levels,) were entirely cut off. A party of some fifty or sixty Shawanese, supposed to have been headed by Cornstalk, penetrated the country under the garb of friendship, and as no recent hostilities had taken place in that region, the inhabitants fondly believed there was no danger. With this fatal security, they received the savages warmly and extended them every reasonable hospitality. Suddenly, they fell upon the men, butchering every one of them, and then made captives of the women and children. They next visited the Levels, where Archibald Clendenin had erected a rude block house, and where were gathered quite a number of families. Here the Indians were again entertained with hospitality. Mr. Clendenin had just brought in three fine elk, upon which the savages feasted sumptuously. One of the inmates was a decrepid old woman, with an ulcerated limb; she undressed the member, and asked an Indian if he could cure it. "Yes," he replied, and immediately sunk his tomahawk into her head. This was the signal, and instantly every man in the house was put to death.

The cries of the women and children alarmed a man in the yard, who escaped and reported the circumstances to the settlement at Jackson's river. The people were loth to believe him, as the character of the Indians had been so peaceable. Soon, however, they were convinced, for the savages appeared and many of the fleeing families were massacred without mercy.

The prisoners were then marched off in direction of the Ohio. Mrs. Clendenin proved herself in that trying moment a woman fit to be one of the mothers of the west. Indignant at the treachery and cowardly conduct of the wretches, she did not fail to abuse them from the chief down, in the most unmeasured manner. The savages, to intimidate her, would flap the bloody scalp of her dead husband against her face, and significantly twirl their tomahawks above her head, but still the courageous woman talked to them like one who felt her injuries, and feeling, resolved to express them. On the day after her captivity, she saw an opportunity to escape, and giving her infant to a woman, slipped unobserved into a thicket. The child soon beginning to cry, one of the Indians inquired concerning the mother, but getting no satisfactory reply, swore he would "bring the cow to the calf," and taking the infant by the heels dashed out its brains against a tree. Mrs. C. returned to her desolate home, and secured the remains of her husband from the rapacious jaws of the wild animals with which the woods abounded.

It is stated that a black woman in escaping from Mr. Clendenin's house, killed her own child to prevent its cries attracting the attention of the savages.

Such were some of the horrid realities felt and endured by the first settlers of Western Virginia.

In October of this year, (1764,) a party of forty or fifty Mingo and Delaware Indians crossed the Ohio, and ascending Great Sandy came over on New river, where they separated, and forming two parties, directed their steps toward different settlements — one party going towards Roanoke and Catawba, the other in the direction of Jackson's river. They had not long passed, when their trail was discovered by three men, (Swope, Pack and Pitman,) who were trapping on New river. These men followed the trail till they came to where the Indian party divided; and judging from the routes taken, that their object was to visit the Roanoke and Jackson's river settlements, they determined to apprize the inhabitants of their danger. Swope and Pack started for Roanoke and Pitman for Jackson's river. But before they could accomplish their object, the Indians had reached the settlements on the latter river, and on Catawba.

The party which came to Jackson's river, travelled down Dunlap's creek and crossed James river, above Fort Young, in the night and unnoticed; and going down this river to William Carpenter's, where was a stockade fort under the care of a Mr. Brown, they met Carpenter just above his house and killed him. They immediately proceeded to the house, and made prisoners of a son of Mr. Carpenter, two sons of Mr. Brown, (all small) and one woman — the others belonging to the house were in the field at work. The Indians then despoiled the house and taking off some horses, commenced a precipitate retreat — fearing discovery and pursuit.

When Carpenter was shot, the report of the gun was heard by those at work in the field; and Brown carried the alarm to Fort Young and Fort Dinwiddie. Captain Paul, commanding the latter, immediately started with twenty men in pursuit. On Indian creek they met Pitman almost exhausted. The pursuit was kept up, but the savages escaped.

As Captain Paul and his men were returning, they accidentally met with the other party of Indians, who had been to Catawba, and committed some depredations and murders there. They were discovered about midnight, encamped on the north bank of New river, opposite an island at the mouth of Indian creek. Excepting some few who were watching three prisoners, (whom they had taken on Catawba, and who were sitting in the midst of them,) they were lying around a small fire, wrapped in skins and blankets. Paul's men not knowing that there were captives among them, fired in the midst, killed three Indians, and wounded several others, one of whom drowned himself to preserve his scalp — the rest of the party fled hastily down the river and escaped.

Several captives were released, and considerable plunder recovered. To show the deadening effect of these terrible scenes upon the human mind, we will copy the reply of a prisoner rescued at this time. She was a Mrs. Gunn, an English woman, and had known Captain Paul years before. Recognizing his voice, she called him by name, just as one of his men, who supposed her to be a squaw, was in the act of tomahawking her. She made no resistance, and when asked the reason replied, "I had as soon be killed as not — my husband is murdered — my children are slain — my parents are dead. I have not a relation in America — everything dear to me here is gone — I have no wishes — no hopes — no fears — I would not have risen to my feet to save my life."

Such were some of the horrors experienced on the frontier in the early settlement of the country. The above facts we derive chiefly from Withers.

1777.

This, the far-famed bloody-year, and the "year of the three sevens," as the old pioneers were accustomed to call it, is full of painful incidents to hundreds of families in North-Western Virginia. It was, indeed, the most terrible year the early settlers ever experienced. Dark, mysterious clouds of malignant spirits hung upon the horizon, threatening every moment to overwhelm and exterminate the half-protected pioneer in his wilderness home. At length the storm broke over them, and scarcely a settlement in the great Valley of the West that did not experience its fatal and terrible effect. The fury of the savages during this year seemed to have no bounds. The wretched inhabitants were massacred with every conceivable cruelty. Men, women, and children were chosen objects of their revenge, and scarcely a settlement west of the Alleghanies that escaped their visits and their fury. The alarm became great, and terror seemed to seize upon the entire population. Block-houses were hastily thrown up, and many who could, moved their families to Red-stone, and other points on the Monongahela; but still, there were hundreds left to endure all the anticipated horrors of an Indian invasion.

The Indians separated into what were termed "scalping parties," and penetrated the country at various points. One of their first acts along the Monongahela was to visit the house of a Mr. Grigsly, on West Fork, and carry off his wife and two children. Mr. Grigsby was absent at the time; but returning soon after, and missing his family, suspected the true cause, although no injury had been done to either the house or furniture. Securing the services of some of his neighbors, pursuit was immediately given. Keeping the trail about six miles, the horror-stricken husband came suddenly upon the ghastly forms of his murdered wife and child. The savages, finding Mrs. Grigsby unable to travel on account of her delicate situation, most inhumanly tomahawked her, together with her youngest child.

The almost frantic husband and parent, burning for revenge, rushed on with a few select men, but the savages suspecting a pursuit, divided into small parties, and so effectually covered their trail, that all efforts to trace them were unsuccessful, and the pursuit had to be given up.

This was but the commencement of such scenes of blood along the Monongahela. A short time after this occurrence, a Miss Coons, whose father erected Coons' fort, went into the field to turn some hemp which lay near the fort. While there engaged, two young men, Thomas Cunningham and Enoch James, approached, and after a short conversation, went on. They had not gone far before the report of a gun was heard, and on looking round saw two Indians standing near Miss Coons, one of whom was in the act of scalping his unfortunate victim. Pursuit was immediately given, but the savages eluded every effort to trace them. One of the young men fired at the retreating murderer, but without success.

Western Pennsylvania suffered in common this year with Western Virginia. Scalping parties overran the settlements along the lower Monongahela and its tributaries. The settlements within the region now embraced in Washington, Alleghany, and Westmoreland counties suffered severely. As it was known that the Indians who committed these depredations crossed the Alleghany river, it was determined to erect a fort at some convenient point on that stream, supposing that the presence of a small garrison would have the effect to check the movements of the enemy in that quarter. Accordingly, Colonel William Crawford, whose melancholy fate a few years later thrilled the whole country with horror, visited the Alleghany for the purpose of selecting a proper location for the proposed fort. He decided to place it near the mouth of Puckety creek, about seventeen miles above Fort Pitt. The fort was immediately built, and called Crawford, in honor of its projector. Several others were erected about this time along the Loyalhanna, Kiskeminitas, Cheat, Ten-mile, Pidgeon creek, &c. &c. The effect of the erection of this fort may have been to force the Indians lower down, and such was doubtless the fact. Large parties of them found their way into Virginia at points below, and their operations in this quarter were more extensive, particularly in the neighborhood of Wheeling, (which we shall presently notice) than was ever before undertaken. The whole combined force of the western confederated tribes seemed directed against this particular section.

Early in April, a man named Rodger McBride, was killed and scalped, about ten miles up Wheeling creek, which caused considerable excitement, and induced Colonel Morgan, United States Indian Agent for the middle department, to communicate the fact by letter to Colonel Crawford, under date April 10. About the same time, another murder was committed near where Bridgeport now stands, (opposite Wheeling).

SIEGE OF FORT HENRY.

The fall of 1777, so memorable in the annals of the West, was remarkable for nothing more than the united and determined attack, by the combined arms of British and Indians, against the stockade at Wheeling, Virginia.

The eloquent Chatham was never more right, than when he denounced the alliance between Britain and the American savages as a "disgrace, — a deep and deadly sin." That act, connected as it was with the execrable scalp

173

bounty, will stand a living stigma upon her name and history as long as time lasts.

Early in the month of August, fears began to be felt by the settlers, as flying reports occasionally reached them, that the Indians were gathering in great numbers, and it seemed certain they meditated an attack during the approaching autumn. Every precaution was taken to guard against an insidious attack. Scouting parties were kept out, who, with the sleepless vigilance of well trained spies, watched all the movements of the enemy. Information had been conveyed to General Hand, commanding at Fort Pitt, by some friendly Moravian Indians, who received it from Isaac Zane, brother of Colonel Ebenezer Zane, that a large army of Indians, composed chiefly of warriors from the great North-Western confederacy, were making vigorous preparations to strike an effective and terrible blow upon some of the settlements on the Ohio. It was further stated, that this chosen body of savages would be under the command of Simon Girty, a man whose known relentless ferocity toward his foresworn countrymen, could not but add to the fearful prospect before them.

General Hand lost no time in widely disseminating the information thus obtained.

As it was uncertain where the expected blow would fall, all was activity, fear and alarm at the several little half-finished fortresses stretching at distances from one to two hundred miles, between Fort Pitt and the Great Kanawha. But it soon became manifest at what point the enemy designed to strike. With apprehensions of dread, the settlers at the mouth of Wheeling, (numbering about thirty families,) betook themselves to their fort, and with calm resolution awaited the issue.

Early in the evening of the 31st of August, Capt. Joseph Ogle, who had been sent out some days before, at the head of ten or fifteen men, to scout along the different routes usually followed by the Indians, returned to Wheeling, and reported no immediate cause of danger.

The Indians, with their accustomed sagacity, suspecting that their movements might be watched, abandoned all the paths usually trodden, and dividing as they approached the river, into small distinct parties, struck out along new lines for the Ohio. Without discovery, they reached the vicinity of Bogg's island, (two miles below Wheeling creek,) and there consolidating their force, crossed the river and proceeded directly to the creek bottom, under cover of night, and completed their plans for movement in the morning.

The Indian army consisted of over three hundred and fifty Mingoes, Shawanese and Wyandotts. It was commanded by the notorious renegade, Simon Girty, and well furnished with arms, ammunition, &c., by the infamous Hamilton, governor of Canada. Girty disposed of his men in two lines across the bottom, stretching from the river to the creek. They were arranged at convenient distances, and effectually concealed by the high weeds and corn.

Posted near the centre of these lines, and close to a path leading from the fort (which they supposed some of the whites would pass along in the morning,) were six Indians.

Shortly after day-break of the 1st of September, Dr. McMechen, who was about returning east of the mountains, sent out a white man named Boyd, and a negro, to catch the horses. The two men had not proceeded far before they discovered the six Indians already referred to. Hoping to escape, they made a hurried retreat, but Boyd was killed. The negro was permitted to return, doubtless to mislead the whites as to the actual number of the foe.

The commandant immediately ordered Captain Samuel Mason, who had brought his company to the fort on the previous evening, to go out and dislodge the enemy. With fourteen of his men, the gallant Captain at once sallied forth, and after proceeding partly across the bottom, discovered the six Indians and fired upon them. Almost simultaneously with this discharge, the entire Indian army arose, and with horrid yells rushed upon the little band of whites. Finding that to stand were madness. Mason ordered a retreat, and in person commenced cutting his way through the Indian line. This he succeeded in doing, but most of his gallant little party perished in the attempt. Out of the fourteen, but two escaped, and they, like Captain Mason, eluded the pursuing savages by concealing themselves beneath brush and fallen timber. The names of those who escaped this general slaughter, were Hugh McConnell and Thomas Glenn. William Shepherd, son of Colonel David Shepherd, had gained the spring near where the market-house now stands, when one of his feet caught in a vine, and falling, the pursuing savage was instantly upon him, and with a war club dispatched him on the spot.

So soon as the disaster to Mason had been ascertained at the fort, Captain Joseph Ogle, with his dozen experienced scouts, advanced to his relief, but not without forebodings of imminent danger, as the yells of the savages, and shrieks of the whites, told too plainly that a terrible massacre was taking place.

With fearless steps Captain Ogle moved on to the scene of conflict, determined to cover the retreat of his unfortunate countrymen, or perish in the attempt. An excited and bloody foe rushed upon them with the fury of demons, and all but two or three shared the fate of the first detachment.

Captain Ogle, Sergeant Jacob Ogle, Martin Wetzel, and perhaps one other, were all who escaped.

The loss of so many brave men at such a time, was a sad blow to this part of the country. Those who fell were the pride of that little fortress. They were heroes in every sense of the word; — men of iron nerve, indomitable courage and devoted patriotism. The valor of either would have done honor to the victors of Marathon. Scarcely had the shrieks of the wounded and dying been quieted, than the army of savages, with reeking scalps just torn from the heads of the ill-fated soldiery, presented themselves in front of the fort, and demanded a surrender.

The appearance of the enemy, as they approached, was most formidable. They advanced in two separate columns, with drum, fife, and British colors.

The morning was calm, warm, and bright, and the sun just rising over the high hill which overlooked the fort, was gently dissipating the heavy fog which covered the bloody scene on the bottom.

As the Indians advanced, a few scattering shots were fired at them from the fort, without, however, doing much execution. Girty, having brought up his forces, proceeded to dispose of them as follows. The right flank, was brought around the base of the hill, and distributed among the several cabins convenient to the fort. The left were ordered to defile beneath the river bank, close under the fort.

Thus disposed, Girty presented himself at the window of a cabin, holding forth a white flag, and offering conditions of peace. He read the proclamation of Hamilton, Governor of Canada, and in a stentorian voice demanded the surrender of the fort, offering, in case they complied, protection; but if they refused, immediate and indiscriminate massacre.

Girty referred, in a very boasting manner, to the great force at his command; and called upon them, as loyal subjects, to give up in obedience to the demand of the king's agent, and that not one of them should be injured.

Although the whole number of men then in the fort did not exceed ten or a dozen, still there was no disposition to yield; but, on the contrary, a fixed determination to defy the renegade, and all the power of King George.

Girty having finished his harangue. Colonel David Shepherd, the commandant, promptly and in the most gallant and effective manner, replied, "Sir, we have consulted our wives and children, and all have resolved — men, women, and children, sooner to perish at their posts than place themselves under the protection of a savage army with you at the head; or abjure the cause of liberty and the colonies." The outlaw attempted to reply, but a shot from the fort put a stop to any further harangue.

A darker hour had scarcely ever obscured the hopes of the west. Death was all around that little fortress, and hopeless despair seemed to press upon its inmates; but still they could not and would not give up. Duty, patriotism, pride, independence, safety, all required they should not surrender, and forswear the cause of freedom.

Unable to intimidate them, and finding the besieged proof against his vile promises, the chagrined and discomfited Girty disappeared from the cabin, but in a few minutes was seen approaching with a large body of Indians, and instantly a tremendous rush was made upon the fort. They attempted to force the gates, and test the strength of the pickets by muscular effort. Failing to make any impression, Girty drew off his men a few yards, and commenced a general fire upon the port-holes.

Thus continued the attack during most of the day and part of the night, but without any sensible effect. About noon, a temporary withdrawal of the enemy took place. During the cessation, active preparations were carried on within the fort to resist a further attack. Each person was assigned some particular duty. Of the women, some were required to run bullets, while others were to cool the guns, load and hand them to the men, &c. Some of them, indeed, insisted upon doing duty by the side of the men, and two actually took their position at the port-holes, dealing death to many a dusky warrior.

About three o'clock, the Indians returned to the attack with redoubled fury. They distributed themselves among the cabins, behind fallen trees, &c. The number thus disposed of, amounted to perhaps one-half the actual force of the enemy. The remainder advanced along the base of the hill south of the fort, and commenced a vigorous fire upon that part of the stockade. This was a cunningly devised scheme, as it drew most of the inmates to that quarter. Immediately a rush was made from the cabins, lead on by Girty in person, and a most determined effort made to force the entrance. The attempt was made with heavy timber, but failed, with the loss of many of their boldest warriors.

Several similar attempts were made during the afternoon, but all alike failed. Maddened and chagrined by repeated disappointment and ill-success, the savages withdrew to their covert until night-fall. Day at length closed; darkness deepened over the waters, and almost the stillness of death reigned around. About nine o'clock, the savages re-appeared, making night hideous with their yells, and the heavens lurid with their discharge of musketry.

The lights in the fort having been extinguished, the inmates had the advantage of those without, and many a stalwart savage fell before the steady aim of experienced frontiermen.

Repeated attempts were made during the night to storm the fort, and to fire it, but all failed through the vigilance and activity of those within.

At length that night of horror passed, and day dawned upon the scene, but to bring a renewal of the attack. This, however, did not last long, and despairing of success, the savages prepared to leave. They fired most of the buildings, killed the cattle, and were about departing, when a relief party of fourteen men, under Colonel Andrew Swearengen, from Holliday's fort, twenty-four miles above, landed in a pirogue, and undiscovered by the Indians, gained entrance to the fort.

Shortly afterwards. Major Samuel McColloch, at the head of forty mounted men, from Short creek, made their appearance in front of the fort, the gates of which were joyfully thrown open. Simultaneously with the appearance of McColloch's men, re-appeared the enemy, and a rush was made to cut off the entrance of some of the party. All, however, succeeded in getting in except the gallant Major, who, anxious for the safety of his men, held back until his own chance was entirely cut off. Finding himself surrounded by savages, he rode at full speed in direction of the hill.

The enemy, with exulting yells, followed close in pursuit, not doubting they would capture one whom of all other men they preferred to wreak their vengeance upon. (For a full account of the sequel, the reader is referred to the biographical sketch of Major McColloch, to be found in its appropriate place in this volume.) Greatly disappointed at the escape of the gallant Major, and knowing the hopelessness of attempting to maintain a siege against such increased numbers, the Indians fired a few additional shot at the fort, and then moved rapidly off in a body for their own country.

It has been conjectured that the enemy lost on this occasion from forty to fifty in killed and wounded. The loss of the whites has been already stated. Not a single person was killed within the fort, and but one slightly wounded.

### DEPLORABLE AMBUSCADE.

By far the most disastrous ambuscade in the settlement of the west, was that at the head of Grave creek narrows, now Marshall county, Virginia, September 27th, 1777.

Captain William Foreman, a brave and meritorious officer, organized a volunteer company in Hampshire county, Virginia, and marched to Wheeling in the fall of 1777. It was known that Patrick Henry, Governor of Virginia, had determined early in the spring of that year, to send an expedition against the Indian towns at the head of the Scioto, and with this view ordered three hundred men to be raised in the counties of Youghioghany, Monongalia and Ohio. Some of the most patriotic of the citizens east of the mountains, thinking the west in this emergency might stand in need of aid, determined to go to her assistance. Of this number was Capt. Foreman, who soon raised a company, and by the middle of September was at Wheeling. A gallant soldier, but wholly unfamiliar with Indian warfare, he proved himself unfit for the service, and in his very first expedition suffered the deplorable ambuscade an account of which we will now give.

After the withdrawal of the Indians from Wheeling, nothing more was seen of them, or heard of their movements up to the time of which we now speak; and the impression became general that they had retired to their towns.

On Sunday morning, September 26th, (1777,) a smoke was noticed by some persons at Wheeling, in the direction of Grave creek, which caused an apprehension that the Indians might be burning the stockade and houses of Mr. Tomlinson. In order to ascertain this fact, and afford protection if any were necessary. Captain Foreman, with his company, and a few experienced scouts, were despatched by Colonel Shepherd for the purpose.

The party proceeded without interruption to Grave creek, and found all safe. Remaining over night, they started early on the following morning to return. When they had reached the lower end of Grave creek narrows, some of the more experienced frontiermen suggested the expediency of leaving the river bottom, and returning by way of the ridge. The commander, however, hooted at the idea of so much caution, and ordered the party to proceed. The order was obeyed by his own men, including several of the volunteer scouts; but some declined to go with him, and of these was a man named Lynn, whose great experience as a spy, added to his sagacity and judgment, should at least have rendered his opinions valuable, and entitled to weight. His apprehensions were, that the Indians, if lurking about, had watched the movements of the party, and would most likely attack them at some point on the river. He said, that in all probability, they had been on the opposite side of the river and noticed the party go down; that they had crossed during the night and most probably were at that time lying in ambush for their return. How fearfully were his apprehensions realized.

During the interchange of opinions between Foreman and Lynn, a man named Robert Harkness, a relative of Mr. Tomlinson, sat on a log near the parties, and often said that the controversy at times ran high. Foreman, who prided himself on being a thoroughly disciplined officer, was not disposed to yield to the suggestions of a rough backwoodman. Lynn, on the other hand, convinced of the fatal error which the other seemed determined to commit, could not but remonstrate with all the power of persuasion at his command. Finally, when the order to march was given, Lynn with some six or eight others struck up the hill side, while Foreman with his company pursued the path along the base.

Nothing of importance occurred until the party reached the extreme upper end of the narrows. Just where the bottom begins to widen, those in front had their attention drawn to a display of Indian trinkets, beads, bands, &c., strewn in profusion along the path. With a natural curiosity, but a great lack of perception, the entire party gathered about those who picked up the articles of decoy, and whilst thus standing in a compact group, looking at the beads, &c., two lines of Indians stretched across the path, one above, the other below, and a large body of them simultaneously arose from beneath the bank, and opened upon the devoted party a most deadly and destructive fire. The river hill rises at this point with great boldness, presenting an almost insurmountable barrier. Still, those of the party who escaped the first discharge, attempted to rush up the acclivity, and some with success. But the savages pursued and killed several.

At the first fire, Captain Foreman and most of his party, including his two sons, fell dead. The exact loss cannot with certainty be ascertained, but is supposed to have been about twenty, including the Captain. We give, (Note C, end Chap. I.,) a list of losses, &c., sustained by members of Captain Foreman's company, but there is nothing to indicate who were killed. The presumption is, however, that most of those whose names are mentioned suffered on the occasion referred to.

When Lynn and his party heard the guns, they rushed down the side of the hill, hallooing as though they were five times as numerous. This had the effect of restraining the savages in pursuit, and perhaps saved the lives of many.

Of those who escaped up the hill were Robert Harkness and John Collins. The former, in pulling himself up by a sapling, had the bark knocked into his face with a ball from an Indian's gun. Collins was shot through the left thigh, breaking the bone, and completely disabling him. Lynn and his companions carried him to a spring said to have been just over the hill, and throwing together their supply of provisions, left him in a sheltered position, promising to send a messenger on the following day with a horse.

Those who were so fortunate as to escape this terrible affair, made their way in safety to Wheeling.

On the second day, a party went down and buried the dead. Col. Shepherd, Col. Zane, Andrew Poe, and Martin Wetzel were of this number. They were thrown into one common grave, and the place of their interment is still pointed out to the passer-by.

Collins, the wounded man, was taken off on horseback, the second night. They carried him to Shepherd's Fort, and the present Mrs. Cruger remembers to have seen him when brought in. He suffered greatly with his wounded limb in riding; but finally recovered, and lived for many years.

The number of Indians engaged in this affair was never known. Some supposed it was the same body that attacked the fort at Wheeling, three weeks previous; but this is all conjecture.

About the last of September, two men (Leonard Petro and William White), who were watching a path that led up the Little Kanawha, killed an elk, and after a hearty supper laid down to sleep. "About midnight. White awakening, discovered by the light of the moon, that there were several Indians near, who had doubtless been drawn by the report of their gun in the evening. He saw at a glance, the impossibility of escape, by flight; and preferring captivity to death, he whispered to Petro to lie still, lest any movement of his might lead to this result. In a few minutes the Indians sprang on them; and White raising himself as one lay hold of him, aimed a furious blow, with his tomahawk, hoping to wound the Indian by whom he was beset, and then make his escape. Missing his aim, he affected to be ignorant of the fact, that he had encountered Indians; professed great joy at meeting with them, and declared that he was then on his way to their towns. They were not deceived by the artifice; for although he assumed an air of pleasantness and gaiety, calculated to win upon their confidence, yet the woful countenance of Petro, convinced them that White's conduct was feigned, that he might lull them into inattention, and thus be enabled to escape. They were both tied for the night; and in the morning. White being painted red, and Petro black, they were forced to proceed to the Indian towns. When approaching their village, the whoop of success brought several to meet them; and on their arrival at it, they found every preparation made for running the gauntlet. White did not, however, remain long in captivity. Eluding their vigilance, he took one of their guns and began his flight homeward. Before he had travelled far, he met an Indian on horseback, whom he succeeded in shooting; and mounting his horse, made his way home. Petro was never heard of afterwards. The painting of him black, had indicated their intention to kill him; and the escape of White probably hastened it."

The inhabitants of the Upper Monongahela continued to observe their usual vigilance until toward the close of November, when a fall of snow occurring, they relaxed somewhat their watchfulness. As a general thing, the Indians withdrew from the settlements on the commencement of winter, and did not reappear until the coming spring. Instances were very rare, in which they disturbed the settlements during winter. The readiness by which they could be tracked, together with the severity of the weather, compelled them to such a course.

The snow to which we have referred, lulled the inhabitants into false security. About twenty Indians had penetrated the settlement in Tygart Valley, and were waiting to make an attack when the snow fell. Not liking to return without some trophy of their valor, the savages concealed themselves until the snow disappeared. On the 15th day of December they came to the house of Darby Connoly, at the upper extremity of the Valley, and killed his wife, himself, and several of their children, taking three others prisoners. Proceeding to the next house, they killed John Stewart, wife and child, .and took Miss Hamilton (sister of Mrs. Stewart) captive. Then changing their direction, with great dispatch, they entered upon their journey homeward, with the captives and plunder.

In the course of the evening, after these outrages were committed, John Hadden passing by the house of Connoly, saw an elk which the family raised, lying dead in the yard, and suspecting that all was not right, entered the house, and with horror saw what had been done. Knowing that the work of blood had been recently committed, he hastened to alarm the neighborhood, and sent an express to Captain Benjamin Wilson, who lived about twenty miles down the Valley. With great promptitude, Capt. Wilson went through the settlement, exerting himself to procure as many volunteers, as would justify going in pursuit of the murderers; and so indefatigable was he in accomplishing this purpose, that, on the day after, he appeared with thirty men, prepared to take the trail, and push forward in pursuit of the savages. For five days they followed through cold and wet, often wading and swimming streams, and then traveling many miles before the icicles could be thawed off. Still there was no appearance of the enemy; and at length, the men positively refusing to go farther, the party returned from its fruitless chase, and the savages escaped with their prisoners and booty.

These were perhaps, the last murders committed in North-Western Virginia, during this fatal and bloody year.

DEATH OF GRANDSTAFF.

Of those who followed the Wetzels, Bennetts, Messers and others, to the west and settled on Wheeling creek, was a man named Grandstaff. He improved the farm now owned by Mr. Buchanan, about three miles above the forks.

On the renewal of Indian hostilities, Grandstaff removed his family to Shepherd's fort. He was in the habit, however, of visiting his improvements almost daily, but returning to the fort in the evening.

In March of this year, Mr. G. went up to his farm, when a party of Indians, who had been lying in wait, shot and scalped him.

1778.

Early in the commencement of this year, it became manifest that the confederated tribes were preparing to renew their attack upon the frontier settlements of the west. On the 8th of February, Gov. Schuyler wrote to Congress, — "There is too much reason to believe that an expedition will be formed against the western frontiers of this state, Virginia and Pennsylvania." The apprehensions of Gen. Schuyler were too well founded. It was in this year the terrible drama of Wyoming took place. Of the savage operations in this section, we shall now proceed to notice. The success of the enemy in the fall previous, seemed to madden them for blood, and at a very early day they moved upon the frontier, spreading alarm and death in almost every direction. The erection of Fort Crawford on the Alleghany, and the contemplated military operations of Gen. Mcintosh on the Ohio, had the effect of restraining the movements of the savages in each of these directions, and forcing them to cross at points farther down. Their failure to take Fort Henry in the previous September, and thinking perhaps that the garrison had been strengthened, they struck the frontier at points below and thence proceeded against the settlements on the Monongahcla. At that time, the entire frontier from Wheeling to Point Pleasant (one hundred and seventy miles) was unprotected, if we except the small and wholly inefficient stations at Grave creek, Baker's, etc. These offered no impediment to the progress of the enemy, and unmolested they struck back to the heart of the mountain settlements.

The inhabitants of the upper Monongahela, not unmindful of the indications which had reached them, commenced busily preparing for the anticipated attack. Harbert's block-house on Ten-mile, was a safe and convenient resort, and thither those living in that quarter took shelter. Notwithstanding these prudential steps, they unhappily suffered themselves to be lulled into false security. The weather being fine, the children were allowed to play outside of the block-house. Suddenly, one of them discovered Indians, and, running in, gave the alarm. "John Murphy stepped to the door to see if danger had really approached, when one of the Indians, turning the corner of the house, fired at him. The ball took effect, and Murphy fell into the house. The Indian springing in, was grappled by Harbert, and thrown on the floor. A shot from without, wounded Harbert, yet he continued to maintain his advantage over the prostrate savage, striking him effectually as he could with his tomahawk, when another gun was fired from without, the ball passing through his head. His antagonist then slipped out at the door, badly wounded in the encounter.

"Just after the first Indian entered, an active young warrior, holding a tomahawk with a long spike at the end, came in. Edward Cunningham instantly drew up his gun, but it flashed, and they closed in doubtful strife. Both were active and athletic; and sensible of the high prize for which they contended, each put forth his strength, and strained every nerve to gain the ascendancy. For awhile, the issue seemed doubtful. At length, by great exertion, Cunningham wrenched the tomahawk from the hand of the Indian, and buried the spike end to the handle, in his back. Mrs.

Cunningham closed the contest. Seeing her husband struggling with the savage, she struck at him with an axe. The edge wounding his face severely, he loosened his hold, and made his way out of the house.

"The third Indian, who had entered before the door was closed, presented an appearance almost as frightful as the object he had in view. He wore a cap made of the unshorn front of a buffalo, with the ears and horns still attached, and hanging loosely about his head, gave a most hideous appearance, and on entering the room, this frightful monster, aimed a blow with his tomahawk at Miss Reece, which alighting on her head, inflicted a severe wound. The mother, seeing the uplifted weapon about to descend on her daughter, seized the monster by the horns; but his false head coming off, she did not succeed in changing the direction of the weapon. The father then caught hold of him; but far inferior in strength, he was thrown on the floor, and would have been killed, but for the interference of Cunningham, who, having succeeded in clearing the house of one Indian, wheeled and struck his tomahawk into the head of the other.

"During all this time the door was kept secured by the women. The Indians from without endeavored several times to force it and would at one time have succeeded; but just as it was yielding, the Indian, who had been wounded by Cunningham and his wife, squeezed out, causing a momentary relaxation of their efforts, and enabled the women again to close it."

The savages on the outside, in the meantime, were busily engaged in securing such of the children as could travel, and murdering in the most inhuman and revolting manner all who could not. Despairing of being able to do further mischief, they moved off.

One white adult only was killed, and four or five wounded. Of the children, eight or ten were killed and carried off. The Indians lost one killed, and had two badly wounded.

Many other depredations of a similar character occurred in that part of Virginia, during the spring of the present year. Our crowded limits will not allow us to give them in detail. We will notice a few as we find them chronicled by the local historian.

"On the eleventh of April, some Indians visited the house of William Morgan, on Dunker's bottom. They there killed a young man by the name of Brain, Mrs. Morgan, (the mother of William) and her grand-daughter, and Mrs. Dillon and her two children; and took Mrs. Morgan (the wife) and her child prisoners. When on their way home, coming near Pricket's fort, they bound Mrs. Morgan to a bush, and went in quest of a horse to have her ride, leaving the child with her. She succeeded in untying with her teeth, the bands which confined her, and wandered the balance of that day and part of the next, before she came in sight of the fort. Here she was kindly treated, and in a few days sent home.

Toward the latter part of the same month, a party of about twenty Indians visited Hacker's creek settlement. The families were generally fortified; but as it was necessary to put in a crop, the men while thus employed carried their rifles with them, and often went in bodies, so as to afford better security against surprise or attack from the Indians.

A company of men, thus engaged about the last week in May, on Hacker's creek, and being a good deal dispersed in various occupations, some fencing, others clearing, and a few ploughing, they were unexpectedly fired upon, and Thos. Hughes and Jonathan Lowther shot down: the others being incautiously without arms, fled for safety. Two of the company, having the Indians rather between them and West's fort, ran directly to Richards', as well for their own security as to give the alarm. They had already been apprized that the enemy were at hand. Isaac Washburn, who had been to mill on Hacker's creek, on his return and near where Clement's now stands, was shot from his horse, tomahawked and scalped. The alarm of this murder had been given before the men arrived. The Indians escaped without pursuit.

Early in June, a few Indians made their appearance in the neighborhood of Fort Randolph (Point Pleasant), and after vainly manoeuvring to draw out an attacking party from the garrison, disappeared, when suddenly a large body of savages arose from their covert and demanded a surrender of the fort, on pain of instant destruction.

Captain McKee, the commandant, asked until morning for consideration. During the night, the besieged made good use of the darkness by carrying water into the fort, and putting all things in readiness for a regular siege.

In the morning. Captain McKee replied, that the demand for a surrender could not be complied with. The Indians (they were mostly Shawanese) then said, they had come expressly for the purpose of avenging the death of their great chief, Cornstalk; that the fort should be reduced, and every soul massacred. The attack was commenced with great fury, and continued, with but little intermission, for several days. Finding they could make no sensible impression, the enemy withdrew and proceeded up the Kanawha, evidently with the intention of attacking the Greenbriar settlements. No recent demonstration of hostility having been made in that quarter. Captain

McKee justly became alarmed for the issue, unless information of their approach could be conveyed to the settlements. Two soldiers were immediately sent in pursuit, but being discovered, were fired upon, and they returned to the fort. Two others then volunteered, Philip Hammon and John Pryor. An Indian squaw present, decorated them in true savage style, so that the native warriors could scarcely have told them from genuine Shawanese. Thus equipped, the intrepid hunters left Fort Randolph, and over hill and dale they sped onward, until finally they reached the settlements. The people were alarmed, and ere night closed in the whole neighborhood were collected at the residence of Colonel Andrew Donally. Everything was put in readiness for an attack. Dr. Campbell, in his Narrative, says, a strict watch was kept through the night, but no enemy appeared. The second day passed off in like manner. That night, most of the men went to the second story, having slept none for nearly forty-eight hours. In the latter part of the night they became drowsy, and when daylight appeared, all were in a profound sleep. Only three men were on the lower floor, — Hammon, and the white and black servants of Colonel Donally. At daybreak the white servant opened the door, that he might bring in some firewood, and had gone but a few steps from the house when he was shot down. The Indians now sprang from their concealment on the edge of the ryefield near the house, and rushing in a body, attempted to enter the door. Hammon and the black servant Dick, made an effort to secure it, but the Indians commenced chopping with their tomahawks, and had actually cut through the door, when Dick, fearing that they might succeed in gaining their purpose, left Hammon at his post, and seizing a musket which stood near, loaded with heavy slugs, discharged it through the opening among the crowd. The Indians now fell back, and the door was secured. Some Of the savages crawled under the floor, and were endeavoring to force their way up; Hammon and Dick, with one or two men from the loft, who had been aroused by the firing, quietly awaited the Indians in their effort. Presently, one of them showing his head through the opening, Hammon aimed a blow with his tomahawk, which placed him beyond the power of doing further injury. A second was killed in the same way, and the rest escaped. In the meantime, all the men in the loft were up, and pouring upon the enemy a most destructive fire, drove them off under cover of the woods. The attack was kept up during most of the day, but at such a distance as to do but little harm. One man was killed by a ball passing through an interstice in the wall. On the alarm being given by

Hammon and his companion, a messenger was sent to the station at Lewisburg, (this messenger was John Pritchett, and was killed on the morning of the attack). By the activity of Colonel Samuel Lewis and Colonel John Stuart, a force of sixty-six armed men was ready to march on the third morning. To avoid an ambush, they left the direct road, and taking a circuitous route, arrived opposite the fort, turned across, and passing through a rye-field, entered in safety. Giving up all hope after the accession of so large a force, the savages withdrew, and moved off in direction of the Ohio. Seventeen of them were found dead in the yard.

About the middle of June, as Captain James Booth and Nathaniel Cochran, were at work in a field on Booth's creek, a party of Indians came upon them, and killing Booth, took the other prisoner. Captain Booth was a brave and meritorious citizen, and his loss was greatly regretted.

A few days subsequent to these transactions, William Grundy, Benjamin Shinn, and Benjamin Washburn, in returning from a lick, were fired upon, and Grundy killed. About the same time Thomas Ryan, brother of the boy killed at the spring, during the meditated attack on Wheeling, in 1781, was murdered on Short creek, on the farm lately owned by R. Hardesty, Esq. Ryan was a man of much energy of character, and had been useful in border service. His death was greatly regretted.

His widow married Silas Zane, and was a second time widowed by savage hands. Zane was killed while crossing the Scioto, a few years after, in company with George Green and one or two other men.

DEATH OF MRS. FREEMAN.

Although the Indians disappeared for a brief period after their attack upon the men at Hacker's, still they lingered through the country, closely watching every opportunity to commit mischief. Had the force been sufficient at any one post, to have gone in pursuit, the savages could have been driven from the country; but, as it was, the settlers could only remain at home and protect their women and children. Notwithstanding the great danger there was known to be in leaving the fort, still persons would occasionally venture out, and unhappily, in many instances, at the sacrifice of their lives. Such are the facts in the case we are now about to give. Three women ventured forth from West's fort to gather greens in an adjacent field. One of these was Mrs. Freeman, another Mrs. Hacker, but the name of the third we have not been able to ascertain. While thus busily engaged, they were furiously attacked by four Indians, and all would undoubtedly have been killed, had not their screams brought the men to their rescue. Three of the savages immediately retreated, but the fourth, who carried a long staff with a spear on its end, ran up and thrust it through the body of the unfortunate Mrs. Freeman. The savage then scalped his victim before the men could drive him off.

Some persons at a distance from the fort, hearing the screams, rushed forward. Of this number were Jesse Hughes and John Schoolcraft, who ran for the fort together, and as they approached, Hughes discovered two Indians standing with their faces towards the fort, and looking very attentively at the movements of the whites. Changing their course they reached the fort in safety. Hughes immediately grasped his rifle and bounded out in pursuit, followed by some half dozen others. Before reaching the place where the two Indians had been seen, a signal resembling the howl of a wolf was heard, which Hughes immediately answered, and moved rapidly on in the direction whence it proceeded. In a short time, the howl was again given and a second time answered. Running to the brow of a hill and cautiously looking around, Hughes and his companions saw two Indians coming towards them. Hughes instantly fired, and one of them fell. The other sought safety in flight, and by running through the thickets, finally escaped.

In the fall of this year, a party of Indians came upon the house of Gilbert Hustead, living on Bartlett's run, and made him prisoner. Hearing a noise in the yard, Hustead opened the door to ascertain the cause, and finding it surrounded by Indians, put on an air of the utmost nonchalance, and walking out, extended his hand, welcoming them to his house and manifesting every degree of pleasure on seeing them. The wild men, not accustomed to so much deception, greeted their new found friend, and stepped in to share his proffered hospitality. Hustead could not be too kind and attentive; and finally, by handsomely abusing the "rebels," as he called his neighbors, and showing them (the Indians) every civility, won their favor and saved his scalp. Inquiring whether they were hungry and would not be glad to have something to eat, he asked one of them to shoot a fat hog in the yard, that they might regale on it that night, and have some on which to subsist whilst travelling to their towns. In the morning, still further to maintain the deception, he broke his furniture to pieces, saying "the rebels shall never have the good of this." He then accompanied them to their towns, acting in the same, apparently contented and cheerful manner, till his sincerity was believed by all, and he obtained leave to return for his family. He succeeded in making his way home, where he remained, sore at the destruction of his property, but exulting in the success of his artifice.

At the time of the above occurrence, a much larger party of Indians made their way to Coburn's creek, and attacked a company of whites returning from a field in the neighborhood of Coburn's fort. John Woodfin and Jacob Miller were both killed and scalped.

They next made their appearance on Danker creek, near to Stradler's fort. Here, as on Coburn creek, they lay in ambush on the road side, awaiting the return of the men who were engaged at work in some of the neighboring fields. Towards evening the men came, carrying with them some hogs which they had killed for the use of the fort people, and on approaching where the Indians lay concealed, were fired upon and several fell. Those who escaped injury from the first fire, returned the shot, and a severe action ensued. But so many of the whites had been killed before the savages exposed themselves to view, that the remainder were unable long to sustain the unequal contest. Overpowered by numbers, the few who were still unhurt, fled precipitately to the fort, leaving eighteen of their companions dead in the road. These were scalped and mangled by the Indians in a most shocking manner, and lay some time before the men in the fort, assured of the departure of the enemy, went out and buried them.

Weakened by the severe loss sustained in this bloody skirmish, had the Indians pushed forward to attack the fort, in all human probability, it would have fallen before them.

One of the last murders committed in the Monongahela country during this year, was that on the person of David Edwards, a worthy and industrious settler. He had been to Winchester for a supply of salt, and while on his return, near Valley river, was shot, tomahawked and scalped. His remains were not discovered for several days, and were so mutilated by wild beasts that they were with difficulty recognized.

1779.

The surrender to Clark of the British "hair-buyer," as Hamilton was very appropriately called, put it out of that functionary's power to purge the west of the "Long-knives," as he had so bravely threatened to do. It also had the effect to restrain the activity of the savages on the Virginia frontier, especially as the trade in scalps had become dull since the bounty patron had gone to Williamsburg, loaded with irons. But the savages were not long quiet; they had injuries of their own which they burned to avenge; and although more prisoners were made and fewer scalps taken, than when

Hamilton was abroad, still their depredations were as great, and the terror which their presence inspired just as all-pervading, as during the previous years. In Virginia, they did not appear by a month so early as usual, but when commenced their operations were quite as extensive. Anticipating increased danger, the settlers on Hacker's creek all removed with their families to the neighboring forts, and placed themselves in proper condition for meeting and resisting the enemy in any number that might come. Several new forts had, in the meantime, arisen; and therefore, when the campaign fairly opened, the settlers were better prepared to encounter their fierce adversaries than ever before. The extreme frontier people had also been busy. Many new stockades were erected, and the old ones repaired. Tomlinson's, at Grave creek, which had been abandoned in 1777, was re-fitted and occupied; Shepherd's, at the forks of Wheeling, which the Indians had burned, was re-built, with many others along the populated vallies in the neighborhood of Wheeling.

MORGAN'S RENCONTRE.

One of the most remarkable instances of personal heroism in the history of the West, is that of the celebrated combat between David Morgan and two Indians. Other instances, exhibiting equal success with even greater disparity of numbers, are upon record; but in none do we find more of true courage, energy, and intrepidity, than in this unequal contest between a man of advanced years and feeble health, struggling with, and finally vanquishing both his powerful adversaries. The settlements along the upper Monongahela, which had suffered so severely during the preceding fall, had not as yet been disturbed by the enemy, and many imagined that there was to be no repetition of them, at least during the present season. They however, still remained shut up in their block-houses, and rarely ventured far without appropriate means of defence. Of those who removed with their families to Prickett's fort, was David Morgan, one of the earliest settlers on the frontier, and a man of great energy of character, and of sterling worth. He was a near relative of General Morgan of Revolutionary memory, and like that distinguished officer, possessed, in a remarkable degree, courage and capacity for almost any emergency.

At the time of which we speak, Mr. Morgan was upwards of sixty years of age, and for some days had been slightly indisposed. Early in April, he desired two of his children, Stephen, sixteen years of age, and Sarah, about fourteen, to feed the stock at his farm, distant about one mile, and on the opposite side of the river. This he did, in consequence of feeling worse that morning than usual. No Indians had yet been seen in the neighborhood, and of course he considered all perfectly safe.

As the weather was fine, the brother and sister concluded to remain and prepare a piece of ground for melons. Soon after they left the fort, Mr. Morgan lay down, and shortly falling to sleep, dreamed that he saw the children walking before him, scalped. This vision awoke him, and finding, upon inquiry, that the children had not returned, he became uneasy, and started immediately in hunt of them. Approaching the premises, he beheld his children busily engaged in the manner already indicated.

Seating himself upon a log close at hand, Morgan watched his children for some time, when suddenly he saw emerge from the house two Indians, who moved rapidly up toward Stephen and his sister. Fearing to alarm the children, Morgan cautiously warned them of their danger, and told them to go at once to the fort. They instantly obeyed, and the Indians, discovering their movements, gave their accustomed whoop, and started in pursuit. Morgan, having hitherto escaped their attention, now arose, and returning their shout, caused the savages to seek behind trees instant protection.

Knowing that the chances of a fair fight were almost hopeless, Morgan thought to escape by running, and so manage as to keep the trees between himself and the enemy. In this, however, he was mistaken; impaired health, and the infirmities of age disabled him from keeping long beyond the reach of the fleet and athletic warriors. Finding, after a run of some two hundred yards, that the savages were rapidly gaining on him, he determined to shoot one, and take his chance with the other. Turning to fire, both Indians sprung behind trees, and Morgan did the same; but finding the one he first gained too small to protect his person, he quitted it and made for another, which was reached in safety.

One of the Indians, hoping to get nearer his intended victim, ran to the tree which Morgan had left, but finding it too small, threw himself behind a log close at hand. This, however, did not conceal him entirely, which Morgan noticing, instantly fired, and shot the savage through the part exposed. Feeling himself mortally wounded, with more than Spartan fortitude, he drew his knife, and inflicted two deep stabs upon his breast. To him death had no fears, save as dealt by the hand of his white antagonist.

The heroic old man, having thus effectually disposed of one of his pursuers, again resorted to flight. The chances were now desperate, as the Indian had the double advantage of tomahawk and rifle. Running fifty or sixty yards, he glanced hurriedly over his shoulder, just in time to see the savage ready to fire. Jumping to one side, the ball passed harmlessly by, and the two now felt that the combat must be brought to close quarters. With all the fury of his nature, the savage rushed upon his adversary with loud yells and uplifted tomahawk. Morgan prepared to meet him with his gun, but the savage aimed a blow with his tomahawk, with such force and effect as to knock the rifle from Morgan's grasp, and cut two of the fingers from his left hand. They now clinched, and the combat became equal, except the savage was the younger and much more powerful of the two. Frantic at the loss of his companion, and his own ill-success, he fought with a desperation rarely known in single combat; Morgan, on the other part, inspirited by the success which had thus far attended him, nerved his arm, and strung every muscle to the conflict, resolved to kill his combatant, or sell his own life as dearly as possible. Our hero, in his younger days, had been a most expert wrestler, and was thus enabled with ease to throw the Indian; but the latter, more active and powerful, readily turned him. With a yell of exultation, the savage now held his adversary down, and began to feel for his knife. Morgan saw the movement, and well knew all would be over if the savage got possession of it.

The Indian was prevented getting the knife by a woman's apron, which he had wrapped around his body in such a manner as to confine the handle. Whilst endeavoring to extricate it, Morgan got one of the Indian's thumbs between his teeth, and so firmly did he hold it, and effectually grind it, that the poor wretch was sadly disconcerted, and more than once screamed with pain. Finally, he grasped his knife, but so close to the blade, that Morgan noticing it, caught the end of the handle, and drew it quickly through the Indian's hand, cutting it severely. The savage was now literally hors de combat, and springing to his feet, endeavored to get away; but the resolute Morgan, not yet having done with him, held on to the thumb, until he had inflicted a mortal thrust in the side of his enemy. Letting go, the Indian sank almost lifeless to the ground, and Morgan made his way to the fort. Before reaching the river, he overtook his children. After hearing his adventure, a party of men left the fort, and proceeded to the place of conflict. On reaching the spot, nothing was to be seen of the wounded Indian; but his trail of blood indicated the place of his concealment. The poor creature had taken the knife from his side, bound up the wound with the apron already alluded to, and as the whites approached him, he feelingly accosted them, with "How do do, broder?" What followed, we would, for the sake of our common humanity, fain screen; but, as the facts have often been published, and the whole affair has become matter of history, we can see no propriety in withholding any part now.

"How do do, broder?" met with no fraternal response from the party who discovered his retreat. He was immediately dispatched; and not satisfied with that, himself and companion were both scalped, and then flayed. Their skins were afterwards tanned and made into shot-pouches, belts, razor-straps, &c. Human nature revolts at the contemplation of such acts of wanton barbarity. The impression has hitherto prevailed that Morgan was one of this party. This, we are assured, is not the fact. He was too much exhausted from loss of blood, and the severe personal conflict, to go out with the men, and of course could not have participated.

AFFAIR AT MARTIN'S FORT.

In June of this year, the humble structure known as Martin's fort, which stood on Crooked run, was the scene of a painful and bloody affair.

On the morning of the attack, most of the men went, as usual, to their respective improvements in the neighborhood. Those who remained, not apprehending an attack, were leisurely engaged outside of the fort, while the women were occupied in milking the cows. A party of Shawanese, who had lain in wait, embraced the favorable opportunity, and rushing upon the whites, killed three men, and made prisoners of seven others. Peter Croase, James Stuart, and James Smalley were the men killed.

Soon after this occurrence, a small party of Indians appeared on Pike run, a tributary to the Monongahela, below Brownsville, and surprised two daughters of Capt. David Scott, who were carrying dinner to some men mowing a meadow, not far from their father's house. The younger, an interesting and beautiful girl, was killed on the spot, as she made some resistance, but her sister was carried into captivity. The murdered sister was not found for several days, and when discovered, presented a most horrible spectacle. Voracious birds had so preyed upon her that she was but with difficulty recognized.

About the last of September, Nathaniel Davisson and his younger brother, living in the vicinity of Clarksburgh, started upon a hunting expedition on the waters of Ten-mile. Hunting separately, as was the custom, Josiah returned to camp at an hour designated for meeting there, but not finding his brother, and after waiting some time, feeling uneasy about his safety, determined to search for him. Unable to see or hear any thing, the other returned home, and prevailed upon several of his neighbors to aid in endeavoring to ascertain his fate. Their search was alike unavailing. In the following March, his remains were found by John Read, while hunting. He had been shot and scalped; and notwithstanding he had lain out nearly six months, yet he was but little torn by wild beasts, and easily recognized.

Tygart's Valley settlement, which had escaped a savage visitation in 1778, was not to be so exempt during the present year. In October, a party of Indians lying in ambush near the road, fired at Lieut. John White, who was riding by, but with no other effect than wounding his horse, and causing him to throw his rider. This was fatal to White, as the ground was open, and he was soon shot, tomahawked and scalped.

So soon as this event was made known, Capt. Benjamin Wilson raised a company, and proceeding by forced marches to the Indian crossing at the mouth of the Sandy fork of Little Kanhawa, he remained there nearly three days with a view to intercept the retreat of the savages. They, however, returned by another rout, and thus his scheme of cutting them off failed.

Some time after this, several families in the Buchanan settlement, left the fort and returned to their homes, under the belief that the season had advanced too far, for the Indians again to come among them. But in this they were deceived. The men being all assembled at the fort, for the purpose of electing a captain, some Indians fell upon the family of John Schoolcraft, and killed the women and eight children, — two little boys only were taken prisoners. A small girl, who had been scalped and tomahawked, a portion of her brains coming from her head, was found the next day alive.

The last mischief done this fall, was perpetrated at the house of Samuel Cottrial, near the present town of Clarksburgh. During the night, considerable fear was excited, both at Cottrial's and at Sotha Hickman's, on the opposite side of Elk creek, by the continued barking of dogs. Cottrial, on going to bed, secured well the doors, and directed that no one should stir out in the morning until it was ascertained that no danger threatened. Just before day, Cottrial being asleep, Moses Coleman, who lived with him, got up, shelled some corn, and giving a few ears to Cottrial's nephew, with directions to feed the pigs around the yard, went himself to an adjoining building and commenced grinding. A single Indian, one of a party who had lain secreted during the night, made his appearance, and first catching the boy, fired and killed Coleman. Running to scalp his victim, the little fellow made good his escape. The other Indians went off without doing further injury.

The above, for which we are indebted to the interesting local history of that region, was followed by numerous other cases of savage cruelty, occurring towards the close of the season of 1779. We regret that our want of room will not allow more copious extracts at the present time.

1781.

Many depreciations were committed during this year on the frontiers of Virginia and Pennsylvania, and it was perhaps mainly to these circumstances that the unfortunate Moravian Indians owe their destruction.

Early in February, a party of Delawares entered the settlement on the waters of Raccoon creek, Washington county, near the present town of Florence, and after committing several acts of violence, made an attack upon the house of Robert Wallace, during his absence from home, making prisoners of Mrs. W., her little son Robert, two-and-a-half years old, another son ten years old, and an infant daughter, also a man named John Carpenter. With their prisoners, and what plunder they could carry off, the savages made their way toward the Ohio; but finding Mrs. Wallace and her infant somewhat troublesome, they were tomahawked and scalped. The two boys were carried to Sandusky, where the elder died. Robert was then sold to the Wyandotts, by whom he was held in captivity about two and a half years. His father hearing of him, sent a man to the Wyandott towns, giving him a certain mark by which the boy could be recognized, and in this way he was rescued, and restored to his friends. He is now living on Raccoon creek, a stout, hearty old man, and bears in distinct recollection the trials, hardships, and privations of his captivity. He thinks his mother and little sister were killed near where Georgetown now stands. About three years subsequent to their captivity, the husband was informed that the remains of a woman and child had been discovered near the place designated. He repaired to the spot, and upon examination recognized the remains as those of his murdered wife and child. They were collected and buried at King's creek Meeting-house.

The clothing of Mrs. Wallace, which were found at the Moravian towns, called down the vengeance of Colonel Williamson's men upon that devoted people.

MURDER OF CAPTAIN THOMAS AND FAMILY.

On the night of the 5th of March, a party of Indians came to the house of Capt. John Thomas, on Booth's creek, one of the branches of the

Monongahela. Capt. Thomas was a man of much piety, and what was perhaps unusual in the early days of our Republic, had regular family devotion. It was whilst thus engaged, surrounded by his wife and seven children, that the Indians approached his cabin. The settlement had felt no apprehension as yet of Indian depredation, as the season had not sufficiently advanced to cause alarm. Anticipating no attack, Capt. Thomas was therefore not prepared, and his house not so well secured as was his custom. He had just repeated the line of the hymn,

"Go worship at Immanuel's feet,"

as the Indians approached and fired. The christian father fell dead at the moment, and a band of savages forcing the door, entered and commenced the work of death. Mrs. Thomas implored their mercy for herself and children; but, alas! the savage knows no mercy for feeble woman or helpless infancy. The tomahawk did its work, until the mother and six children lay weltering in blood, by the side of the slaughtered father. They then proceeded to scalp the fallen, and plunder the house, and then departed, taking with them one little boy, a prisoner.

"Elizabeth Juggins, (daughter of John Juggins, who had been murdered in that neighborhood, the preceding year) was at the house of Capt. Thomas, when the Indians came, but as soon as she heard the report of the gun and saw Capt. Thomas fall, she threw herself under the bed, and escaped observation of the savages. After they had completed the work of blood and left the house, fearing that they might be lingering near, she remained in that situation until the house was found on fire. When she crawled forth from her asylum, Mrs. Thomas was still alive, though unable to move; and casting a pitying glance towards her murdered infant, asked that it might be handed to her. Upon seeing Miss Juggins about to leave the house, she exclaimed, "Oh, Betsey, do not leave us!" Still anxious for her own safety, the girl rushed out, and taking refuge for the night between two logs, in the morning early, spread the alarm.

"When the scene of these enormities was visited, Mrs. Thomas was found in the yard, much managled by the tomahawk and considerably torn by hogs — she had, perhaps in the struggle of death, thrown herself out at the door. The house, together with Captain Thomas and the children, was a heap of ashes."

The fate of this pious family is but one in the long catalogue of bloody doings which mark the pages of our western history. It required a christian's heart, and the christian's hope, to live amid such scenes unmoved and unawed. Who can contemplate the fate of that unfortunate family without emotions of poignant sorrow. How happy was the morning which dawned upon them, but, alas, how terrible the evening!

In April of this year, three brothers, Mathias, Simon and Michael Schoolcraft, left Buchanan's Fort, and went to the head of Stone-coal creek, for the purpose of hunting. On their way back, a party of Indians fired upon them, killing the first-named brother, and taking the others prisoners. These, with other members of the family previously taken never returned. A singular fatality seemed to attend this family. The three brothers whose names we have just given, constituted the last of fifteen, who either fell before the rifle or tomahawk, or suffered, perhaps, a more dreadful fate in the hands of their captors.

The founder of this Virginia branch of the Schoolcraft family, was one of the earliest settlers on the upper Monongahela. He emigrated from central New York, mainly induced by the prospect of acquiring for a large family, suitable landed properties. Unfortunately, his family early fell a prey to the relentless and ever vigilant savage. The founder of the Virginia family was, we believe, distantly connected with the distinguished author, Henry R. Schoolcraft, whose magnificent work just issued (1851) is alike creditable to himself, the government (by whose munificence it has been published,) and the cause of American literature. It seems not a little remarkable, that while one member of the family branch should have been devoting almost his whole life to studying means for bettering and promoting the condition of the Indians, members of another branch, and they constituting a numerous family, should have been totally exterminated by the same savage hands.

MEDITATED ATTACK ON WHEELING.

In September of this year, occurred what may be called the second attempt upon Wheeling.

Fortunately, the purpose of the Indians was frustrated by the timely information communicated by Colonel Brodhead, then commanding the western division of the army. The despatch of Colonel B. was as follows:
—

"Fort Pitt, August 24, 1781.

Sir :—

I have this moment received certain intelligence that the enemy are coming in great force against us, and particularly against Wheeling. You will immediately put your garrison in the best posture of defence, and lay in as great a quantity of water as circumstances will admit, and receive them coolly. They intend to decoy your garrison, but you are to guard against stratagem, and defend the post to the last extremity. You may rely upon every aid in my power to frustrate the designs of the enemy; but you must not fail to give the alarm to the inhabitants in your reach, and make it as general as possible, in order that every man may be prepared at this crisis.

I am, sir, your most obedient servant,

(Signed) Daniel Brodhead,

Col. Commanding W. D.

To the Commanding Officer at Fort Henry Wheeling."

This information, as may well be supposed, startled the inhabitants at Wheeling; but, not unmindful of the notice, they put themselves in readiness to meet and resist any attack the enemy might make. The fort was immediately placed in proper condition for defence, and nothing left undone to ensure their safety.

About ten days after the reception of the despatch of Col. Brodhead, a party of over one hundred Indians suddenly appeared in the vicinity of the fort. The first intimation those within the stockade had of the presence of the enemy, was by a boy named George Reikart, reaching the fort almost exhausted, who stated that a large party of Indians were at the spring, (near the hill,) and that they had killed his companion, John Ryan, and taken David Glenn prisoner.

The approach of the Indians had been so sudden and noiseless, that Ryan was shot down, and Glenn taken prisoner, but Reikart, who was some distance off, gathering walnuts, escaped. Just as he entered the fort-gate, a rifle-ball struck him on the wrist.

In a moment, those within were ready to receive them; but, it is supposed, that the savages, from information of Glenn, anticipated a warm reception, and deemed it better valor to make off at once. This they did, after demanding in a pompous manner, the surrender of the fort, which request the inmates very politely declined acceding to.

Thus, owing to the timely information of Col. Brodhead, the settlement at Wheeling was, doubtless, saved from what might have been a bloody visitation.

MURDER AT LINK'S BLOCK-HOUSE.

Of the many primitive places of defence which sprung up at an early day in the forests of North-western Virginia, was that of Link's block-house, on middle Wheeling creek. It was built by Jonathan Link, in 1780, and served to shelter the defenceless settlers of the neighborhood. This rude structure stood a few miles from the present town of Triadelphia, and early became the scene of a bloody occurrence.

In the fall of 1781, a party of fifteen or twenty Indians, returning from an excursion to the interior, made an attack upon this block-house so suddenly, that Link and two of his men were instantly killed, and several taken prisoners. The men had been at a shooting match, and it is supposed may have indulged rather too freely to present a vigorous defence.

Of those taken prisoner, was William Hawkins, who lived within a few miles, but who had gone to attend the shooting match. Hawkins told the Indians, if they did not kill him he would go quietly to his house. This they agreed to, but his family hearing their approach, (Hawkins spoke loud so as to give the alarm,) secreted themselves in time. A daughter, however, was discovered and taken prisoner, and another member of the family killed.

The savages, after plundering the house, marched their prisoners in front, and proceeding a mile or two, ordered the daughter on ahead. They then took Hawkins and another prisoner, named Presly Peak, to the summit of a ridge, tied them to separate trees, and tomahawked them.

1782.

This was a fatal and trying year to the frontier settlements of Virginia. The enemy were early in the field, and almost ceaseless in their attacks upon the comparatively defenceless inhabitants. The expeditions of Williamson, Crawford, &c., seemed but to arouse the savages to increased acts of barbarity. They penetrated some distance to the interior, and waged their ruthless and indiscriminating warfare with an energy and ferocity rarely equalled.

Family after family fell before their approach, until the whole country became aroused to the extent of their depredations. Their blows fell with particular severity upon the settlements along the upper Monongahela.

In the neighborhood of Clarksburgh many acts of hostility were committed, which greatly alarmed the adjacent settlements.

The following, which we extract from Mr. Withers' sketches, cannot but be interesting to most readers of western history. We much regret the instance of human depravity which it details; but for the credit of our nature, we can say, such instances were very rare in the early days of the west.

"On the 8th of March, as William White, Timothy Dorman and his wife, were going to, and within sight of Buchanan fort, some guns were discharged at them, and White being shot through the hips, fell from his horse, and was then tomahawked, scalped and mutilated in the most frightful manner. Dorman and his wife were taken prisoners. The people in the fort heard the firing, and flew to arms; but the river intervening, the savages cleared themselves before the whites crossed over.

"After the death of White (one of their most active, cautious, and vigilant spies) and the capture of Dorman, it was resolved to abandon the fort, and seek elsewhere security from the greater ills which it was found would befall them if they remained. This apprehension arose from the fact, that Dorman was then with the savages, and that to gratify his enmity to particular individuals in the settlement, he would unite with the Indians, and from his knowledge of the country, he enabled to conduct them the more securely to blood and plunder. He was a man of a sanguinary and revengeful disposition, prone to quarrelling, and had been known to say that if he caught particular individuals with whom he was at variance, in the woods alone, he would murder them and attribute it to the savages. The fearful apprehensions of increased and aggravated injuries after taking him prisoner, were well founded. Subsequent events fully proved, that but for the evacuation of the fort, and the removal of the inhabitants, all would have fallen before the fury of savage warriors, with this white miscreant at their head.

"While some of the inhabitants of that settlement were engaged in moving their property to a fort in Tygart's valley (the others moving to Nutter's fort and Clarksburg), they were fired upon by a party of savages, and two of them, Michael Hagle and Elias Paynter, fell. The horse which a man named Bush rode, was shot through; yet Bush succeeded in extricating himself, and escaped, though closely pursued by one of the savages. Several times the Indian following him, called out, "Stop, and you shall not he hurt. If you do not, I will shoot you!" and once. Bush, nearly exhausted and in despair of getting off, actually relaxed his pace for the purpose of yielding himself a prisoner, when turning round he saw the savage stop, and commence loading his gun. This inspired Bush with fear for the consequences, and renewing his flight, finally escaped. Edward Tanner, a youth, was taken prisoner, and in going to their towns, met between twenty and thirty savages, headed by Timothy Dorman, proceeding to attack Buchanan fort. Learning from him that the inhabitants were moving from it, and that it would be abandoned in a few days, the Indians pursued their journey with so much haste, that Dorman had well nigh failed from fatigue. They arrived, however, too late for the accomplishment of their bloody purpose; the settlement had been deserted, and the inhabitants were safe within the walls of other forts.

"A few days after the evacuation of Buchanan fort, some of its former inmates went from Clarksburg for grain which had been left at Buchanan. They found a heap of ashes where the fort had stood, and other signs convinced them that the savages were yet lurking about. They, however, continued to go from farm to farm collecting the grain, but with the utmost vigilance, and at night went to an out-house, near where the fort had stood. Here they found a paper, with the name of Timothy Dorman attached to it, dated at the Indian towns, and containing information of those who had been taken captive in that part of Virginia.

"Early in the morning, as some of the men went from the house to mill, they saw the savages crossing the river, Dorman being with them. Thinking it best to impress them with a belief that they were able to encounter them in open conflict, the men advanced towards the foe, calling to their companions in the house, to come on. The Indians fled hastily to the woods, and the whites, not so rash as to pursue them, returned to the house, and secured themselves in it, as well as they could. At night, Capt. George Jackson went privately from the house, and at great hazard of being discovered, proceeded to Clarksburg, and obtained such aid as enabled him to escort his companions in safety to that place.

"Disappointed in their hopes of involving the inhabitants of Buchanan settlement in destruction, the savages went on to the Valley. Between Westfall's and Wilson's forts, they came upon John Bush and his wife, Jacob Stalnaker and his son Adam. The latter were riding in the rear of Bush and his wife; Adam was killed. The old gentleman rode briskly on, but some of the savages were before, and endeavored to catch his bridle-reins. He, however, escaped in safety. The horse from which Adam Stalnaker had fallen, was caught by Bush, and both he and Mrs. Bush got safely away on him."

SECOND SIEGE OF FORT HENRY.

The last beleaguerment of the fort at Wheeling, was certainly one of the most important events in the settlement of the north-west, — one, upon which it may emphatically be said, the very existence of the frontier of Virginia depended.

On the eleventh day of September, 1782, a body of three hundred and fifty Indians and whites; the former, Shawanese and Delawares, under the command of George Girty, and the latter, a company known as the "Queen's Rangers," commanded by Captain Pratt, made their appearance in front of the little stockade at Wheeling, and peremptorily demanded a surrender. The besiegers marched up in regular file, headed by a fife and drum, with the British flag flying over them.

Girty, upon whom the whole command devolved, defiled his men by the spring near where the market-house now stands, and in the name of the British Governor demanded a surrender. He promised to all who would give up, "the best protection King George could afford." To this, the brave and dauntless inmates of the fort returned contemptuous answers, and defied the savages, both white and red, to do their worst.

Girty, deeming it imprudent to commence the attack in daylight, kept his men at a convenient distance until nightfall. The conversation, however, was continued between the besieged and besiegers, the former delighting to load the renegade with the most opprobrious epithets. Shots were occasionally fired at him, but the distance was too great for effect.

Fortunately for the inmates, that the attack had not commenced half an hour earlier. For some days previous to the appearance of the savages, scouts had been across the Ohio, but discovering no traces of the enemy, returned on the afternoon of Saturday, and reported accordingly. This news had the effect of lulling the inmates into a feeling of security, so that it was scarcely deemed necessary to fasten the gates at night.

A day or two previous to the time of which we write, Andrew Zane had gone to Catfish, for a supply of liquor. Returning with two kegs, (one in each end of a bag,) he discovered, as he supposed, when near the present site of Mount Wood Cemetery, indications of Indians. Concealing his kegs, he hurried to the fort with all haste, and gave the alarm. Those who had just returned from the Indian country, laughed at his fears, but most of the men said they would go along, and have a "spree."

Nearly the whole efficient force of the garrison accompanied Zane, and finding no Indians, repaired to the spring already alluded to, and there treated themselves to a glorious "blow out." Before starting with Zane, it was deemed advisable, with the characteristic caution of experienced frontiermen, to send across the river two spies, who might give the alarm in case of danger. As the party at the spring were busy with their "grog," the alarm guns of the scouts were fired on the island, and at the same moment, a large body of Indians were crossing the creek, just above backwater. A simultaneous rush was made for the fort; and scarcely had the last man entered, when the Indians appeared in large numbers crossing the bottom.

All at once became activity and bustle within the fort. The men prepared for an energetic defence, each arming himself with a rifle, tomahawk, scalping knife and spear. The women were busy in running bullets, securing the children, etc. The whole number of fighting men within the stockade did not exceed eighteen, while the number of women and children was about forty.

Shortly before the enemy appeared, a pirogue loaded with cannon-balls, designed for Gen. Clark, at Louisville, in charge of a man named Sullivan, and two others, landed at Wheeling, to remain over night. Sullivan was a shrewd and experienced soldier, well versed in Indian cunning; and on this account was selected to manage the affairs of the fort during the siege, as the commandant, Captain Boggs, had gone for succor immediately on the alarm of the enemy's approach. Sullivan was a man of discrimination and courage, and well qualified for the post of commander. His shrill voice could be heard at all hours, urging on the men, and consoling the women. But at length he was wounded, and for a time had to give way.

About sundown, Girty made a second demand for surrender, declaring that should be his last summons, and swearing, if they refused, that the fort would be stormed, and every soul massacred. He was answered by taunts of defiance; said they remembered too well the fate of Col. Crawford, to give up, and be butchered like dogs. Girty replied, that their doom was sealed — he had taken their express, and all hope of safety might be given up. Sullivan inquired what kind of looking man the messenger was? "A fine, smart, active young fellow," answered the outlaw chief. "That's a d—d lie," said Sullivan, "he is an old gray-headed man."

Finding all attempts to intimidate in vain, Girty led on his white and red army of savages, and attempted to carry out his threat of storming the fort.

Near the centre of the stockade, and at a point sufficiently elevated to clear the pickets, was a small French cannon, which the enemy could at times see, but which they tauntingly said was "wood," and dared them to "shoot." Having approached within a convenient distance, and just as the whole party was pressing up in deep columns, the "bull-dog" was let off, cutting a wide passage through the ranks of wondering and affrighted savages. Captain Pratt, who had heard guns, and knew how they sounded, cried out to his swarthy comrades, "Stand back; by G——, there's no wood about that!"

The Indians and the "Rangers" gave way at the first discharge, but soon rallied and returned. Girty divided his force into small parties, and attacked the fort at different points; now attempting to storm it; and again to fire it. In this manner the siege was kept up during the whole night; and but few such nights were ever passed upon the frontier.

One of the bastions having given way, but two were of use, and these the men occupied in turn. The women, during the whole of that long and perilous night, proved themselves heroines of no ordinary type. They stood at their posts like soldiers of a dozen campaigns, cooling and loading the rifles of their husbands, brothers, and lovers. Such women were worthy the love and devotion of men like these. No timid shrieks escaped them; no maidenly fears caused them to shrink from their self-imposed and most onerous task. Such were the pioneer mothers of the west — women whose souls and bodies were so sorely tried in the fierce fire of our Indian wars. Through the whole of that long and terrible night, without food and without rest, did these brave and noble women stand to their duty, regardless of fatigue, but nerving their hearts to the contest, and animating the men with hope and courage. The Greek matron, who urged her son to the conflict, charging him to return with his shield or upon it, displayed no more zeal, devotion, and true courage, than these hero-women of the west. History is full of examples of female heroism. Israel had her Judith and Deborah; France glories in her Joan and Lavalette; — two of them unsexed themselves in the excitement of battle; one ingloriously stained her hands in human gore, and the other had nothing to lose by her successful efforts; but the western heroines, without the eclat of female warriors, displayed more true courage throughout the long and stormy days of our Indian warfare, and exhibited more of the true spirit of heroism, than any example in ancient or modern history.

At an early hour in the evening, the Indians descried the pirogue already referred to, and at once resolved to try the sport of cannonading. Procuring a stout log of sufficient size and length, these simple-minded men split it open, and having cut out the centre with their tomahawks, fastened the parts together with iron bands, and chains, found in a smith-shop belonging to a man named Reikart. They then charged it heavily with powder and ball, and first announcing that their artillery had arrived, applied the torch, when instantaneously a half-dozen of the gaping savages, who had clustered around to witness the discharge, were blown into eternity. Their frail gun had bursted, scattering death and consternation all around.

During the night, a large number of Indians posted themselves in the loft of a house which stood thirty or forty yards north of the fort. These amused themselves by dancing, shouting, and yelling, making night hideous with their horrid noise. Thinking to dislodge them, several ineffectual attempts were made to do so with grape shot; but failing, a full-sized ball was fired, which cut off a sleeper, and let the whole mass down together. This disaster frightened the assailants off for a time.

The cannon was fired sixteen times during the first night, doing more or less execution at each discharge. It was managed by a man named John Tait, shortly afterwards killed and partly eaten by the savages, on Dillie's bottom, opposite Grave creek.

At the time of the Indian visitation in 1777, it will be remembered, they burned all the houses, killed the cattle, etc. Similar outrages were again attempted in 1781, and then Colonel Ebenezer Zane resolved, that should the savages again visit the settlement, he would remain in his house and perish, sooner than abandon it to the torch of the enemy. On the re-appearance of the Indians, Colonel Zane continued at his house, and declared his fixed determination to defend it to the last. In the house with him were several members of his family, including his brother Silas. There were also two brothers by the name of Green, and a black servant, by the name of Sam. So constantly did these four keep up the fire against the enemy, that they were slow to approach within range of the guns.

The fortunes of the night were often variable. The enemy at one time appeared to have the vantage, but again, their schemes were frustrated by the energy and skill of those within the fort. More than twenty times did they attempt to fire the stockade, by heaping bundles of hemp against the walls, and kindling them at different points. Most fortunately, however, the hemp was wet, and could not be made to burn. Dry wood and other combustibles were tried, but all in vain. Day at length dawned upon the hopes of that almost despairing people; and never did Aurora display her beauties to a more admiring or a more rejoicing group. The night had been long, and full of gloomy terror. They knew not at what moment the formidable enemy would crush the walls of their frail enclosure; but come what might, they resolved to stand firm to the last.

Immediately after day-break the Indians and British withdrew to the spring, and a cessation of hostilities for several hours ensued.

It was about noon of this day that an incident occurred which has been the theme of history, poetry and romance. We allude to the "gunpowder exploit," as it is familiarly known in border story.

As we have already stated, Colonel Zane remained in his cabin near the fort, during the whole siege. Finding that his supply of powder was likely to run out, he proposed to those present, that some one of them would have to visit the fort and renew the stock. It was known to be a hazardous undertaking, and unwilling to order either of the white men to so perilous an enterprise, Colonel Zane submitted the matter to their own devotion and courage. One of them instantly proffered his services, but a female member of Col. Zane's family came forward and said, "No! I will go; should I be killed, I can be better spared than one of these men." That woman, according to the traditionary accounts of the country, was Elizabeth Zane, sister to Colonel Zane. She is represented to have been a young woman of great resolution and much energy of character, and those who knew her intimately say unhesitatingly, that she was just the person for such an exploit. Preparing herself for the feat, the intrepid girl stepped from the cabin and bounded to the fort with the speed of a deer. A number of Indians concealed in the neighborhood, saw her emerge from the cabin, but did not attempt to shoot, only exclaiming with contemptuous epithets, "Squaw, squaw." She reached the fort, and tying about her person eight or ten pounds of powder, again ventured forth and moved rapidly towards the cabin of Colonel Zane. Suspecting all was not right, the savages opened upon her a volley of rifle balls, but unscathed, the courageous girl bounded into the arms of those who stood ready to receive her.

That act of the heroic and single-hearted female saved the inmates of Colonel Zane's house from certain destruction. Their ammunition had been exhausted, and every soul would have fallen a sure prey to the fury of the savages, had not a supply been obtained.

Night closing in, the enemy renewed the attack, and maintained it without intermission until daybreak.

Shortly after sunrise, the enemy despairing of success, commenced killing the cattle, burning the vacant cabins, &c.

About ten o'clock a. m., an Indian spy, who had been sent out to watch the approach of a relief, returned, and when within sight of the fort, gave a long, deep, peculiar whoop, which the well-trained Indian hunters fully understood as a signal to be off. Scarcely had the echoes of his shout ceased reverberating along the valley than the entire hostile army moved rapidly toward the river, which they crossed near where the North-Western Bank now stands. In less than half an hour after their retreat, Captain Williamson with seventy mounted men rode up to the fort, and great was the rejoicing at the appearance of his gallant band. Thus ended the final investment of Fort Henry. The Indians never again attempted to molest it, but gave the place as wide a latitude as convenient in their expeditions against the back settlements.

RICE'S FORT ATTACKED.

After raising the siege at Wheeling, a division of the enemy visited the settlements on Short and Buffalo creeks, but the people had all taken the precaution to shut themselves up in block-houses. Determined, however, to effect a massacre somewhere, out of revenge for their failure at Fort Wheeling, the party made a descent upon Rice's Fort. Information had luckily reached the inmates of the Indians' design, and they were prepared for them. The Indians surrounded the fort and demanded a surrender, saying, "Give up, give up; too many Injun — Injun too big; no kill." But the sturdy frontiermen thought differently, and answered with shouts of defiance: "Come on, cowards, we are ready for you; show us your yellow skins, and we'll make holes in them for you!" This was what may be considered brag, however, as the fort was but illy defended, many of their men having gone to Hagerstown, Md., to exchange their peltries for ammunition, salt, &c. The savages finding they could make no impression upon the inmates, withdrew until nine or ten o'clock at night, when they fired a large and well filled barn which stood within thirty yards of the fort. The position of the building and the course of the wind saved the fort from destruction, and its inmates from massacre.

After the barn was set on fire, the Indians collected on the side of the fort opposite, so as to have the advantage of the light, and kept up a pretty constant fire, which was as steadily answered by those in the fort, until about two o'clock, when the Indians left the place and made a hasty retreat.

The names of those who defended this little fortress were Jacob Miller, George Lefler, Peter Fullenweider, Daniel Rice, George Felebaum and Jacob Lefler, Jr. George Felebaum was shot in the forehead, through a port-hole, at the second fire of the Indians, and instantly expired, so that in reality the defence of the place was made by only five men.

The ascertained loss of the Indians was four, three of whom were killed at the first fire from the fort, the other was killed about sundown. There can be no doubt but that a number more were killed and wounded in the engagement, but concealed or carried off.

FATE OF THE PIATT FAMILY.

In the year 1782, rumor having reached Dillie's blockhouse, a small stockade opposite Grave creek, on the farm now owned by Col. John Thompson, that an attack was meditated upon Ryerston's station, which was near the line between Virginia and Pennsylvania, it was deemed expedient to send a detachment to the relief of the station. During the absence of the men, a party of Indians took possession of a corn field near the block-house. The night being extremely warm, one of the inmates, named Piatt, said he would go and sleep in the cabin, as he could not endure the fleas. His wife and five children, went along. The cabin stood about three hundred yards from the block-house. At the break of day, the Indians attacked, and murdered every member of that ill-fated family. A woman at the block-house heard the guns, and expressed fears that the Indians were attacking the cabin, but others said it was the men returning from Ryerston's.

The savages soon presented themselves before the blockhouse, brandishing the bloody scalps of their victims, and demanded a surrender. Old Mr. Winter tauntingly replied, they had plenty of men, and would give them cold lead in abundance if they remained any longer. Fearing they might meet with warm work, the savages made off without further delay. There were not six fighting men in the house at that time.

Early in the fall, a party of Indians came upon the premises of a man named Yates, living not far from the residence of the late Colonel Woods, and succeeded in getting between a young man named Peter Starnator and Yates' house. Starnator was a few hundred yards in advance when he discovered the Indians, and finding it unsafe to attempt to return, started at full speed down the bottom. The savages, however, proved too fleet for him, as he was overtaken and shot in the Narrows, near where Mr. Steenrod now lives. The Indian who killed him was so close that the shot made a hole in the skull large enough to admit a man's hand.

He was taken to Wheeling, and interred in the old burial ground, upon which the North-Western Bank now stands.

MURDER OF THE TAIT FAMILY.

During the same fall, another family, named Tait, living about half a mile below the block-house, was attacked by a party of Indians, and four of them killed. A son, fifteen years of age, in attempting to bar the savages out, was severely wounded by a ball in the mouth. His father at length was shot down, and the youth secreted himself behind a barrel. The door was then forced open, and the savages entered. The father and two small children were immediately tomahawked and scalped. Mrs. Tait had concealed herself on the "log pole," but was soon discovered and dispatched. The cannibals then commenced the revolting work of cutting pieces from the old man's breasts and thighs, which were roasted and eaten! During the time they were thus engaged, the boy managed to drag his mother off the fire without being noticed.

As many writers have denied the existence of American cannibalism, it may not be inopportune to cite here some authority in proof of it. At a recent meeting of the American Academy of Arts and Sciences, Professor Shepherd, who has lately spent some time in exploring the mining regions on the shores of Lake Superior, related an instance of the most horrible cannibalism among the Ojibbeway tribe of Indians, on the north shore of the Lake. "He frequently passed on foot, alone and unarmed, by the hut of an Indian, who had killed and eaten his wife and two children. The personal appearance of this savage monster, as might naturally be supposed, was horrible beyond description."

Another important witness is Hon. Lewis Cass, of Michigan. In his oration, delivered at Fort Wayne, Indiana, July 4, 1843, on the occasion of celebrating the opening of the Wabash and Erie canal, the distinguished orator said:

"The line of your canal was a bloody war-path, which has seen many a deed of horror. And this peaceful town has had its Moloch, and the records of human depravity furnish no more horrible examples of cruelty than were offered at his shrine.

The Miami Indians, our predecessors in the occupation of this district, had a fearful institution, whose origin and objects have been lost in the darkness of aboriginal history, but which continued to a late period, and whose orgies were held upon the very spot where we now are. It was called the Man-eating Society, and its was the duty of its associates to eat such prisoners as were preserved and delivered to them for that purpose. The members of this society belonged to a particular family, and the dreadful inheritance descended to all the children, male and female. The duties it imposed could not be avoided, and the sanctions of religion were added to the obligations of immemorable usage. The feast was a solemn ceremony, at which the whole tribe was collected, as actors or spectators. The miserable victim was bound to a stake, and burned at a slow fire, with all the refinements of cruelty which savage ingenuity could invent. There was a traditionary ritual, which regulated, with revolting precision, the whole course of procedure at these ceremonies. Latterly the authority and obligations of the institution had declined, and I presume it has now wholly disappeared. But I have seen and conversed with the head of the family, the chief of the society, whose name was White Skin. With what feelings of disgust, I need not attempt to describe. I well knew an intelligent Canadian, who was present at one of the last sacrifices made to this horrible institution. The victim was a young American, captured in Kentucky, during the revolutionary war. Here, we are now assembled in peace and security, celebrating the triumph of art and industry. Within the memory of the present generation, our countrymen have been thus tortured, and murdered, and devoured. But, thank God, that council fire is extinguished. The impious feast is over."

## DEATH OF HUGH CAMERON.

In February of this year, a man named Hugh Cameron, in company with another person, both of whom had been employed by Captain Boggs, (living at that time on his farm near the mouth of Boggs' run,) went out to the camp, which was a short distance from the house, to boil sugar. Although so early in the season, the Indians had commenced their depredations, and Captain B., a few days previously, removed his family to the fort at Wheeling. Cameron and his companion had been cautioned by Captain B. and others to be on their guard, and that one should watch while the other slept. The men, however, as was too often the case in those days, disregarded the admonition, and one of them at least paid for the temerity with his life.

At night, the savages stole upon their tent and killed Cameron, but in the darkness his companion escaped. The remains of the unfortunate man were found some years after, those of the body lying near the mouth of Boggs' run, and the skull half a mile up that stream, carried there, it was supposed, by some wild animal: they were identified by a peculiar tooth.

## NOTE A.

The stockade at Wheeling, of which a most perfect representation is given in our drawing, was one of the earliest built in the west, and is memorable for having undergone two distinct sieges which, for duration, severity, and manly resistance, are unequalled in the annals of the west. It was built in 1774, and stood upon the spot now occupied by "Zane's row," and the present residence of Colonel Charles D. Knox. It was considered one of the most substantial structures of the kind, in the valley of the Ohio, and is said to have been planned by no less a personage than George Rogers Clark, certainly one of the first military genius in the land. (The reader will notice elsewhere, that Clark was at Wheeling in the spring of 1774, at which time the fort was projected, and it is not therefore improbable, his master mind may have suggested the plan of this celebrated stockade.) Fort Henry' was a parallelogram, having its greatest length along the river. The pickets were of white oak, and about seventeen feet in height; it was supported by bastions, and thus well adapted for resisting a savage force, however powerful. It contained several cabins, arranged along the western wall. The commandant's house, store-house, etc., were in the centre; the captain's house was two stories high, and the top so adapted as to be used for firing a small cannon from: this, the artist has caught, and shown in his drawing. The store-house was but one story, and very strong, so as to answer for a lock-up. No regular garrison was maintained at this post, or at least, only for a very brief period. When Lord Dunmore returned from Camp Charlotte, he left some twenty or thirty men at the fort, who remained during most of the following year. Towards the close of 1776, the Virginia Convention, apprehending renewed outbreak on the part of the Indians, since the repudiation of Dunmore's government, ordered the post at Wheeling to be garrisoned by fifty men; this order, however, was not fulfilled.

In the fall of the same year, (1776), three new counties having been created in the west, (Ohio, Youghiogheny, and Monongahela,) the authorities of the first named lost no time in preparing to meet any force that might be sent against them. Their militia were organized, and other steps taken for a vigorous and successful resistance.

NOTE B.

There seems to be a wide-spread error, as to the date of this occurrence. Within recent years, several writers have sprung up who pertinaciously insist that the "first battle of Wheeling," was on the twenty-sixth of September, 1777. Another gentleman, delving among the old records of Ohio county, thought he had discovered the true and unquestionable date in one of the early order books of said county, and says that the siege commenced on the 27th of September. Convinced, from information in our possession, that these were both wrong, we determined to right the matter, and establish the truth. This we have found a most difficult task. To upset an authenticated record, we knew would be a troublesome matter; but feeling not unlike Sir Walter Raleigh when he burned his history, because a fact which he was personally cognizant of had been contradicted, we resolved to go no further until we had investigated the case most thoroughly, and could satisfy ourselves most fully. All the evidence at hand tended most conclusively to prove that the first, and not the twenty-sixth or twenty-seventh of September was the day upon which the siege commenced. But how would this evidence weigh against the order referred to, was the question? With much labor and investigation, we are at length able to reconcile the apparent discrepancy. Sergeant Jacob Ogle was not killed at Wheeling, as the record would seem to imply, although it does not say so; but was one of the two who escaped with his kinsman. Captain Ogle. Here then, the mystery ceases, and the record and the facts perfectly agree. Sergeant Jacob Ogle, we repeat, escaped the terrible massacre in front of the fort at Wheeling, on the first day of September, only to fall in the deplorable ambuscade at Grave creek narrows, September twenty-seventh, 1777!

These facts we have derived from an undoubted source. The late Mr. Hedges of this county frequently stated that Sergeant Ogle was one of the party who fell with Foreman.

NOTE C.

"The undersigned, having been applied to for a statement of facts respecting the memorable achievement at the attack on Fort Henry, (Wheeling,) in September, 1782, known as the 'Gunpowder exploit,' would state as follows, viz.:

On Monday afternoon, September 11, 1782, a body of about 300 Indians, and 50 British soldiers, composing part of a company known as the 'Queen's Rangers,' appeared in front of the fort, and demanded a sui-render. These forces were commanded respectively by the white renegade Girty, and a Captain Pratt.

The demand for a surrender was of course uncomplied with, and the attack then commenced.

During the forenoon of Tuesday, September 12th, the enemy having temporarily withdrawn from the attack, but occupying a position within gunshot of the fort, those within the stockade observed a female leave the residence of Colonel Zane, and advance with rapid movements towards the fort. She made for the southern gate, as it was less exposed to the fire of the enemy. The gate was opened immediately, and she entered in safety.

That person was none other than Molly Scott, and the object of her mission, was to procure powder for those who defended the dwelling of Colonel Zane! The undersigned was at that time in her 17th year, and remembers with perfect distinctness every circumstance connected with the incident. She saw Molly Scott enter the fort, assisted her in getting the powder, and saw her leave, and avers most positively that she, and she alone, accomplished the feat referred to, and deserves all the credit there may be attached to it.

The ammunition at that time was kept in the 'store-house,' adjoining the residence of my father, known as the 'Captain's house.' My father having left for help on the commencement of the attack, and I being the oldest child under the paternal roof, was directed by my mother to go with the messenger (Molly Scott), to the store-house, and give her whatever ammunition she needed. This the undersigned did, and will now state without the fear of contradiction, that the powder was given to Molly Scott, and not to Elizabeth Zane.

The undersigned assisted said Molly Scott in placing the powder in her apron, and to this she is willing to be qualified at any time.

Elizabeth Zane, for whom has long been claimed the credit of this heroic feat, was at that time at the residence of her father, near the present town of Washington, Pa.

At the time of its occurrence, the achievement was not considered very extraordinary. Those were emphatically times when woman's heart was nerved to deeds of no ordinary kind; — we all felt it was then 'to do or die;' and the undersigned does not hesitate to say, that more than one within the little stockade at Wheeling, would have accomplished the feat with as much credit as the one whose name seems destined to an immortality in border warfare.

But undersigned does not wish to detract any from the heroism of that feat, she only desires to correct a gross error — to give honor to whom honor is due. This she deems imperative, that the truth and justice of history may be maintained.

The undersigned disclaims all unkind feelings towards any one, in relation to this statement. Elizabeth Zane was one of her earliest acquaintances, whom she knew to be a woman brave, generous and single-hearted. Given under my hand and seal, this 28th day of November, 1849.

Lydia S. Cruger. [seal.]
NOTE D.

The names of those who were known to have been in the fort at the time, we have with great pains collected, and give below. The list comprises twenty-seven men and six boys. Of the men, not more than eighteen were able to do efficient service; the balance were either disabled by injuries sustained in warfare, or labored under autumnal fevers. Stephen Burkam, Silas, Jonathan, and Andrew Zane; Copeland Sullivan, Jacob and George Reikart; James Smith and his two sons, Henry and Thomas; Conrad Stroop, John Tait, Wright, old Mr. Mills, Edward Mills, and Thomas Mills, Hamilton Kerr, Alexander M'Dowell, Harry Clark, James Saltar, James Clark, Casper French, Conrad Wheat and four sons, James Boggs, (son of Captain Boggs), Martin and George Kerr, Peter Nisewanger, and two men, companions of Sullivan.

Two-thirds of the above persons had families in the fort. We cannot name all the female soldiers of that little stockade, but trust we may not be considered invidious for particularizing a few. There was Mrs. Ebenezer Zane, a skilful nurse and courageous woman; the fort would have suffered without her ministering and tender care to the sick and wounded. Next was Betsy Wheat, an Amazon in strength, and a Lucretia in ferocity. Her loud voice, and stern word of command, to those whom she thought laggard, could be heard all over the fort. We have heard it said that the courage, energy, and devotion of this woman, did more to encourage and revive the drooping spirits of the despondent, than that of any other person. Next, and not least, was Miss Lydia Boggs, now Mrs. Cruger.

# CHAPTER II.

1783.

MIRACULOUS ESCAPE.

One of the most remarkable escapes upon record, is that of Thomas Mills. The circumstances were these. On the 30th day of July, Mills and two other men, Henry Smith and Hambleton Kerr, started on a fishing excursion up the river from Wheeling. When near Glenn's run, a party of Indians, who had watched the movements of the whites, fired upon them, killing Smith, and wounding Mills in fourteen places. He had that many distinct bullet-holes in him, and yet not one of them was mortal. Kerr escaped. Just before the attack, Mills and his companions had caught an enormous cat-fish, (weighing 87 pounds,) and when the men were taken from the canoe at Wheeling, their appearance was truly frightful; they were literally covered with blood and sand. Mills recovered from his wounds, and was recently living on the Ohio, near Shade river. He was in his time, a most useful man on the frontier, possessing great experience as a hunter and scout.

The men were gigging by torch light, and thus became fair objects for the aim of the savages.

In the summer of this year, John Nieswanger and Joseph Heffler, two very efficient spies, started on a hunting expedition down the Ohio. They were dressed in Indian fashion, as was often the custom on such occasions, so as the better to elude detection. They descended the river in a canoe, and on the evening of the day they left, put into Little Grave creek. A party of Indians had watched their movements, and during the night attacked them with fury. Nieswanger was killed, but his companion succeeded in getting off, with the loss of two fingers. He escaped to Wheeling, and thence went to Pittsburgh, to have an operation performed upon his maimed hand. Returning, and when near the present residence of Hamilton Woods, lie was attacked and killed by the Indians. While in pursuit of Heffler, at Grave creek, the canoe floated off, and thus the savages lost the chance of scalping the unfortunate Nieswanger. Some months afterwards the canoe was found lodged at the head of Captina Island, with the remains of the hunter and his gun still in it.

1784 was a year of comparative quiet on the frontier. The treaty of peace between the United States and Great Britain had the effect to restrain the western Indians for the time being.

1785.

## CAPTIVITY OF MRS. CUNNINGHAM.

In the latter part of June, a small party of Indians visited the house of Edward Cunningham, an enterprising settler on Bingamon, a branch of West Fork. Thomas Cunningham, a brother of Edward, lived in a house almost adjoining. The two families affording thus protection one to the other. At the time spoken of, Edward and his family were in one cabin, and the wife of Thomas, with her four children, (her husband having gone east on a trading expedition) were in the other, both families eating their dinners, when in stepped before the astonished mother and children, a huge savage, with drawn knife and uplifted tomahawk. Conscious of his security with the mother and children, but fearing danger from Edward Cunningham, who had seen him enter, the savage quickly glanced around for some means of escape in an opposite direction. Edward watched the movements of the savage through an opening in the wall. In the other house was a similar hole, (made to introduce light), and through it the Indian fired, shouting the yell of victory. It was answered by Edward, who had seen the aim of the savage just in time to escape, — the bark from the log close to his head was knocked off by the Indian's ball, and flew in his face. The Indian seeing that he had missed his object, and observing an adze in the room, deliberately commenced cutting an aperture in the back wall, through which he might pass out, without being exposed to a shot from the other building.

Another of the Indians came into the yard just after the firing of his companion, but observing Edward's gun pointing through the port hole, endeavored to retreat out of its range. Just as he went to spring the fence, a ball struck him, and he fell forward. It had, however, only fractured his thigh bone, and he was yet able to get over the fence, and take shelter behind a quilt suspended on it, before Edward could again load his gun. Meantime the Indian in the house was engaged in cutting a hole through the wall, during which Mrs. Cunningham made no attempt to get out, well aware it would only draw upon her head the fury of the savage; and that if she escaped this one, she would most probably be killed by some of those who were watching outside. She knew, too, it would be impossible to take the children with her. She trusted to hope that the one inside would withdraw without molesting any of them. A few minutes served to convince her of the hopeless folly of trusting to an Indian's mercy. When the opening had been made sufficiently large, the savage raised his tomahawk, sunk it deep into the brains of one of the children, and throwing the scarcely lifeless body into the back yard, ordered the mother to follow him. There was no alternative but death, and she obeyed his order, stepping over the dead body of one of her children, with an infant in her arms, and two others screaming by her side. When all were out he scalped the murdered boy, and setting fire to the house, retired to an eminence, where two of the savages were with their wounded companion, — leaving the other two to watch the opening of Edward Cunningham's door, when the burning of the house should force the family from their shelter. They were disappointed in their expectation of that event by the exertions of Cunningham and his son. When the flame from the one house communicated to the roof of the other, they ascended to the loft, threw off the loose boards which covered it, and extinguished the fire; — the savages shooting at them all the while; their balls frequently striking close by.

Unable to force out the family of Edward Cunningham, and despairing of doing further injury, they beat a speedy retreat. Before leaving, however, the eldest son of Mrs. Thomas Cunningham was tomahawked and scalped in presence of the shuddering mother. Her little daughter was next served in the same way; but, to make the scene still more tragical, the child was dashed against a tree, and its brains scattered about. The mother, during the whole of these bloody acts, stood motionless in grief, and in momentary awe of meeting a similar fate. But, alas, she was reserved for a different, and, to a sensitive woman, a far more dreadful fate. With her helpless babe she was led from this scene of carnage. The savages carried their wounded companion upon a litter. Crossing the ridge, they found a cave near Bingamon creek, in which they secreted themselves until after night, when some of the party returned to Edward Cunningham's, but not finding any one at home, fired the house, and made a hasty retreat towards their own country.

Mrs. Cunningham suffered untold mental and physical agony during her march to the Indian towns. For ten days her only nourishment was the head of a wild turkey and a few paw-paws. After a long absence she was returned to her husband, through the intercession of Simon Girty, who ransomed her, and sent her home. This one single act should redeem his memory from a multitude of sins.

After the savages had withdrawn, Cunningham went with his family into the woods, where they remained all night, there being no settlement nearer than ten miles. In the morning the alarm was given, and a company of men soon collected to go in pursuit of the Indians. When they came to Cunningham's, and found both houses heaps of ashes, they buried the bones of the boy who was murdered in the house, with the bodies of his brother and little sister, who were killed in the field; but so cautiously had the savages conducted their retreat, that no traces of them could be discovered, and the men returned to their homes.

Subsequently, a second party started in pursuit, and traced them to the cave; but it was found the enemy had left the night previous, and all hope of effecting a successful pursuit was given over. After her return from captivity, Mrs. Cunningham stated, that at the time of the search on the first day, the Indians were in the cave, and that several times the whites approached so near, that she could distinctly hear their voices; the savages standing with their guns ready to fire, in the event of being discovered, and forcing her to keep the infant to her breast, lest its cry might indicate their place of concealment.

CAPTIVITY OF TWO BOYS.

In the spring of this year, the Indians early re-appeared in the neighborhood of Wheeling. One of their first acts on Wheeling creek, was the captivity of two boys, John Wetzel, Jr., and Frederick Erlewyne, the former about sixteen years of age, and the latter a year or two younger. The boys had gone from the fort at Shepherd's, for the purpose of catching horses. One of the stray animals was a mare, with a young colt, belonging to Wetzel's sister, and she had offered the foal to John, says the account which we follow, as a reward for finding the mare. While on this service, they were captured by a party of four Indians, who, having come across the horses, had seized and secured them in a thicket, expecting the bells would attract the notice of their owners, as they could kill them. The horse was ever a favorite object of plunder with the savages; as not only facilitating his own escape from pursuit, but also assisting him in carrying off the spoil. The boys, hearing the well-known tinkle of the bells, approached the spot where the Indians lay concealed, congratulating themselves on their good luck in so readily finding the strays, when they were immediately seized by the savages. John, in attempting to escape, was shot through the wrist. His companion hesitating to go with the Indians, and beginning to cry, they dispatched him with the tomahawk. John, who had once before been taken prisoner and escaped, made light of it, and went along cheerfully with his wounded arm. The party struck the Ohio river early the following morning, at a point near the mouth of Grave creek, and just below the clearing of Mr. Tomlinson. Here they found some hogs, and killing one of them, put it into a canoe they had stolen. Three of the Indians took possession of the canoe with their prisoner, while the other was busied in swimming the horses across the river. It so happened that Isaac Williams, Hambleton Kerr, and Jacob, a Dutchman, had come down that morning from Wheeling, to look after the cattle, etc., left at the deserted settlement. When near the mouth of Little Grave creek, a mile above, they heard the report of a rifle. "Dod rot 'em," exclaimed Mr. Williams, "a Kentuck boat has landed at the creek, and they are shooting my hogs." Quickening their pace, in a few minutes they were within a short distance of the creek, when they heard the loud snort of a horse. Kerr being in the prime of life, and younger than Mr. Williams, was several rods ahead, and reached the bank first. As he looked into the creek, he saw three Indians standing in a canoe; one was in the stern, one in the bow, and the other in the middle. At the feet of the latter, lay four rifles and a dead hog; while a fourth Indian was swimming a horse, a few rods from shore. The one in the stern had his paddle in the edge of the water in the act of turning and shoving the canoe from the mouth of the creek into the river. Before they were aware of his presence, Kerr drew up and shot the Indian in the stern, who instantly fell into the water. The crack of his rifle had scarcely ceased, when Mr. Williams came up .and shot the one in the bow, who also fell overboard. Kerr dropped his own rifle, and seizing that of the Dutchman, shot the remaining Indian. He fell over into the water, but still held on to the side of the canoe with one hand. So amazed was the last Indian at the fall of his companions, that he never offered to lift one of the rifles which lay at his feet in self-defence, but acted like one bereft of his senses. By this time the canoe, impelled by the impetus given to it by the first Indian, had reached the current of the river, and was some rods below the mouth of the creek. Kerr instantly reloaded his gun, and seeing another man lying in the bottom of the canoe, raised it to his face as in the act of firing, when he cried out, "Don't shoot, I am a white than!" Kerr told him to knock loose the Indian's hand from the side of the canoe, and paddle to the shore. In reply he said his arm was broken and he could not. The current, however, set it near some rocks not far from land, on which he jumped and waded out. Kerr now aimed his rifle at the Indian on horseback, who by this time had reached the middle of the river. The shot struck near him, splashing the water on his naked skin. The Indian seeing the fate of his companions, with the utmost bravery, slipped from the horse, and swam for the canoe, in which were the rifles of the four warriors. This was an act of necessity, as well of daring, for he well knew he could not reach home without the means of killing game. He soon gained possession of the canoe, unmolested, crossed with the arms to his own side of the Ohio, mounted the captive horse, which had swam to the Indian shore, and .with a yell of defiance escaped into the woods. The canoe was turned adrift to spite his enemies, and was taken up near Maysville with the dead hog still in it, the cause of all their misfortunes.

THE DOOLIN MURDER.

Edward Doolin was one of the earliest settlers near the mouth of fishing creek. He improved the farm now partly owned by Samuel McEldowney, about one mile above New Martinsville, Virginia. Most of the settlers on Fishing creek had, on the opening of spring, moved into Tomlinson's fort; but Doolin, not apprehending danger, refused to go. The circumstances of this murder are thus given by General Butler, who was one of the Commissioners appointed to hold treaties with the northern and western Indians. His Journal, from which we extract, was kept during his visit to the Miami, in 1785:

"I saw one Irvine, who had come from Cumberland river in a boat; he arrived at Fort Mcintosh just the evening before I set out. He says he met General Clark below Sciota a small distance, the 13th inst., on his way to the falls of the Ohio. He says he met with the wife of one Doolin, whose husband and two children were murdered by the Indians on Fish creek, on the 20th instant. Their conduct was very extraordinary. They came to the door and knocked, very early in the morning; the man rose out of bed and was shot through the door, which broke his thigh; on his falling, the door was broke in by the Indians, who tomahawked him and two children; the woman in fright lay still. They told her not to be uneasy, that they would not hurt her or the child she had in her arms, and desired she would not leave the house, as they would soon be back again, but did not intend to injure her; that they were Cherokees, and would never make peace. She asked why they troubled her, that the Indians had made peace with General Clark last fall; they said, not they; that if they could meet General Clark they would kill him also. He says he does not think the Indians mean to do any mischief generally, that it is a few banditti, who are a collection of Cherokees, Shawanese, etc."

Mrs. Doolin afterwards married Edmund Martin, and moved with her husband to Kentucky.

## CAPTIVITY OF MRS. FRANCES SCOTT.

Mr. Scott, a citizen of Washington county, Virginia, had his house attacked on Wednesday night, June 29th, 1785, and himself, with four children, butchered upon the spot.

Early in the evening, a considerable body of Indians passed his house and encamped within a couple of miles. Himself and family had retired, with the exception of Mrs. Scott, who was in the act of undressing, when the painted savages rushed in, and commenced the work of death. "Mr. Scott, being awake, jumped up, but was immediately fired at: he forced his way through the midst of the enemy and got out of the door, but fell. An Indian seized Mrs. Scott, and ordered her to a particular spot, and not to move: others stabbed and cut the throats of the three younger children in their bed, and afterwards lifting them up, dashed them upon the floor, near the mother; the eldest, a beautiful girl of eight years old, awoke, escaped out of the bed, ran to her parent, and, with the most plaintive accents, cried, 'mamma! mamma! save me!' The mother, in the deepest anguish of spirit, and with a flood of tears, entreated the savages to spare her child; but with a brutal fierceness, they tomahawked and stabbed her in the mother's arms. Adjacent to Mr. Scott's dwelling house another family lived, of the name of Ball. The Indians attacked them at the same time; but the door being shut, the enemy fired into the house through an opening between two logs, and killed a young lad; they then tried to force the door, but a surviving brother fired through and drove them off; the remaining part of the family ran out of the house and escaped. In Mr. Scott's house were four good rifles, well loaded, and a good deal of clothing and furniture, part of which belonged to people that had left it on their way to Kentucky. The Indians, being thirteen in number, loaded themselves with the plunder, then speedily made off, and continued travelling all night. Next morning their chief allotted to each man his share; and detached nine of the party to steal horses from the inhabitants on Clinch river. The eleventh day after Mrs. Scott's captivity, the four Indians who had her in charge, stopped at a place of rendezvous to hunt. Three went out, and the chief, being an old man, was left to take care of the prisoner, who, by this time, expressed a willingness to proceed to the Indian towns, which seemed to have the desired effect of lessening her keeper's vigilance. In the day time, as the old man was graning a deer skin, the captive, pondering on her situation, and anxiously looking for an opportunity to make her escape, took the resolution, and went to the Indian carelessly, asked liberty to go a small distance to a stream of water, to wash the blood off her apron, that had remained besmeared since the fatal night of the murder of her little daughter. He told her, in the English tongue 'Go along!' she then passed by him, his face being in a contrary direction from that she was going, and he very busy. After getting to the water, she went on without delay towards a high, barren mountain, and travelled until late in the evening, when she came down into the valley, in search of the track she had been taken along; hoping thereby to find the way back, without the risk of being lost, and perishing with hunger in uninhabited parts.

"That night she made herself a bed with leaves, and the next day resumed her wanderings. Thus did that poor woman continue from day to day, and week to week, wandering in the trackless wilderness. Finally, on the 11th of August, she reached a settlement on Clinch river, known as New Garden.

"Mrs. Scott related, that during her wandering from the tenth of July to the eleventh of August, she had no other subsistence but chewing and swallowing the juice of young cane, sassafras, and some plants she did not know the names of; that, on her journey, she saw buffaloes, elk, deer, and frequently bears and wolves, not one of which, although some passed very near, offered to do her the least harm. One day a bear came near her, with a young fawn in his mouth, and, on discovering her, he dropped his prey and ran off. Hunger prompted her to try and eat the flesh; but, on reflection, she desisted, thinking that the bear might return and devour her: besides, she had an aversion to raw meat,

"Mrs. Scott long continued in a low state of health, and remained inconsolable at the loss of her family, particularly bewailing the cruel death of her little daughter."

MURDER OF TWO SISTERS.

Next to the Tush murder, perhaps the most melancholy occurrence on Wheeling creek, was that of two sisters — the Misses Crow. The parents of these girls lived about one mile above the mouth of Dunkard, or lower fork of the creek. According to the statement of a third sister, who was an eye-witness to the horrid tragedy, and herself almost a victim, the three left their parents' house for an evening walk along the deeply shaded banks of that beautiful stream. Their walk extended over a mile, and they were just turning back, when suddenly, several Indians sprung from behind a ledge of rock, and seized all three of the sisters. With scarcely a moment's interruption, the savages led the captives a short distance up a small bank, when a halt was called, and a parley took place. It seems that some of the Indians were in favor of immediate slaughter, while others were disposed to carry them into permanent captivity. Unfortunately, the arm of mercy was powerless. Without a moment's warning, a fierce-looking savage stepped from the group with elevated tomahawk, and commenced the work of death. This Indian, in the language of the surviving sister, "Began to tomahawk one of my sisters — Susan by name. Susan dodged her head to one side, the tomahawk taking effect in her neck, cutting the large neck vein, [jugular] the blood gushing out a yard's length. The Indian who had her by the hand, jumped back to avoid the blood. The other Indian then began the work of death on my sister Mary. I gave a sudden jerk and got loose from the one that held me, and ran with all speed, and took up a steep bank, gained the top safe — (but just as I caught hold of a bush to help myself up, the Indian fired, and the ball passed through the clump of hair on my head, slightly breaking the skin;) the Indian taking round, in order to meet me as I would strike the path that led homeward. But I ran right from home, and hid myself in the bushes, near the top of the hill. Presently I saw an Indian passing along the hill below me; I lay still until he was out of sight; I then made for home."

1786.

In the autumn of this year, James Snodgrass and John Ice were killed while looking for their horses, which had strayed from their owners when on a buffalo hunt on Fishing creek.

A few days subsequent to this occurrence, a party of Indians came to Buffalo creek, and meeting Mrs. Dragoo and her son in a field gathering beans, took them prisoners, and supposing that their detention would induce others to look for them, waylaid the path leading from the house. "According to expectation, uneasy at their continued absence, Jacob Strait and Nicholas Wood went to ascertain the cause. As they approached, the Indians fired, and Wood fell. Strait taking to flight, was soon overtaken. Mrs. Strait and her daughter, hearing the firing and seeing the savages in pursuit of Mr. Strait, betook themselves also to flight, but were discovered by some of the Indians, who immediately ran after them. The daughter concealed herself in a thicket and escaped. Her mother sought concealment under a large shelving rock, and was not afterwards discovered, although those in pursuit of her husband, passed near and overtook him not far off. Indeed she was at that time so close as to hear Mr. Strait say, when overtaken, 'Don't kill me, and I will go with you;' and the savage replying, 'Will you go with me?' she heard the fatal blow which deprived her husband of life.

"Mrs. Dragoo being infirm and unable to travel to their towns, was murdered on the way. Her son (a lad of seven) remained with the Indians upwards of twenty years, — he married a squaw, by whom he had four children, two of whom he brought home with him, when he forsook the Indians."

1787.

## THE BEVANS' MURDER.

Clark's block-house was, in July of this year, the scene of a painful occurrence. Of those who had resorted there, was a family by the name of Bevans, embracing six members in all, two sons and two daughters. Not apprehending danger, these four visited, on the occasion referred to, their farm, which was within a mile of the fort, for the purpose of pulling flax. Reaching the field, they all seated themselves upon the fence and were looking at the flax, when the Indians fired upon them. John, one of the sons, received a ball through his body, but not so as to disable him from running for the blockhouse. An Indian followed close in pursuit, but the unfortunate young man kept ahead until within sight of the blockhouse, when he sunk down dead. The Indian had just given up the chase, as he saw him fall. Cornelius, the other brother, ran a different direction, with an Indian after him, tomahawk in hand. The little fellow ran down a steep hill, leaping over a large prostrate tree, in the top of which he hid himself. The two girls were tomahawked and scalped, and both found lying together. They were buried on the spot and in the same grave.

Clark told Rodefer that he saw John Bevans fall over the fence a short distance below the fort. One of the daughters was married, and an additional account says, that her husband, James Anderson, was with her and was killed.

## FEMALE HEROISM.

The women of the west were Spartans in every sense of the word. They possessed in a remarkable degree a union of strength, courage, love, devotion, simplicity and shrewdness which well fitted them for the severe and often terrible trials through which they had to pass. These noble qualities, called forth, perhaps, by the circumstances with which they were surrounded, distinguished the women of the heroic age of the west. Disregarding danger, and alone devoted to the safety of her little household, the western mother nerved her arm and steeled her heart to the severe duties which surrounded her.

A young girl braves the danger of an Indian army, and rushes forth from a place of safety to procure the means of defending those whom she loves more tenderly than life. Another bares her breast to the knife of the savage rather than disclose the hiding place of her friends; while yet another throws herself upon the person of her father, to receive the impending blow of the uplifted tomahawk.

Again, the fond wife, who has seen her husband shot dead by a rifle levelled over her own shoulders, watches over his blood-stained corpse, in her desolate home, surrounded by fierce savages, rather than attempt to escape and leave his precious remains subject to farther outrage. Such were the women of the west — the hero-mothers of the Revolution.

The case of our Virginia matron, which should have been noticed in its appropriate chronological order, will now be given.

On Dunkard creek, now within the limits of Monongalia county, lived a Mr. Bozarth, his wife, and three children.

The alarm which had caused the settlers to resort to Prickett's fort, (elsewhere noticed), induced two or three families living convenient to Mr. Bozarth, to collect at his house. About the 1st of April, (1789), when hut two men were in the house, with Mrs. Bozarth, the children, who had been out playing, ran suddenly in, crying that "Indians were coming!"

In order to ascertain the true cause of this alarm, one of the men stepped to the door and was struck upon the breast with a rifle ball, which knocked him back into the house. A savage sprung in after him and attacked the other white man with all the fury of his nature. The man being unarmed, called for a knife, but Mrs. Bozarth not seeing one at the instant, picked up an axe, and killed the savage on the spot. While the courageous woman was thus engaged, a second Indian presented himself at the door, and firing, killed the man who had been struggling with his companion. Quick as thought, the intrepid matron turned upon this new comer, and at one blow ripped open his abdomen, causing the savage to yell most lustily for help. Immediately, several of his companions rushed to the rescue, but the invincible woman was ready for them. The first who attempted to enter was struck upon the head, and his skull cleft, making the third victim to the axe of this Virginia Amazon. The others having drawn out the wounded savage, and learning the strength of the house, attempted to force the door, but Mrs. Bozarth had so securely fastened it, as to defy all their efforts. The savages then killed the children in the yard and made off.

In connection with this, and as illustrative of our subject, we will give one more case, which, although not occurring within the present limits of our state, was, at the time the transaction took place, strictly a part of Virginia.

"During the summer of this year, the house of Mr. John Merrill, of Nelson county, Ky., was attacked by Indians, and defended with singular address and good fortune. Merril was alarmed by the barking of a dog about midnight, and upon opening the door in order to ascertain the cause of the disturbance, received the fire of six or seven Indians, by which his arm and thigh were both broken. He instantly sunk upon the floor and called upon his wife to close the door. This had scarcely been done, when it was violently assailed by the tomahawks of the enemy, and a large breach soon effected. Mrs. Merrill, being a large woman, possessing both strength and courage, guarded the door with an axe, and successively killed or badly wounded four of the enemy as they attempted to force their way into the cabin.

"The Indians then ascended the roof and attempted to enter by way of the chimney, but here again they were met by the same determined enemy. Mrs. Merrill seized the only feather bed which the cabin afforded, and hastily ripping it open, poured its contents upon the fire. A furious blaze and stifling smoke instantly ascended the chimney, and brought down two of the enemy, who in a few moments were at the mercy of the woman. Seizing the axe, she quickly dispatched them, and was instantly afterwards summoned to the door, where the only remaining savage now appeared, endeavoring to effect an entrance, while Mrs. Merrill was engaged at the chimney. He soon received a gash on the cheek, which compelled him, with a loud yell, to relinquish his purpose, and return hastily to Chillicothe, where, from the report of a prisoner, he gave an exaggerated account of the fierceness, strength, and courage of the "Long-knife squaw!'"

THE BECHAM MURDER.

Of those who settled on Little Wheeling, after the cessation of hostilities in 1783, was a family named Becham. They lived near what is now known as the Scotch ridge. In October, 1787, two of the sons of Mr. Becham left home to hunt their horses, and look for bee trees. They had not gone far before a small party of Indians fell upon them, and took them prisoners. The Indians had caught one of the horses and tied him to a tree, and when the boys approached they were made captives without any resistance. The Indians then caught another horse, and placing a boy each before them, rode off. They made for the Ohio at Grave creek. That night they encamped about four miles from the river, and after securing their prisoners, fell asleep. During the night, something caused them to believe they were pursued; and without a moment's hesitation tomahawked and scalped the unfortunate prisoners, and then made off as speedily as possible. Happily, in the hurry and confusion of the moment, they did not do up the work of death in an effective manner, as neither boy was killed, and the eldest but slightly injured, saving the loss of his scalp. Thomas sat by the side of his brother for some time, but finding his head bleeding freely, took from the Indian's plunder a check apron, and tied it around his head. Deeming it imprudent to remain there, Thomas took some of the plunder, among which were a few pewter spoons, and mounting one of the horses, rode off for help. He travelled about three miles down Grave creek, where he left the horse, and proceeded on foot to the Flats. He went directly to the house of Mr. Masters, father of Dr. Z. Masters, living at that time on the farm now owned by Mr. Lewis D. Purdy, where his wound was dressed, and himself taken care of. A party went out on the morning to look for the other boy, but the savages had been back and made fatal work. It was supposed they had waited at some convenient point of observation until daylight, and discovering no pursuing party, returned to camp and dispatched the poor boy who had still survived. Thomas lived to a good old age, and for many years resided in Belmont county, Ohio. The Indians engaged in this expedition returned to the neighborhood of West Alexandria, and killed a Scotch woman, also a man named Ageo. They then escaped to the Ohio, and crossed near Yellow creek. Ageo was killed in going to the fort, after the murder of the woman referred to. He was shot from his horse.

1788.

THE JOHNSON BOYS.

All who have read anything of western history, will remember the thrilling feat of the two Johnson boys. As many very contradictory accounts have been given of that occurrence, which so links their name with the heroic age of the west, we were anxious to procure the full facts, and for this purpose consulted the surviving brother, now a hale old man of seventy-four, living in Monroe county, Ohio. In answer to our inquiry, he has written out a detailed statement of the whole transaction, which it affords us sincere pleasure to herewith submit:

Antioch, Monroe County, Ohio,

January 18th, 1851.

Dear Sir: — Yours of the 8th instant has just come to hand, and I with pleasure sit down to answer your request, which is a statement of my adventure with the Indians. I will give the narrative as found in my sketch book. I was born in Westmoreland county, Pennsylvania, February 4th, 1777. When about eight years old, my father, James Johnson, having a large family to provide for, sold his farm, with the expectation of acquiring larger possessions further west. Thus he was stimulated to encounter the perils of a pioneer life. He crossed the Ohio river, and bought some improvements on what was called Beach Bottom Flats, two and a half miles from the river, and three or four miles above the mouth of Short creek, with the expectation of holding by improvement right under the Virginia claim. Soon after we reached there, the Indians became troublesome; they stole horses, and killed a number of persons in our neighborhood. When I was between eleven and twelve years old, in the month of October, 1788, I was taken prisoner by the Indians, with my brother John, who was about eighteen months older than I. The circumstances were as follows: — On Saturday evening, we were out with an older brother, and came home late in the evening. The next morning one of us had lost a hat, and about the middle of the day, we thought that perhaps we had left it where we had been at work, about three-fourths of a mile from the house. We went to the place and found the hat, and sat down on a log by the road-side, and commenced cracking nuts. In a short time we saw two men coming toward us from the house. By their dress, we supposed they were two of our neighbors, James Perdue and J. Russell. We paid but little attention to them, until they came quite near us, when we saw our mistake: they were black. To escape by flight was impossible, had we been disposed to try. We sat still until they came up. One of them said, "How do, brodder?" My brother asked them if they were Indians, and they answered in the affirmative, and said we must go with them. One of them had a blue buckskin pouch, which we gave my brother to carry, and without further ceremony, he took up the line of march for the wilderness, not knowing whether we should ever return to our cheerful home; and not having much love for our commanding officers, of course we obeyed orders rather tardily. The mode of march was thus — one of the Indians walked about ten steps before, the other about ten behind us. After travelling some distance, Ave halted in a deep hollow and sat down. They took out their knives and whet them, and talked some time in the Indian tongue, which we could not understand. My brother and me sat eight or ten steps from them, and talked about killing them that night, and make our escape. I thought, from their looks and actions, that they were going to kill us; and, strange to say, I felt no alarm. I thought I would rather die than go with them. The most of my trouble was, that my father and mother would be fretting after us — not knowing what had become of us. I expressed my thoughts to John, who went and began to talk with them. He said that father was cross to him, and made him work hard, and that he did not like hard work; that he would rather be a hunter, and live in the woods. This seemed to please them; for they put up their knives, and talked more lively and pleasantly. We became very familiar, and many questions passed between us; all parties were very inquisitive. They asked my brother which way home was, several times, and he would tell them the contrary way every time, although he knew the way very well. This would make them laugh; they thought we were lost, and that we knew no better. They conducted us over the Short creek hills in search of horses, but found none; so we continued on foot until night, when we halted in a hollow, about three miles from Carpenter's fort, and about four from the place where they first took us; our route being somewhat circuitous, we made but slow .progress. As night began to close in, I became fretful. My brother encouraged me, by whispering that we would kill them that night. After they had selected the place of our encampment, one of them scouted round, whilst the other struck fire, which was done by stopping the touch-hole of his gun, and flashing powder in the pan. After the Indian got the fire kindled, he re-primed the gun and went to an old stump, to get some tinder wood, and while he was thus employed, my brother John took the gun, cocked it, and was about to shoot the Indian: alarmed lest the other might be close by, I remonstrated, and taking hold of the gun, prevented him shooting; at the same time I begged him to wait till night, and I would help him kill them both. The other Indian came back about dark, when we took our supper, such as it was, — some corn parched on the coals, and some roasted pork. We then sat and talked for some time. They seemed to be acquainted with the whole border settlement, from Marietta to Beaver, and could number every fort and block-house, and asked my brother how many fighting men there were in each place, and how many guns. In some places, my brother said, there were a good many more guns than there were fighting men. They asked what use were these guns. He said the women could load while the men fired. But how did these guns get there? My brother said, when the war was over with Great Britain, the soldiers that were enlisted during the war were discharged, and they left a great many of their guns at the stations. They asked my brother who owned that black horse that wore a bell? He answered, father. They then said the Indians could never catch that horse. We then went to bed on the naked ground, to rest and study out the best mode of attack. They put us between them, that they might be the better able to guard us. After awhile, one of the Indians, supposing we were asleep, got up and stretched himself on the other side of the fire, and soon began to snore. John, who had been watching every motion, found they were sound asleep. He whispered to me to get up, which we did as carefully as possible. John took the gun with which the Indian had struck fire, cocked it, and placed it in the direction of the head of one of the Indians. He then took a tomahawk, and drew it over the head of the other Indian. I pulled the trigger, and he struck at the same instant; the blow falling too far back on the neck, only stunned the Indian. He attempted to spring to his feet, uttering most hideous yells, but my brother repeated the blows with such effect that the conflict became terrible, and somewhat doubtful. The Indian, however, was forced to yield to the blows he received on his head, and in a short time he lay quiet at our feet. The one that was shot never moved; and fearing there were others close by, we hurried off, and took nothing with us but the gun I shot with. They had told us we would see Indians about to-morrow, so we thought that there was a camp of Indians close by; and fearing the report of the gun, the Indian hallooing, and I calling to John, might bring them upon us, we took our course towards the river, and on going about three-fourths of a mile, came to a path which led to Carpenter's fort. My brother here hung up his hat, that he might know where to take off to find the camp. We got to the fort a little before daybreak. We related our adventure, and the next day a small party went out with my brother, and found the Indian that was tomahawked, on the ground; the other had crawled off, and was not found till some time after. He was shot through close by the ear. Having concluded this narrative, I will give a description of the two Indians. They were of the Delaware tribe, and one of them a chief. He wore the badges of his office — the wampum belt, three half-moons, and a silver plate on his breast; bands of silver on both arms, and his ears cut round and ornamented with silver; the hair on the top of his head was done up with silver wire. The other Indian seemed to be a kind of waiter. He was rather under size, a plain man. He wore a fine beaver hat, with a hole shot through the crown. My brother asked him about the hat. He said he killed a captain and got his hat. My brother asked him if he had killed many of the whites, and he answered, a good many. He then asked him if the big Indian had killed many of the whites, and he answered, a great many, and that he was a great captain — a chief.

[Signed] Henry Johnson.

In connection with the above, and to still further show of what material the boys were made, in the great heroic age of the west, we give the following, which we find in a recent communication from Major Nye, of Ohio. The scene of adventure was within the present limits of Wood county, Virginia.

"I have heard from Mr. Guthrie, and others, that at Bellville a man had a son, quite a youth, say twelve or fourteen years of age, who had been used to firing his father's gun, as most boys did in those days. He heard, he supposed, turkeys on or near the bank of the Ohio, opposite that place, and asked his father to let him take the gun, and kill one. His father, knowing that the Indians frequently decoyed people by such noises, refused, saying it was probably an Indian. When he had gone to work, the boy took the gun and paddled his canoe over the river, but had the precaution to land some distance from where he had heard the turkey all the morning, probably for fear of scaring the game, and perhaps a little afraid of Indians. The banks were steep, and the boy cautiously advanced to where he could see without being seen. Watching awhile for his game, he happened to see an Indian cautiously looking over a log, to notice where the boy had landed. The lad fixed his gun at a rest, watching the place where he had seen the Indian's head, and when it appeared again, fired, and the Indian disappeared. The boy dropped the gun and ran for his canoe, which he paddled over the river as soon as possible. When he reached home, he said, 'Mother, I killed an Indian!' and the mother replied, 'No, you have not.' 'Yes, I have,' said the boy. The father coming in, he made the same report to him, and received the same reply; but he constantly affirmed it was even so; and, as the gun was left, a party took the boy over the river to find it, and show the place where he shot the Indian, and behold, his words were found verified. The ball had entered the head, where the boy had affirmed he shot, between the eye and ear."

Such "boys" made the men of the Republic in after years — men whom neither tyranny nor oppression could subdue.

CAPTIVITY OF MRS. GLASS.

Early on the morning of the 27th of March, two Indians appeared on the premises of Mr. Glass, residing a few miles back of the present town of Wellsburgh. At the time, Mrs. G. was alone in her house, with the exception of an infant and a small black girl. Mrs. Glass was spinning, and had sent her negro woman to the woods for sugar water. In a few moments she returned, screaming at the top of her voice, "Indians! Indians!" Mrs. Glass jumped up, and running, first to the window, then to the door, attempted to escape. But an Indian met her, and presented his gun; Mrs. Glass caught hold of the muzzle, turned it aside, and begged him not to kill her. The other Indian, in the meantime, caught the negro woman, and brought her into the house. They then opened a chest and took out a small box and some articles of clothing, and without doing any further damage, departed with their prisoners. After proceeding about a mile and a half, they halted, and held a consultation, as she supposed, to kill the children. This she understood to be the subject by their gestures. To one of the Indians, who could speak English, she held out her little boy, and begged not to kill him, as he would make a fine chief after awhile. The Indian made a motion for her to walk on with her child. The other Indian then struck the negro child with the pipe end of his tomahawk, which knocked it down, and then, by a blow with the edge, across the back of the neck, dispatched it.

"About four o'clock in the evening they reached the river, a mile above the creek, and carried a canoe, which had been thrown up in some drift wood, into the river. They got into this canoe, and worked it down to the mouth of Rush run, a distance of about five miles. They pulled the canoe into the mouth of the stream, as far as they could; going up the run about a mile, encamped for the night. The Indians gave the prisoners all their own clothes for covering, and one of them added his own blanket. Shortly before daylight the Indians got up, and put another blanket over them. The black woman complained much on account of the loss of her child, and they threatened, if she did not desist, to kill her.

"About sunrise they commenced their march, up a very steep hill, and at two o'clock halted on Short creek, about twenty miles from the place whence they set out in the morning. The spot had been an encampment shortly before, as well as a place of deposite for the plunder, which they had recently taken from the house of a Mr. Vanmeter, whose family had been killed. The plunder was deposited in a sycamore tree. They had tapped some sugar trees when there before, and now kindled a fire, and put on a brass kettle, with a turkey, which they had killed on the way, to boil in sugar water.

"Mr. Glass was working, with a hired man in a field, about a quarter of a mile from the house, when his wife and family were taken, but knew nothing of the event until noon. After searching about the place, and going to several houses in quest of his family, he went to Wells' fort, collected ten men, and that night lodged in a cabin, on the bottom on which the town of Wellsburg now stands.

"Next morning they discovered the place where the Indians had taken the canoe from the drift, and their tracks at the place of embarkation. Mr. Glass could distinguish the track of his wife by the print of the high heel of her shoe. They crossed over the river, and went down on the other side, until they came near the mouth of Rush run; but discovering no tracks of the Indians, most of the men concluded that they would go to the mouth of the Muskingum, by water, and therefore wished to turn back. Mr. Glass begged of them to go as far as the mouth of Short creek, which was only two or three miles. To this they agreed. When they got to the mouth of Rush run, they found the canoe of the Indians. This was identified by a proof, which goes to show the presence of mind of Mrs. Glass. While passing down the river, one of the Indians threw into the water several papers, which he had taken out of Mr. Glass' trunk; some of these she carelessly picked up, and under pretence of giving them to the child, dropped them into the bottom of the canoe. These left no doubt. The trail of the Indians, and their prisoners, up the run to their camp, and then up the river hill, was soon discovered.

"About an hour after the Indians had halted, Mr. Glass and his men came within sight of their camp. The object then was to save the lives of the prisoners, by attacking the Indians so unexpectedly, as not to allow time to kill them. With this view, they crept along until they got within one hundred yards of the camp. Fortunately, Mrs. Glass' little son had gone to a sugar-tree, but not being able to get the water, his mother had stepped out to get it for him. The negro woman was sitting some distance from the two Indians, who were looking attentively at a scarlet jacket, which they had taken some time before. On a sudden they dropped the jacket, and turned their eyes towards the men, who, supposing they were discovered, immediately discharged several guns, and rushed upon them, at full speed, with an Indian yell. One of the Indians, it was supposed, was wounded the first fire, as he fell and dropped his gun and shot pouch. After running about one hundred yards, a second shot was fired after him, by Maj. M'Guire, which brought him to his hands and knees; but there was no time for pursuit, as the Indians had informed Mrs. Glass that there was another encampment close by. They therefore returned with all speed, and reached Beech Bottom fort that night.

"The other Indian, at the first fire, ran a short distance beyond Mrs. Glass, so that she was in a right line between him and the white men; here he halted for a moment, to put on his shot pouch, which Mr. Glass mistook for an attempt to kill his wife with a tomahawk."

This artful manoeuvre, no doubt, saved the life of the savage, as his pursuers could not shoot at him, without risking the life of the woman.

The above we have slightly altered from the account already published, and think it is entirely correct as now given. Mrs. Glass subsequently married a Mr. Brown, and was long a resident of Brooke county.

The Monongahela settlements suffered somewhat severely from savage visitation during most of this year. The tomahawk and scalping knife found their victims in almost every neighborhood.

"In August, five Indians on their way to the Monongahela, met with two men on Middle Island creek, and killed them. Taking their horses, they continued on until they came to the house of William Johnson, on Ten-mile, and made prisoners of Mrs. Johnson and some children, plundered the house, killed part of the stock, and taking with them one of Johnson's horses, returned towards the Ohio. When the Indians came to the house, Johnson had gone to a lick not far off, and on his return in the morning, seeing what had been done, and searching until he found the trail of the savages and their prisoners, ran to Clarksburg for assistance. A company of men repaired with him to where he had discovered the trail, and keeping it about a mile, found four of the children lying dead in the woods. The savages had tomahawked and scalped them, and placing their heads close together, turned their bodies and feet out so as to represent a cross. The dead were buried, and further pursuit given over."

In the same month, two lads were surprised and killed at Neil's station, a small stockade which stood on the Kanawha, about a mile back of the present town of Parkersburg. The boys were twelve and fifteen, sons of a German who lived within a few hundred yards of the block-house. They had been to the station late in the evening, and returning, went out of their path to hunt the cows. The savages had watched them go down, and at a favorable moment fell upon them with their tomahawks and killed both on the spot. Alarmed at their delay, the parents made a search for them on the following morning and found their bodies as described. That night, the Indians attempted to burn the block-house by means of straw and hay, which they thrust through the port-holes; but in this they were foiled by the vigilance of those within.

### ROBERT CARPENTER.

A nephew of Joseph Tomlinson, named Robert Carpenter, came near losing his life under the following circumstances. He had gone out early in the morning for the horses, and while hunting near Grave creek, was fired on by a party of Indians who were concealed near the bank. The ball took effect in his shoulder, breaking the bone, and inflicting a severe wound. Thus disabled, the Indians soon overtook and made him prisoner. Anxious to get possession of the horses, but unable to catch them, the Indians concluded to let Carpenter try it, as the animals knew him and would be less difficult to capture. Accordingly, Carpenter was untied and started in pursuit. Going about two hundred yards, he determined to escape, and instead of catching the horses ran towards the house of a friend. But his flight was so greatly impeded by the old shoes which he wore, and his disabled arm, that the savages soon overtook him. Another attempt was then made by the Indians to get the horses, but utterly failing, Carpenter ventured to offer his services, declaring that he would not again try to escape, but do his best to catch the horses, and go along with them to their country. Finding they could not get near the animals, they concluded to trust Carpenter once more, threatening him with all manner of horrid deaths if he attempted again to escape. This time he adroitly drove the horses before him a considerable distance, and then kicking off his shoes, and taking a firm hold of his maimed limb, started on the race of life or death. He safely escaped to the house of Nathan Master, living on the farm now owned by Lewis D. Purdy, Esqr.

### MURDER OF THE GRICE FAMILY.

This occurrence, which should have gone with the preceding chapter, was unavoidably omitted, but is now given as possessing interest to the inhabitants in the region where the tragedy took place.

Of the families gathered at Shepherd's fort was one by the name of Grice. When it was determined to evacuate the fort, this family, instead of seeking shelter elsewhere, concluded to return to their improvement, distant about two miles from the forks. The family consisted of Grice, his wife and five children. When near the mouth of Peter's run, a party of Indians, who had watched the movements at the fort, fell upon them and murdered, or supposed they had, all but one, whom they took prisoner. Rachel, a girl of eleven years of age, was knocked down with a war-club and her skull fractured, but she was not killed. Dr. Moore, of Catfish, was called upon, and trepanned her. She recovered, and afterwards married Captain Henry Jolly, a well known citizen of Ohio. One of the victims was a married daughter, who at the time was enceinte. The eldest son, John, was made prisoner, who remained with them eleven years, but at last got an opportunity, while in Kentucky, to escape. The Indians who committed this depredation were eleven in number. Rachel said, the man who scalped her had blue eyes and light hair.

MURDER OF THE PURDY FAMILY.

One of the most bold and bloody murders perpetrated in the neighborhood of Wheeling, during this year, was that on the family of James Purdy, a worthy and industrious settler on the hill just above Bedelion's mill. The family consisted of Mr. and Mrs. Purdy and their four children.

The cabin in which they lived was unfinished; a blanket supplying the place of a door. But this was not deemed unsafe, as no Indians had appeared in the settlement for some months. Shortly after dark, four Indians stepped into the cabin, and without uttering a word commenced butchering the defenceless family. Two of them fell upon Purdy, who called to his wife for a knife, which she handed him; but he was then too much exhausted from the repeated blows of the tomahawk to use it, and the next moment after receiving it sunk lifeless to the floor. Mrs. Purely was knocked down with a war club; one child was dashed against the door-way, and its brains scattered over the room, while an interesting little boy, who was screaming with fright, had both his fears and his pains quieted by a blow from the tomahawk. The two remaining children, daughters, were then made prisoners, and after plundering the house, effected a hurried retreat across the Ohio. The girls were released after ten years' captivity. Mrs. Purdy was only stunned by the blow with the war club, and falling near the door, crawled off and secreted herself while the Indians were eating.

## ATTACK UPON KIRKWOOD'S CABIN.

Early in the spring of this year, a large body of Indians made an attack upon the settlement at the mouth of Indian Wheeling creek, opposite Wheeling, Virginia. A block-house was in course of erection, but not in a condition to be occupied; the cabin of Captain Robert Kirkwood was used as a place of resort for the neighborhood. On this occasion. Captain Joseph Biggs, who commanded a company of scouts, was in the cabin with fourteen of his men. About four o'clock in the morning, Captain Biggs, feeling restless, arose and went out into the air. Returning, he closed the door, and what was unusual, rolled a barrel of pork against it, in order to make it more secure. He had scarcely time to get into bed, when the attack was commenced, and a furious assault made upon the door by means of rails, logs, &c. The besieged placed themselves under Captain Biggs, by whom the defence was maintained in a manner highly creditable to him as a brave and skilful officer. He ordered every particle of light to be extinguished, and so stationed his men as to fire upon the enemy from every direction. The night was clear and beautiful; the moon being nearly full, gave those within great advantage over the enemy, as they were enabled by the light, to shoot the savages whenever they presented themselves. Early in the engagement. Captain Biggs received a serious wound, but with the courage of a true soldier concealed the nature of it until day-light. In noticing the movements of the enemy through one of the windows of the cabin, an Indian, who had slipped close under the side of the house, suddenly thrust his rifle through the window at which Captain Biggs was standing, and discharging it, lodged the ball in the left arm of the captain, just below the shoulder. The bone was badly fractured, and parts of it afterwards came away.

Foiled in their attempt to effect an entrance at the door, (which had been well secured by puncheons from the floor,) the savages determined to try the effect of fire; and accordingly hurled burning fagots upon the roof, which, in a few minutes, was enveloped in flames. But again they were unsuccessful, for the whites pushed off the roof. The Indians now became furious, and commenced piling brush against the sides of the house, which they fired. At one time that noble little band thought their fate was sealed, as the flames would often mount to the top of the walls. With perseverance and caution, however, they succeeded in subduing the fire, and finally extinguishing it. This they did first with water, milk, and such other liquids as could be commanded, and finally with sand from beneath the cabin floor. Early in the attack, the mortar was removed from the chinks of the wall, and the savages having suffered severely from the steady aim of the scouts through these convenient port-holes, retired behind the half-finished block-house.

Shortly before day-break, the boom of a cannon was heard echoing among the hills, which the besieged hailed as the harbinger of help. The firing had been heard at Wheeling, and the gun announced that assistance would soon be at hand. The savages, too, understood it, and without delay gathered up their wounded and disappeared in the forest. Five of the whites were severely wounded, one mortally. These were. Captain Joseph Biggs, John Walker, Elijah Hedges, John Barrett, and Joseph Van Meter. Walker was shot through the hip, severing the urethra, and causing his death early next day. He was removed to the residence of Colonel Zane, Wheeling, where he died, and was buried with military honors. A coat belonging to some of the inmates, which had been suspended by the centre-log, and was left hanging after the roof had been thrown off, was found, on examination, to be completely riddled with bullets. The number of Indians was never fully ascertained, nor the extent of their killed and wounded. They were supposed to have been the same concerned in the engagement with Captain Van Buskirk's company at the mouth of Brush run, an account of which is elsewhere given.

FATAL DECOY.

One of the most common, and at the same time, most successful decoys practised by the wily savage, was that of the turkey call. The case we are about to record belongs to that class.

Of those forted at Grave creek, was a William Mcintosh, wife and child. Early one morning, the cry of a turkey was heard against the hill-side, across the river. Mcintosh, although warned against the deceptions of the enemy, started over with his gun and dog. He landed his canoe at a point nearly opposite the fort, and commenced ascending the bank. Before taking ten steps, the "turkey," from his concealed position, fired and shot his victim through the head.

Mcintosh remaining much longer than was thought right, some men from the fort went over on the third day, and there found the unfortunate man scalped, with his faithful dog sitting by his side.

SURPRISE OF A HUNTER'S CAMP.

On the 28th of January, (1791,) a hunting party, composed of Joseph Biggs, James Boggs, (son of Captain Boggs,) James and Alexander Mitchell, Thos. Barr, Thos. Richards, Elijah Whittaker, Joshua Williamsom, (brother of Colonel Williamson,) and some others whose names cannot be obtained, crossed the Ohio from Short creek, on a hunt in the Indian country. They went out as far as Stillwater, and having killed considerable game were about returning. As the party lay around their camp fire at night, a body of Indians rose up from beneath the creek bank, and fired directly into their midst. Boggs was shot through both hips with a large musket ball; the rest of the party escaped unhurt and eluded pursuit, but lost all their guns, blankets, game, etc. The Indians scalped their unfortunate victim, — almost denuding the entire skull, then stretched him out and placed an old musket across his breast. His arms were extended at full length, and frozen so firmly in that position, that when the men went out from Wheeling to bury him, they had to amputate the limbs to get him in a convenient sized grave. The ground was so frozen that the men could not bury the body at any great depth, and the result was, as afterwards ascertained, that the bears scented out the spot and devoured the remains. These facts we have derived from Mrs. Cruger, who was sister-in-law to Mr. Boggs. The unfortunate man had, during the night previous to his horrible death, what was called a "bad dream," It was that of a swarm of black bees, some of which stung him. His companions said he spoke frequently of the circumstance during the day, and that he regarded it as a fatal presentiment.

One of the latest, and perhaps the very last Indian murder committed on the river near Wheeling, was that of Uriah McCutcheon, who was killed by a small party of Indians near the present Harris' Ferry. According to B. McMechen, Esq., from whom we have obtained this fact, the unfortunate man was found shortly afterwards, tomahawked and scalped.

DEATH OF THREE HUNTERS.

In the fall of this year, three young men, Thomas Swearengen, son of Captain Van Swearengen, John L. Masters, and a third whose name we have not been able to ascertain, crossed the Ohio, and commenced hunting up the valley of Short creek. The day was very fine, and as no Indian depredations had been committed for some time in that immediate neighborhood, the hunters believed they were perfectly safe. But their hopes proved a vain delusion. They had not gone far, when a party of Indians, doubtless attracted by the report of the hunters' rifles, fired upon them, killing Swearengen on the spot, and so wounding the others, that they were easily overtaken and dispatched. The bodies of all three were afterwards found and identified. The scene of this disaster was some four or five miles back from the river and creek. Some men from the Ohio side gave information of the discovery of the bodies, and a party of Virginians from the neighborhood of Beech bottom went over and buried them. Similar expeditions to the one we have just spoken of, frequently went from this side into the Indian country, and they generally paid for their temerity. We have already noticed two or three, and now have to speak of another. Not long after the last mentioned occurrence, a party of seven, from the neighborhood of West Liberty, including one of the Biggs' and also one of the Hedges', crossed the river, and after one day's hunt, were attacked by a considerable body of Indians, and put to rout with the loss of three of their number.

MASSACRE OF JOLLY'S FAMILY.

Among the earlier settlers in the neighborhood of Wheeling, was Daniel Jolly. His improvement was on the hill, about three miles from the mouth of the creek. The land is, we believe, now occupied by Mr. McEnall, and the site of his cabin is still pointed out not far from the road which crosses the hill from the old toll-gate to the river. The family of Jolly consisted of himself, wife and four children, with one grand-child.

On the 8th day of June, a small party of Indians, who had secreted themselves behind some gooseberry bushes in the garden, fired upon the family, killing Mrs. Jolly instantly and wounding a son, daughter and grand-son. Her eldest son, John, had just reached the house from the corn-field, and was in the act of wiping the perspiration from his brow with the sleeve of his shirt as the ball struck him in the mouth. He fell, badly wounded, and the next instant the savages were tomahawking him. Killing and scalping the other wounded ones, and taking prisoner one son and a nephew of Mr. Jolly, named Joseph McCune, they pillaged, then fired the house and made a rapid retreat. Joseph McCune was killed after proceeding a short distance because he could not travel fast, as he suffered from phthisic.

Mrs. Jolly was standing in the door at the moment she was shot, looking in direction of the spring, to which she had sent one of her children. The boy at the spring, whose name was James, escaped, also another member of the family in the field. A daughter, Mary, was absent at her uncle Joseph McCune, who lived on the ridge road, about five miles from the forks of

Wheeling. Mr. Jolly had gone on a journey to the Monongahela to receive a payment for some property which he had sold previous to moving out.

The boy made prisoner remained in captivity seven years, and was then regained by his brother at Pensacola. He was discovered trading at Nashville; and on being questioned, the facts of his captivity were elicited, whereupon a gentleman wrote to Colonel Zane, who communicated the intelligence to the boy's father. These particulars we have derived principally from Mrs. Cruger, Mr. McIntyre, and Mr. Darby.

## DEATH OF CAPTAIN VAN BUSKIRK

Early in June of this year occurred the last conflict on the upper Ohio, between an organized party of Virginians and Indians. In consequence of the numerous depredations on the settlements now embraced in Brooke and Hancock counties, it was determined to summarily chastise these marauders; and accordingly, a party of men organized under the command of Captain Lawson Van Buskirk, an officer of tried courage and acknowledged efficiency. A party of Indians had committed sundry acts of violence, and it was believed they would endeavor to cross the Ohio on their retreat, at some point near Mingo Bottom. The party of Captain Van Buskirk, consisted of about forty experienced frontiermen, some of whom were veteran Indian hunters. The number of the enemy was known to be about thirty. The whites crossed the river below the mouth of Cross creek, and marched up the bottom, looking cautiously for the enemy's trail. They had discovered it along the run, but missing it, they concluded to take the ridge, hoping thus to cross it. Descending the ridge, and just as they gained the river, the Indians fired upon them, killing Captain Van Buskirk, and wounding John Aidy. The enemy were concealed in a ravine amidst a dense cluster of paw-paw bushes. The whites marched in single file, headed by their captain, whose exposed situation will account for the fact that he was wounded with thirteen balls. The ambush quartered on their flank, and they were totally unsuspicious of it. The plan of the Indians was to permit the whites to advance in numbers along the line before firing upon them. This was done; but instead of each selecting his man, every gun was directed at the captain, who fell, with thirteen bullet holes in his body. The whites and Indians instantly tree'd, and the contest lasted more than an hour. The Indians, however, were defeated, and retreated towards the Muskingum, with the loss of several killed, while the Virginians, with the exception of their captain, had none killed and but three wounded.

Captain Van Buskirk's wife was killed just eleven months previous to the death of her husband. They lived about three miles from West Liberty. She had been taken prisoner by the Indians, and on their march towards the river, her ancle was sprained so that she could not walk without pain. Finding her an incumbrance, the wretches put her to death on the hill, just above where Wellsburg now stands. On the following day the body of this unfortunate woman was found by a party who had gone in pursuit.

1794.

## THE TUSH MURDER.

The valley of Wheeling creek, one of the most beautiful and productive in the state, was the theatre of many a painful and bloody drama. Scarcely a quiet bend, or a surrounding hill, or a rippling tributary, that is not memorable as connected with the wars of the Indians. To one unacquainted with its tragic history, it would indeed be difficult to imagine that these clear waters were once tinged with the blood of helpless women and children, and these stern old hills ever echoed to the terrible whoop of the savage. Such, however, is the melancholy fact, as our pages abundantly attest. The case which we are about to detail was, perhaps, the most dreadful that occurred in the settlement of the valley.

Of those who settled at an early day in this region, was George Tush. His residence was about twelve miles from the river, on the farm now owned by Mr. Albert Davis. The family consisted of himself, wife, and five children. During the spring and summer of 1794, the settlements on Wheeling creek had been almost entirely exempt from Indian visitation, and many of the inhabitants began to console themselves with the reflection, that day was about to dawn upon their long night of terror. But, alas, their fondly imagined security was soon to be dispelled. On the evening of Saturday, September 6th, (1794,) as George Tush was in the act of feeding his hogs, in a sty close to his cabin, he was fired upon by three savages, who had concealed themselves, and waited until he should leave the house. A ball struck him transversely upon the breast, cutting a deep gash, and inflicting a serious and painful wound, as it carried off a portion of the bone. It lodged in the shoulder blade. Tush, losing entirely his presence of mind, or, in all charitableness, we may allow that his pain deprived him of self-control, rushed madly by his own door, in direction of the forest, leaving his helpless family to the mercy of relentless savages. The next moment the Indians were in the house. The mother was instantly made prisoner, and in powerless but quivering agony, compelled to witness the horrid butchery of her innocent children. In an instant the youngest born was dashed against a tree, and the other four fell beneath the reeking tomahawk. Pillaging the house of such articles as they could carry off, a hurried retreat was made, lest the escaped husband should follow in pursuit. The feeble woman was brutally urged on before them. But, alas, the scenes which she had just witnessed, together with her own situation, rendered her movements both slow and painful. Fearing discovery, the wretches tomahawked their helpless victim, and left her at a point about eight miles from the place of captivity. Her remains were found some years afterwards by her husband, while hunting. He recognized them by the bones of an infant with which she was at the time largely enceinte.

Of the children tomahawked and scalped, one, a little girl of four years, recovered, and the infant, whose brains were supposed to have been dashed out, was found alive on the following day, lying upon its dead sisters and brothers. That child still lives, and is the wife of George Goodrich, residing near Shelbyville, la. The children had, a few days before, gathered a quantity of acorns, which, it is supposed, prevented the hogs disturbing the remains.

Tush, in his fright, ran some distance, and jumped from a ledge of rocks fifteen feet in height. This so disabled him that he could not get to Jacob Wetzel's house, which was just across the creek, until late at night. He was taken to Wheeling a day or two after, and there remained until his wound was healed. (See letter of Mr. Darby, in a Note at the end of present chapter, for some interesting facts connected with this case.)

DEATH OF TWO BROTHERS.

Late in the fall of 1794, two brothers, named John and Joseph Scott, accompanied by a man named Thomas Manning, started on a hunting expedition to Stillwater. They believed the season so far advanced that no danger need be apprehended from Indians. The three men traversed the country lying between Wheeling and Stillwater without molestation, or indication of Indians. On the first night of their arrival out, they kindled a fire, and after supper prepared for rest. Manning, who was an experienced hunter, attempted to dissuade the Scotts from remaining near the fire. They, however, disregarded the advice, and laughed at his fears. But Manning declared he would not sleep there, and accordingly moved off a short distance. Scarcely had he changed his position, when a party of Indians opened a fire upon them, killing the brothers instantly, and wounding Manning severely, by breaking his left arm. Reserving his fire, the Indians did not rush upon him, and supposing he was mortally wounded, ran upon the Scotts, and plied the tomahawk, that the work of death might be complete. Manning escaped, and made his way to Wheeling. Immediately a party of whites went out and buried the unfortunate brothers. The savages had singularly maimed one of the ill-fated men.

The Scotts were active and industrious men, good hunters, and much respected by all who knew them. Joseph married Debby Hardesty. He lived on the point where the warehouse of Anderson & Pancoast now stands, in Bridgeport. John lived on the island.

BLOODY EXPLOIT.

Jonathan Zane was perhaps one of the best shots in the west. He prided himself particularly upon his skill in this respect. The following incident shows that he was not only a good shot, but a dead shot. We derive the facts from Mr. Reuben Miller, of Bridgeport, Ohio, long a personal friend of Mr. Zane.

About the year 1808, the two (Miller and Zane) were walking near where Phillips' foundry now stands, in Wheeling, when Zane remarked, "About here, I once killed five Indians. I was returning home from hunting my horses, and in passing through the high weeds which at that time grew all around, I saw five Indians jump into the river, and swim for the island. I fired, and one of them sunk. Loading and firing three times in quick succession, three others were killed before reaching the opposite bank." The fifth and last, seeing the fate of his companions, concealed himself behind a sawyer, near the island shore, hoping thus to escape the deadly aim of the white man. After several ineffectual attempts to dislodge him, the effort was about to be given over, when Zane noticed a portion of his abdomen protruding below the log. Drawing a fine aim on the exposed part, he fired, and the savage rolled into the stream.

ATTACK ON MR. ARMSTRONG.

A Mr. Armstrong, one of the early settlers at Belpre, having secured some land on the Virginia side, built a mill and cabin near the head of Blannerhasset's Island, and in the spring of 1794 moved over his family, consisting of his wife and five children. Shortly after their change of residence, a party of Indians concealed themselves on the river hill immediately back of Armstrong's house, and in full view of the stockade at Belpre. At early dawn, Mr. Armstrong heard that so often fatal decoy, the turkey-call, and taking his dog and gun, sallied forth to secure a shot before they should leave the roost. One of the sons, taken prisoner, and now living near Columbus, Ohio, relates what followed. "After proceeding a short distance, either from the dog, or some other circumstance, Armstrong became alarmed, retreated to the house and barred the door. The Indians pursued, and endeavored to get it open, but failing on the first attempt, they took a rail to effect their purpose. While they were endeavoring to gain entrance, Mr. Armstrong snapped his gun, in an attempt to shoot, but it did not go off; he then ascended the loft, and removing some of the roof, escaped through the opening, while the Indians were breaking down the door. The alarm was given to the stockade in upper Belpre, and a party went over. They met Mr. Armstrong and the two eldest sons, who had been in the mill. Mrs. Armstrong they found dead on the outside of the cabin. It appeared as if she had attempted to escape from the roof, as her husband did; but being a heavy woman, had probably fallen and broken her leg. Two children were dead, and a little girl still alive, but insensible, though when disturbed, she would say, 'What's that?' Mrs. Armstrong and two children were scalped; one child about two years of age was not. Two sons who were in the cabin were taken prisoners, and carried to their towns, where they remained until the close of the war, when their elder brothers brought them from the Indian country."

Between the years 1784 and 1793, several murders were committed along the river below Grave creek; the exact dates of some of these we have not been able to ascertain, but will nevertheless give a brief notice of the occurrences. Adam Roe and family, who had been forted at Tomlinson's, considering it safe to return to their improvement, and becoming very tired of fort life, determined to start for the mouth of Fishing creek, and were all killed ten miles below.

Proctor was an early settler near the mouth of a stream now known as Proctor's run. Finding the Indians becoming troublesome, he proposed to remove his family to Wheeling, but the savages were likely to intercept him, and he was compelled to look for some other place. A few miles up the run is a remarkable rock, presenting a concealed entrance, but opening out into a fine large chamber, perfectly dry, and spacious enough to contain thirty or forty persons. Into this Proctor moved with his family, and for some time succeeded in eluding the wily savages. He however, continued imprudently to venture out, and the Indians discovering his tracks, stationed a spy to ascertain his place of abode. This once done, they made an attack, killing the occupant with two of his children. Mrs. Proctor having a child in her arms, elicited the sympathy of an old Indian who stood by, and declared that she should not be killed. She was then made prisoner, but succeeded that night in eluding their vigilance, and making her escape. She reached Wheeling the next day in safety.

NOTE.

There being some discrepancy between the accounts of Mrs. Cruger and Mr. Darby, as to the time of certain occurrences in the settlement of the west, we addressed the latter a note, and in reply, received the following interesting letter, which will fully explain itself.

W. De Hass, Esq. :—

Dear Sir, — Your note of this day I have duly received, and with sincere pleasure proceed to comply with your requisitions; especially, as the facts will have a more fitting and enduring place of record, than if stated in a public print — which it was my intention to have done, had you not presented a superior vehicle.

Though not offered as material to the historical facts, I preface my recollections, with a statement of my position at the time of their occurrence, and my age when brought on the theatre. I was born on the 14th August, 1775, and arrived with my parents on the ground where Washington, Pennsylvania, now stands, December 25th, 1781, of course in my seventh year. Though so young, I very distinctly remember such striking circumstances as attended Indian war, and to which I was either an ear or eye-witness.

In the summer previous to the removal of his family, my father came to Washington county, and built a cabin, and made a crop on William Wolf's farm, on one of the head branches of Buffalo, about five miles west of where the borough of Washington now stands. We had come out, and were living in the cabin, when early in 1782, the Indians committed some murders, and the people took refuge in their block-houses, and we, with others, were, through part of February and March, forted in Jacob Wolf's block-house. The Great Western road traverses the site of this once rude fortress, in which, sixty-eight years past, the writer of these words was sheltered from the fury of savages.

Simultaneous with the above stated circumstances, was planned and carried into effect, the campaign under the nominal command of Colonel David Williamson, and which led on to the deplorable massacre of the Moravian christianized Indians, on the Tuscarawas. In afterlife, I personally knew several men who participated in this affair, and particularly Colonel Williamson; and are now constrained to express my full conviction, that the fatal issue was not premeditated, but the effect of some momentary impulse. You will have, no doubt, means more ample than any in my power to supply, to set this part of frontier history in correct points of view.

As the season or summer of 1782 advanced, another, and much more important expedition against the Indians was planned, and mustered under the joint commands of Colonels David Williamson and William Crawford. This little army penetrated the Indian country, was met, and utterly defeated. Colonel Crawford was made captive, and burned by the savages. In the very neighborhood where I was then living, about two miles from Catfish, (Washington). John Campbell, William Nimmons, William Huston, and William Johnston, never returned, though their individual fate was, I believe, never revealed. I mention the facts from their tendency to fix their memory on my mind; the more, as they influenced all my after life. My parents never returned to their cabin near Wolf's fort. Through 1782, and into 1783, we resided on land as already stated. In 1783,1784, and into 1785, we resided on the land long known as Officers' farm, then owned by James Brownlee. Early in 178-5, my father purchased from Thomas Goudy, the farm, afterwards long owned by Benedict Reynolds, and on which my parents, with their children, resided from early in 1785 to 1793.

In my father's first visit to the west, and before the removal of his family, of the many persons he made acquaintance with, one was Mr. Becham, and a second, ]Mr. Crow, the fathers of the victims whose fate you have to record. I do not remember to have seen the former, but the latter was frequently at our house on the Reynold farm, and spent great part of a day with us, only a few days before the murder of his two daughters, and the astonishing escape of his other daughter, Christina, as you have found stated by Colonel Lewis Bonnett.

I had a half-brother, five years older than myself, and while life remains, I must remember his return home, and communicating to his parents, the murder of two sons, and the scalping and tomahawking of a third, named Thomas, who survived; the children of Mr. Becham. I had then never been, or expected to be, west of our long-deserted cabin on Buffalo. The year, I cannot attempt to state, but can decidedly say, it was not later than 1788, and I think was in 1787.

My first residence on Wheeling waters, was commenced early in 1 793, in the Bonnett, Wetzel, Keller, Mercer, &c. neighborhood, about five or six miles above Shepherd's fort, now Mrs. Cruger's farm. Amongst other persons, I became acquainted with in this neighborhood, was George Tush, who resided with his family near Bonnetts and Wetzels.

Late in 1793, I went to, and opened a school in the then very small, but as on the extreme frontier, the very important village of Wheeling; in which, and in its immediate neighborhood, I remained until 1795. Thus, I was there, during the important year of 1794, important in an especial manner to the long distressed frontier on the Ohio. The power of the savages was broken; fear of their inroads was in great part effaced; but the lapse of time was too brief to permit the horrors of their inroads to be forgotten. The confidence of safety was still felt, and it was in this state of mind, that the people of Wheeling received the fearful news of the murder of Mrs. Tush and her children. The wounded and still bleeding husband and father was brought to our midst, and placed under the care of George Cookis and his wife. I have already stated that I had a previous personal acquaintance with Tush; and by a curious coincidence, the Becham murder, the Crow murder, and other similar tragedies acted years before, were all brought up to our most vivid remembrance, and we had, beside the Tush family, other events to give activity to our recollections.

In conclusion, I must say, that if any one more than another, desires complete success to your work, I am that man. The deepest fountains of my heart are opened, when mentally scanning the scenes of former years — of days long gone by. You will have the credit of aiding in the preservation of names of persons, the value of whose services in life, the present generation can but faintly estimate. They were the heroes and martyrs who braved the danger, and endured the hardships of a savage frontier — they prepared the way which led to the smiling country which now blooms in plenty and peace. When in my old age I can, by the exercise of a sacred duty, have my name associated with those you will place on record, I must sincerely thank Eternal Power for the greatest of earthly favors. My path through life has yet had strewn along it more thorns than roses; but your book, when I receive it, will cure the pain of many sharp thorns, and sweeten the remaining years of a long and changeful existence. Such reading will recall deeds of heroism, and manly traits of character which no other section of earth can give examples to excel. With sentiments of sincere gratitude for your confidence, and hope of your success,

I am, &c., &c.,

William Darby.

Washington City, March 20, 1850.

# PART VII. SKETCHES OF BIOGRAPHY, AND PERSONAL ADVENTURE.

# CHAPTER I. COLONEL EBENEZER ZANE.

Biography has, with much truth, been styled the most interesting, as well as the most entertaining species of literature. It is the only way in which individuality can be exhibited. What a fund of knowledge is found in Plutarch; what an invaluable treasure to the future will be Sparks' Life and Writings of our incomparable Washington.

Cicero has eloquently observed, that —

"The life of the dead is placed in the memory of the living."

This, however, is unhappily not strictly true in the west. The memories of our pioneer fathers are passing away; and unless some attempt speedily be made to rescue them from impending oblivion, they will soon be forgotten. The heroes who flourished before Agamemnon, says the great Roman lyric poet, passed into forgetfulness for want of a recording pen. Shall such be the fate of the gallant men, who devoted their energies and their lives to building up, in the great valley of the west, the noble Republican structure, now the heritage of us all? It has long been charged upon us, that we are culpably neglectful of the memories of our great men; that we seem to despise glory, or despise the means of perpetuating it; and trust to tradition for "transmitting the story of our birth, growth, and struggle for independence." This is a severe, but not an unmerited reflection; and henceforward we hope to have no more cause for reproach. The character of every man in the west, who took any active part in the settlement of the country, contains abundant material for a most interesting biography. What can possess more of interest to the people of the present day, and of this particular region, than a narrative of the toils, struggles and adventures of the men, whose unshod feet tracked in blood the snows of the upper Ohio; whose single-handed combats with the fierce and relentless savage, are unsurpassed in the annals of border warfare?

With this brief introductory notice, we shall proceed to give a sketch of one who took no ordinary part in reclaiming and settling North-Western Virginia.

Col. Ebenezer Zane was born October 7th, 1747, in the county of Berkeley, Virginia. The family is of Danish origin, but at an early day moved to France, thence to England, and, towards the latter end of the seventeenth century, emigrated to America. One branch of the family settled in New Jersey, nearly opposite Philadelphia; the other in Virginia. The subject of our notice sprung from this latter branch. The spirit of restless energy, which so distinguished the old Norseman, was not long in exhibiting itself in some of his Virginia descendants. At the age of twenty-three, with no friend but his faithful dog, and no weapons but his knife and gun, our intrepid hero struck out into the untrodden wilderness, to hunt himself a home, and make himself a name in the immense regions stretching far out toward the setting sun. On a bright morning in June, 1770, he stood upon the high bank of the Ohio, just above the confluence of Wheeling creek, and gazing upon the outspread landscape of island, hill and river, his enraptured vision comprehended all, and more than realized his most extravagant expectations. The scene before him was one of perfect repose. The morning mist just lifted from the bosom of the clear, calm river, was gliding slowly upward, revealing to the lone pioneer a panorama of unsurpassed loveliness. Not a breath of air disturbed the glittering dew drops which hung upon the forest leaves, but all was the unbroken stillness of nature, save when an occasional feathered songster sent his shrill notes through the echoing vale. But our young adventurer was not the man to look upon such a scene with a painter or a poet's eye. He saw at a glance the great advantage of the point, and at once resolved to make there his home. This act showed him to be a man of much judgment and sagacity. At that early day, he saw all the advantages presented by the locality. He clearly realized in his mind's eye the prophetic line of Bishop Berkeley; and that some point on the Ohio, near where he stood, must eventually become an important place through the trade and travel of the west. How well that conception has been fulfilled, let the most flourishing city in the State attest.

Building a cabin, and remaining one season on the Ohio, Mr. Zane returned for his family, and having induced a few resolute friends to accompany him, moved west in the spring of 1772. Deeming it unsafe to carry his family direct to their new abode, he left them at Bedstone; and, in company with his brothers, Jonathan and Silas, and two or three others, proceeded to take possession of his rights in the west. At that time there was not a permanent Anglo-Saxon settlement from the source to the mouth of the Ohio. The little band at Wheeling stood alone in the immense solitude stretching out for thousands of of miles, now the abode of millions of freemen! What a change in one single life-time! What miracles of beneficent and glorious, social and political changes, have been wrought in that interval! Seventy-nine years ago the valley of the Mississippi, with its mighty river sweeping through an immensity of space, was as little known as when Ponce de Leon sought there for the fountain of perennial life, which was to restore to his veteran limbs the vigor and freshness of youth. Behold it now! Did the magic wand of the magician ever work greater wonders in the kaleidoscope of his mystic art? With their sturdy arm, the Zanes soon opened a "clearing," letting the sunlight into the heart of the forest, and in due time had the satisfaction of gathering a good crop of corn. Completing his cabin, and making other preparations for the safety of his family, Mr. Zane visited Redstone, and that fall effected a final removal. With the opening of 1773, came quite a number of settlers from the South-branch, and then was permanently formed a settlement which has grown to a city of many thousands.

Mr. Zane married Elizabeth McColloch, sister to the daring borderers whose services on the frontier we have already had occasion so often to mention. She bore him thirteen children, Catharine, Ann, Sarah, Noah, John, Samuel, Hetty, Jesse, and Daniel, with four who died early, bearing names afterwards given respectively to some of those enumerated above. Of this sterling matron, about whose generosity, devotion, and zeal so much has been said, we regret that our limits will preclude the possibility of adding more. Suffice it, her whole life was the best commentary upon, and her children the best illustration of, what such a wife should be.

The clearing of Col. Zane embraced about ten acres, comprehending that portion of the present city of Wheeling, lying along Main and Market streets, from the brow of the hill to a point above where the Suspension Bridge crosses. It was girdled on every side by the dark green forest, save on the west, where swept the beautiful river.

Col. Zane's intercourse with the natives having been marked by mildness, courtesy, and honorable dealing, his hamlet escaped the fury of the savages, and nothing occurred to mar the pleasure of his western life, until the fall of 1777. Having elsewhere noticed in detail the attack on Fort Henry, in September of that year, it will be unnecessary to say more at this time, but pass on to the consideration of our personal history.

Col. Zane received, from time to time, various marks of distinction, from the Colonial, State, and National governments. He was a disbursing officer under Dunmore, and enjoyed under the commonwealth numerous civil and military distinctions. He always preferred, however, the peace and quietude of his own home to the bustle and pomp of public place. He was as generous as brave; strictly honorable to all men, and most jealous of his own rights. He possessed, in an eminent degree, the constituents of a true gentleman — the disposition to render unto all their due — the quick, delicate, accurate perception of others' rights and others' claims. His temperament was nervous-bilious — quick, impetuous, and hard to restrain when excited. He was, in short, a plain blunt man, rude of speech but true of heart, knowing nothing of formalities, and caring about little else than his family, his friends, and his country.

The personal appearance of Colonel Zane was somewhat remarkable: dark complexion, piercing black eyes, huge brows, and prominent nose. Not very tall, but uncommonly active and athletic, he was a match for almost any man in the settlement, and many are the incidents, in wood and field, told of his prowess and his strength. He was a devoted hunter, and spent much of his time in the woods. But few men could out-shoot, and fewer still out-run him. In illustration of his skill with the rifle, we will give an incident. About the year 1781, some of the whites in the fort observed an Indian on the island going through certain personal movements for the especial benefit of those within the fort. Colonel Zane's attention having been drawn to the indelicate performances, declared he would spoil the sport, and charging his rifle with an additional ball, patiently waited for the chap to re-appear. In a moment his naked body was seen emerging from behind a large sycamore, and commencing anew his performances, Colonel Zane drew upon him a practised aim, and the next instant the native harlequin was seen to go through a peculiar gyration, believed not to have been "in the bills."

Colonel Zane was a man of true courage, as is exemplified by his almost single-handed defence of his own dwelling, in the fall of 1782.

The government of the United States, duly appreciating his capacity, energy and influence, employed him by an act of Congress, May, 1796, to open a road from Wheeling to Limestone, (Maysville.) This duty he performed in the following year, assisted by his brother Jonathan, and son-in-law John McIntyre, aided by an Indian guide, Tomepomehala, whose knowledge of the country enabled him to render valuable suggestions. The road was marked through under the eye of Colonel Zane, and then committed to his assistants to cut out. As a compensation for opening this road. Congress granted Colonel Zane the privilege of locating military warrants upon three sections of land; the first to be at the crossing of the

Muskingum, the second at Hock-hocking, and the third at Scioto. Colonel Zane thought of crossing the Muskingum at Duncan's falls, but foreseeing the great value of the hydraulic power created by the falls, determined to cross at the point where Zanesville has since been established, and thus secure this important power. The second section was located where Lancaster now stands, and the third on the east side of the Scioto opposite Chillicothe. The first he gave principally, to his two assistants for services rendered. In addition to these fine possessions. Colonel Zane acquired large bodies of land throughout Western Virginia, by locating patents for those persons whose fear of the Indians deterred them undertaking personally so hazardous an enterprise.

After a life full of adventure and vicissitude, the subject of our notice died of jaundice, in 1811, at the age of sixty-four.

NOTE A.

In the spring of 1771, Jonathan and Silas Zane visited the west, and made explorations during the summer and fall of that year. Jonathan was perhaps, the most experienced hunter of his day in the west. He was a man of great energy of character, resolution, and restless activity. He rendered efficient service to the settlements about Wheeling, in the capacity of spy. He was remarkable for an earnestness of purpose, an energy and inflexibility of will, which often manifested itself in a way truly astonishing. Few men shared more of the confidence, and more of the respect of his fellow-men, than Jonathan Zane. He was one of the pilots in Crawford's expedition, and it is said, strongly admonished the unfortunate commander against proceeding; as the enemy were very numerous, and would certainly defeat him. He died in Wheeling, at his own residence, a short distance above the present site of the first ward public school. He left large landed possessions, most of which were shared by his children. The late Mrs. Ebenezer Martin, Mrs. Wood, and Mrs. Hildreth, of Belmont county, Ohio, were children of his; also, the late Mrs. Daniel Zane, of the island.

Of Colonel Zane's other brothers, Silas and Andrew, little can be gathered of their personal history. The latter was killed by the Indians, while crossing the Scioto; Isaac was a somewhat more conspicuous character. He was taken captive when but nine years of age, and carried to the Indian towns, where, he afterwards stated, he remained four years without seeing a white man. He became thoroughly Indian in habits and appearance, and married the sister of a distinguished Wyandott chief, by whom he raised a family of eight children. He acquired, with his tawny bride, large landed property, and became an important man in the confederacy. But, notwithstanding all this, he remained true to the whites, and often was the means of communicating important intelligence, which may have saved the settlements from most bloody visitations. In consideration of these services, the government granted him a patent for ten thousand acres of land, on Mad river, where he lived and died.

# CHAPTER II. MAJOR SAMUEL M'COLLOCH.

The story of McColloch's ride, is as familiar to most readers as that of Putnam's, or the famed leap of Curtius; but very few beyond the neighborhood where he lived, know anything of his personal history. Indeed, until very recently, it was a question of doubt who the rider was, — which of the Major McColloch's. It is to supply this desideratum, as well as to do justice to the memory of a brave and meritorious man, that the present memoir has been prepared.

At the time of issuing our prospectus, we believed that Major John McColloch was the person who accomplished this wonderful feat; but soon after learned that the true hero was Major Samuel, (an elder brother of the other.) We were led into this error by injudicious friends of the first named officer, whose opportunities for knowing the facts we supposed were abundant, and whom we presumed would not attempt to warp history for selfish purposes. The mistake we shall now attempt to rectify.

Most writers on the border history of the west, have given the credit of this achievement to the younger brother, for the reason, perhaps, that the first was killed at a very early day, and the other was long known as "Major McColloch."

Unfortunately for the annals of the west, but few written memoranda were made by the first settlers, and these are so vague and unsatisfactory as to be of little service to the biographer or historian. Very few of the old pioneers were able to commit their thoughts to paper; and those who could, did not deem the daily occurrences of life of sufficient importance to place upon record. This, doubtless, would at that time, have been regarded as a most extravagant waste of stationery. Thus it was, that no permanent records were made; and thus it is, we have but little tangible means at command to work upon. The want of such reliable records, is one of the greatest difficulties in the way of the historian. Major John McColloch, as we have learned from some members of his family, kept a regular journal of his personal movement; but this cannot now be found, and the presumption is, it was destroyed. The family were long under the impression that the record had fallen into the hands of Dr. Doddridge, who was a brother-in-law to Major McColloch. Learning this, we addressed a note of inquiry to a member of Dr. D.'s family, and received in reply the information that no such paper could be found.

The McColloch family was one of the earliest that settled on Short creek, where different branches of it still continue to reside. There were originally three brothers, Abraham, Samuel and John, and two sisters. The men were brave, active and generous; the sisters in every respect worthy of such brothers. Colonel Ebenezer Zane married Elizabeth, whose whole life was a model of gentleness, virtue and love. Of the brothers, no men were more respected by their neighbors, or more dreaded by the Indians. Abraham was the elder, Samuel next, and John the third.

At a very early age, the hero of our sketch distinguished himself as a bold and efficient borderer. As an "Indian hunter," he had few superiors. He seemed to track the wily red man with a sagacity as remarkable as his efforts were successful. He was almost constantly engaged in excursions against the enemy, or "scouting" for the security of the settlements. It was mainly to these energetic operations that the frontier was so often saved from savage depredation, and by cutting off their retreat, attacking their hunting camps, and annoying them in various other ways, he rendered himself so great an object of fear and hatred. For these they marked him, and vowed sleepless vengeance against the name.

In consideration of his many very efficient services, Samuel McColloch was commissioned Major in 1775. The daring feat to which allusion has been made, and an account of which we have elsewhere said should be given, was performed September 2d, 1777. The circumstances connected with this remarkable achievement, having been noticed in an account of the first siege of Wheeling, it now alone remains to give the sequel, as then promised. The Indians, it will be remembered, drove the gallant major to the summit of a lofty hill, which overhangs the present city of Wheeling. Knowing their relentless hostility toward himself, he strained every muscle of his noble steed to gain the summit, and then escape along the brow in direction of Van Metre's fort. At length he attained the top, and galloping ahead of his pursuers, rejoiced at his lucky escape. As he gained a point on the hill near where the Cumberland Road now crosses, what should he suddenly encounter but a considerable body of Indians, who were just returning from a plundering excursion among the settlements.

In an instant, he comprehended the full extent of his danger. Escape seemed out of the question, either in the direction of Short creek or back to the bottom. A fierce and revengeful foe completely hemmed him in, cutting off every chance of successful retreat or escape. What was to be done? Fall into their hands, and share the most refined torture savage ingenuity could invent? That thought was agony, and in an instant the bold soldier, preferring death among the rocks and bramble to the knife and fagot of the savage, determined to plunge over the precipice before him. Without a moment's hesitation, for the savages were pressing upon him, he firmly adjusted himself in his saddle, grasped securely the bridle with his left hand, and supporting his rifle in the right, pushed his unfaltering old horse over! A plunge, a crash, — crackling timber and tumbling rocks were all that the wondering savages could see or hear. They looked chagrined but bewildered, one at another; and while they inwardly regretted that the fire had been spared its duty, they could not but greatly rejoice that their most inveterate enemy was at length beyond the power of doing further injury. But, lo! ere a single savage had recovered from his amazement, what should they see but the invulnerable major on his white steed, galloping across the peninsula. Such was the feat of Major McColloch, certainly one of the most daring and successful ever attempted. The place has become memorable as McColloch's leap, and will remain, so long as the hill stands, and the recollections of the past have a place in the hearts of the people. Our engraver has given a very effective and correct representation of this "leap."

It is to us a matter of great regret, that more of the stirring incidents in this man's life have not been collected and preserved. We have heard of many daring feats of personal prowess, but they come to us in such a mixed and unsatisfactory form, as to render their publication, at this time, unsafe. We trust, however, to embody many new incidents in a future edition.

We come now to the most painful duty of the biographer — the catastrophe — the death of his hero. Towards the latter end of July, 1782, indications of Indians having been noticed by some of the settlers. Major McColloch and his brother John, mounted their horses, and left Van Metre's fort, to ascertain the correctness of the report. They crossed Short creek, and continued in the direction of Wheeling, but inclining towards the river. They scouted closely, but cautiously, and not discovering any such "signs" as had been stated, descended to the bottom at a point on the farm now owned by Alfred P. Woods, about two miles above Wheeling. They then passed up the river to the mouth of Short creek, and thence up Girty's Point in the direction of Van Metre's. Not discovering any indications of the enemy, the brothers were riding leisurely along, (July 30, 1782,) and when a short distance beyond the "point," a deadly discharge of rifles took place, killing Major McColloch instantly. His brother escaped, but his horse was killed. Immediately mounting that of his brother, he made off, to give the alarm. As yet no enemy had been seen; but turning in his saddle, after riding fifty yards, the path was filled with Indians, and one fellow in the act of scalping the unfortunate Major. Quick as thought, the rifle of John was at his shoulder, and an instant more, the savage was rolling in the agonies of death. John escaped to the fort unhurt, with the exception of a slight wound on his hip.

On the following day, a party of men from Van Metre's went out and gathered up the mutilated remains of Major McColloch. The savages had disemboweled him, but the viscera all remained except the heart. Some years subsequent to this melancholy affair, an Indian, who had been one of the party on this occasion, told some whites that the heart of Major McColloch had been divided and eaten by the party! This was done, said he, that "We be bold, like Major McColloch." On another occasion, an Indian, in speaking of the incident, said, "The whites (meaning John McColloch) had killed a great captain, but they (the Indians) had killed a greater one."

Before closing this hasty sketch, it may, perhaps, be well enough to advert again to the question of identity.

In the first place, then, it seems generally conceded that the person who accomplished the feat was Major McColloch: and the year of its occurrence 1777. Well, Samuel McColloch was commissioned major in 1775, John not until 1795. Let the candid reader say which could have been the man. But, further; in 1775-6-7, etc., Samuel McColloch was one of the most active and distinguished borderers in Virginia — the pride of the settlements, and a terror to the savages. John was born in 1759, and, therefore, in 1777 was only eighteen years of age; — quite too young a man to have rendered himself so odious to the fierce old Shawanee warriors. But there need be no necessity for depending upon doubtful conjecture, or uncertain data. Without one single exception, all the older citizens agree in saying that it was Major Samuel. The late Colonel Woods said so, unhesitatingly; and we believe, stated very positively, that Major John never claimed the credit, although he (W.) often talked to him of the exploit.

The story in favor of Major John is clearly of modern origin; the result of a mistake in a writer of romance, who gave the credit without knowing the facts.

Major John McColloch was, perhaps, quite as brave and true as his brother. He did ample service in the cause of our long struggle for independence, and a more devoted patriot could not be found. He filled many important posts of honor and trust, and was greatly respected. The early records of Ohio county show that he acted a conspicuous part on the bench and otherwise.

The death of Major Samuel McColloch occurred at the most unfortunate period of our history. It was in the summer of that year, (1782,) so memorable in the annals of the west. The united tribes of the north and west were meditating an attack upon the frontier posts of Virginia, and many feared some of the weaker ones might yield. Amid such perilous scenes as these, the death of such men as Major McColloch could not but be greatly deplored.

Major McColloch married a Miss Mitchell, and had only enjoyed the wedded life six months at the time of his death. His widow married Andrew Woods.

LEWIS WETZEL.

Who in the west, has not heard of Wetzel — the daring borderer, — the brave and successful Indian hunter; the Boone of North-Western Virginia? Within the recollection of many of our readers, Lewis Wetzel was regarded by many of the settlers in the neighborhood of Wheeling, as the right arm of their defence. His presence was considered as a tower of strength to the infant settlements, and an object of terror to the fierce and restless savages who prowled about and depredated upon our frontier homes. The memory of Wetzel should be embalmed in the hearts of the people of Western Virginia; for his efforts in defence of their forefathers, were without a parallel in border warfare. Among the foremost and most devoted, he plunged into the fearful strife which a bloody and relentless foe waged against the feeble colonists. He threw into the common treasury a soul as heroic, as adventurous, as full of energy, and exhaustless of resources, as ever animated the human breast. Bold, wary and active, he stood without an equal in the pursuit to which he had committed himself, mind and body. No man on the western frontier was more dreaded by the enemy, and none did more to beat him back into the heart of the forest, and reclaim the expanseless domain which we now enjoy. Unfortunately for the memory of

Wetzel, no reliable account of him has ever been published. The present generation know little of his personal history, save as gathered from the exaggerated pages of romance, or the scarcely less painted traditions of the day. With many, he is regarded as having been very little better than a semi-savage; a man whose disposition was that of the enraged tiger, and whose only propensity was for blood. Our information warrants us in stating that these conceptions are all false. Lewis Wetzel was never known to inflict unwonted cruelty upon women and children, as has been charged upon him; and he never was found to torture or mutilate his victim, as many of the traditions would indicate. He was revengeful, because he had suffered deep injury at the hands of that race, and woe to the Indian warrior who crossed his path. Lewis Wetzel was literally a man without fear. He was brave as a lion, cunning as a fox, "daring where daring was the wiser part, — prudent when discretion was valor's better self." He seemed to possess, in a remarkable degree, that intuitive knowledge, which can alone constitute a good and efficient hunter, added to which, he was sagacious, prompt to act, and always aiming to render his actions efficient. Such was Lewis Wetzel, the celebrated Indian hunter of Western Virginia.

John Wetzel, the father of Lewis, was one of the first settlers on Wheeling creek. He had five sons and two daughters, whose names were respectively, Martin, Lewis, Jacob, John, George, Susan, and Christina.

The elder Wetzel spent much of his time in locating lands, hunting and fishing. His neighbors frequently admonished him against exposing himself thus to the enemy; but disregarding their advice, and laughing at their fears, he continued to widen the range of his excursions, until finally he fell a victim to the active vigilance of the tawny foe. He was killed near Captina, in 1787, on his return from Middle Island creek, under the following circumstances. Himself and companion were in a canoe, paddling slowly near the shore, when they were hailed by a party of Indians, and ordered to land. This, they of course, refused, when immediately they were fired upon, and Wetzel shot through the body. Feeling himself mortally wounded, he directed his companion to lie down in the canoe, while he (Wetzel) so long as strength remained, would paddle the frail vessel beyond reach of the savages. In this way, he saved the life of his friend while his own was ebbing fast. He died soon after reaching the shore, at Baker's station, and his humble grave can still be seen near the site of that primitive fortress. The author, anxious to ascertain with undoubted certainty, the date of Wetzel's death, and learning from a reliable source that the place of his burial was indicated by a stone inscribed with the initials and year, visited the spot in the summer of 1849. With great difficulty he found the place, and identified the grave of the elder Wetzel. A rough stone marks the spot, bearing in rude, but perfectly distinct characters, "I. W., 1787."

At the time of his father's death, Lewis was about twenty-three years of age, and in common with his brothers, or those who were old enough, swore sleepless vengeance against the whole Indian race. Terribly did he and they carry that resolution into effect. From that time forward, they were devoted to the wood; and an Indian, whether in peace or war, at night or by day, was a doomed man in the presence of either. The name of Wetzel sent a thrill of horror through the heart of the stoutest savage, before whom a more terrible image could not be conjured up than one of these relentless "long-knives." But to the personal history of Lewis.

The first event worthy of record in the life of our hero, occurred when he was about fourteen years of age. The Indians had not been very troublesome in the immediate vicinity of his father's, and no great apprehensions were felt, as it was during a season of comparative quietude. On the occasion referred to, Lewis had just stepped from his father's door, and was looking at his brother Jacob playing, when suddenly turning toward the corn-crib, he saw a gun pointing around the corner. Quick as thought, he jumped back, but not in time to escape the ball: it took effect upon the breast-bone, carrying away a small portion, and cutting a fearful wound athwart the chest. In an instant, two athletic warriors sprang from behind the crib, and quietly making prisoners of the lads, bore them off without being discovered. On the second day they reached the Ohio, and crossing near the mouth of McMahon's creek, gained the big lick, about twenty miles from the river. During the whole of this painful march, Lewis suffered severely from his wound, but bore up with true courage, knowing, if he complained, the tomahawk would be his doom. That night, on lying down, the Indians, contrary to their custom, failed to tie their prisoners. Lewis now resolved to escape; and in the course of an hour or two, satisfying himself that the Indians were asleep, touched Jacob, and both arose without disturbing their captors. Lewis, leading the way, pushed into the woods. Finding, however, that he could not travel without moccasins, he returned to camp, and soon came back with two pair, which, having fitted on, Lewis said, "Now I must go back for father's gun." Securing this, the two boys started in the direction of home. Finding the path, they travelled on briskly for some time; but hearing a noise, listened, and ascertained the Indians were in pursuit. The lads stepped aside, as the pursuers came up, and then again moved on. Soon they heard the Indians return, and by the same plan effectually eluded them. Before day-light, they were again followed by two on horseback, but resorting to a similar expedient, readily escaped detection.

On the following day, about eleven o'clock, the boys reached the Ohio, at a point opposite Zane's island. Lashing together two logs, they crossed over, and were once more with their friends.

As this sketch will not allow us to notice in full his various youthful exploits, we will pass over a series of years, and take up the thread of narrative at such points in our hero's perilous career, as we may deem most interesting to the reader at large. Reaching the years of manhood, this remarkable person spent most of his time in the woods. He was truly, a genuine child of the forest, and seemed to worship the grand old trees with more than Pagan devotion. To him the wilderness was full of charms, but the enjoyment of these was not without great personal danger. A dark, insidious foe prowled upon his track, and closely watched every opportunity to waylay and destroy him. Wetzel roamed abroad, delighted with every fresh grove, hill, dale, and rippling stream. To him the swelling of the breeze, "the repose of the leaf, the mysterious quiet of the shade, the chant of birds, the whoop of the savage, and the long melancholy howl of the wolf," were sights and sounds which stirred his most lively sensibilities. Rising from his couch of leaves, by the side of some moss-covered log, the lone hunter made his hurried meal, and then moved on, careless of fatigue, until night again closed around him. Such was the woodman's life; such the fascinations which bound him to the wilderness.

Shortly after Crawford's defeat, a man named Thomas Mills, in escaping from that unfortunate expedition, reached the Indian Spring, about nine miles from Wheeling, on the present National road, where he was compelled to leave his horse, and proceed to Wheeling on foot. Thence he went to Van Metre's fort, and after a day or two's rest, induced Lewis Wetzel to go with him to the spring for his horse. Lewis cautioned him against the danger, but Mills was determined, and the two started. Approaching the spring, they discovered the horse tied to a tree, and Wetzel at once comprehended their danger. Mills walked up to unfasten the animal, when instantly a discharge of rifles followed, and the unfortunate man fell, mortally wounded. Wetzel now turned, and knowing his only escape was in flight, plunged through the enemy and bounded off at the very extent of his speed. Four fleet Indians followed in rapid pursuit, whooping in proud exultation of soon overhauling their intended victim. After a chase of half a mile, one of the most active savages approached so close that Wetzel was afraid he might throw his tomahawk, and instantly wheeling, shot the fellow dead in his tracks. In early youth, Lewis had acquired the habit of loading his gun while at a full run, and now he felt the great advantage of it. Keeping in advance of his pursuers during another half mile, a second Indian came up, and turning to fire, the savage caught the end of his gun, and for a time, the contest was doubtful. At one moment the Indian, by his great strength and dexterity, brought Wetzel to his knee, and had nearly wrenched the rifle from the hands of his antagonist, when Lewis, by a renewed effort, drew the weapon from the grasp of the savage, and thrusting the muzzle against the side of his neck, pulled the trigger, killing him instantly.

The two other Indians by this time had nearly overtaken him, but leaping forward, he kept ahead, until his unerring rifle was a third time loaded. Anxious to have done with that kind of sport, he slackened his pace, and even stopped once or twice, to give his pursuers an opportunity to face him. Every time, however, he looked round, the Indians tree'd, unwilling any longer to encounter his destructive weapon. After running a mile or two further in this manner, he reached an open piece of ground, and wheeling suddenly, the foremost Indian jumped behind a tree, but which not screening his body, Wetzel fired, and dangerously wounded him. The remaining Indian made an immediate retreat, yelling, as he went, "No catch dat man, him gun always loaded." Our artist has happily caught the spirit of the incident, and very well shown it in the accompanying illustration.

In the summer of 1786, the Indians having become troublesome in the neighborhood of Wheeling, particularly in the Short creek settlement, and a party having killed a man near Mingo bottom, it was determined to send an expedition after the retreating enemy of sufficient force to chastise them most effectually. One hundred dollars were offered to the man who should bring in the first Indian scalp. Major McMahon living at Beech bottom, headed the expedition, and Lewis Wetzel was one of his men. They crossed the river on the 5th of August, and proceeded by a rapid march to the Muskingum. The expedition numbered about twenty men, and an advance of five were detailed to reconnoitre. This party reported to the commander that they had discovered the camp of the enemy, but that it was far too numerous to think of making an attack. A consultation was thereupon held, and an immediate retreat determined on. During the conference, our hero sat upon a log, with his gun carelessly resting across his knees. The moment it was resolved to retreat, most of the party started in disordered haste, but the commander observing Wetzel still sitting on the log, turned to inquire if he was not going along. "No," was his sullen reply; "I came out to hunt Indians, and now that they are found, I am not going home, like a fool, with my fingers in my mouth. I am determined to take an Indian scalp, or lose my own." All arguments were unavailing, and there they were compelled to leave him — a lone man, in a desolate wilderness, surrounded by an enemy vigilant, cruel, blood-thirsty, and of horrid barbarity, with no friend but his rifle, and no guide but the sure index which an all-wise Providence has deep set in the heavens above. Once by himself, and looking around to feel satisfied that they were all gone, he gathered his blanket about him, adjusted his tomahawk and scalping knife, shouldered his rifle, and moved off in an opposite direction, hoping that a small party of Indians might be met with. Keeping away from the larger streams, he strolled on cautiously, peering into every dell and suspicious covert, and keenly sensitive to the least sound of a suspicious character. Nothing, however, crossed his path that day. The night being dark and chilly, it was necessary to have a fire; but to show a light in the midst of his enemy would be to invite to certain destruction. To avoid this, he constructed a small coal-pit out of bark, dried leaves, etc., and covering these with loose earth, leaving an occasional air-hole, he seated himself, encircling the pit with his legs, and then completed the whole by covering his head with the blanket. In this manner he would produce a temperature equal, as he expressed it, to that of a "stove room." This was, certainly, an original and ingenious mode of getting up a fire, without, at the same time, endangering himself by a light.

During most of the following day, he roamed through the forest without noticing any "signs" of Indians. At length, smoke was discovered, and going in the direction of it, found a camp, but tenantless. It contained two blankets and a small kettle, which Wetzel at once knew belonged to two Indians, who were doubtless out hunting. Concealing himself in the matted undergrowth, he patiently awaited the return of the occupants. "About sunset, one of the Indians came in and made up the fire, and went to cooking his supper. Shortly after, the other came in; they then ate their supper, and began to sing and amuse themselves by telling comic stories, at which they would burst into roars of laughter. Singing, and telling amusing stories, was the common practice of the white and red men, when lying in their hunting camps. These poor fellows, when enjoying themselves in the utmost glee, little dreamed that Lewis Wetzel was so close. About nine or ten o'clock, one of the Indians wrapped his blanket around him, shouldered his rifle, took a chunk of fire in his hand, and left the camp, doubtless, with the intention of going to watch a deer-lick. The fire and smoke would serve to keep off the gnats and musquitoes. It is a remarkable fact, that deer are not alarmed at seeing fire, from the circumstance of meeting it so frequently in the fall and winter seasons, when the leaves and grass are dry, and the woods on fire. The absence of the Indian was a cause of vexation and disappointment to our hero, whose trap was so happily set, that he considered his game secure. He still indulged the hope, that the Indian would return to camp before day, but in this he was disappointed. There are birds in the woods which commence chirping just before break of day; and like the cock, give notice to the woodman that light will soon appear. Lewis heard the wooded songsters begin to chatter, and determined to delay no longer the work of death, for the return of the other Indian. He walked to the camp with a noiseless step, and found his victim buried in profound sleep, lying upon one side. He drew his butcher-knife, and with the utmost force, impelled by revenge, sent the blade through his heart. He said the Indian gave a short quiver, a convulsive motion, and then laid still in the sleep of death. Lewis scalped him, and set out for home. He arrived at the Mingo bottom only one day after his unsuccessful companions. He claimed, and as he should, received his reward."

A most fatal decoy on the frontier, was the turkey-call. On several different occasions, men from the fort at Wheeling had gone across the hill in quest of a turkey, whose plaintive cries had elicited their attention, and on more than one occasion the men never returned. Wetzel suspected the cause, and determined to satisfy himself. On the east side of the creek hill, and at a point elevated at least sixty feet above the water, there is a capacious cavern, the entrance to which at that time was almost obscured by a heavy growth of vines and foliage. Into this the alluring savage would crawl, and could there have an extensive view of the hill front on the opposite side. From that cavern issued the decoy of death to more than one incautious soldier and settler. Wetzel knew of the existence and exact locality of the cave, and accordingly started out before day, and by a circuitous route, reached the spot from the rear. Posting himself so as to command a view of the opening, he waited patiently for the expected cry. Directly the twisted tuft of an Indian warrior slowly rose in the mouth of the cave, and looking cautiously about, sent forth the long, shrill, peculiar "cry," and immediately sunk back out of view. Lewis screened himself in his position, cocked his gun, and anxiously awaited for a re-appearance of the head. In a few minutes up rose the tuft, Lewis drew a fine aim at the polished head, and the next instant the brains of the savage were scattered about the cave. That turkey troubled the inhabitants no longer, and tradition does not say whether the place was ever after similarly occupied. A singular custom with this daring borderer was to take a fall hunt into the Indian country. Equipping himself, he set out and penetrated to the Muskingum, and fell upon a camp of four Indians. Hesitating a moment whether to attack a party so much his superior in numerical strength, he determined to make the attempt. At the hour of midnight, when naught was heard, but the long dismal howl of the wolf,

"Cruel as death and hungry as the grave,
Burning for blood, bony, gaunt and grim,"

he moved cautiously from his covert, and gliding through the darkness, stealthily approached the camp, supporting his rifle in one hand and a tomahawk in the other. A dim flicker from the camp-fire faintly revealed the forms of the sleepers, wrapped in that profound slumber, which, to part of them, was to know no waking. There they lay, with their dark faces turned up to the night-sky, in the deep solitude of their own wilderness, little dreaming that their most relentless enemy was hovering over them. Quietly resting his gun against a tree, he unsheathed his knife, and with an intrepidity that could never be surpassed, stepped boldly forward, like the minister of Death, and quick as thought cleft the skull of one of his sleeping victims. In an instant, a second one was similarly served; and as a third attempted to rise, confused by the horrid yells with which Wetzel accompanied his blows, he, too, shared the fate of his companions, and sunk dead at the feet of this ruthless slayer. The fourth darted into the darkness of the wood and escaped, although Wetzel pursued him some distance. Returning to camp, he scalped his victims, and then left for home. When asked on his return, what luck, "Not much," he replied. "I tree'd four Indians, but one got away." This unexampled achievement stamped him as one of the most daring and, at the same time, successful hunters of his day.

The distance to and from the scene of this adventure could not have been less than one hundred and seventy miles.

During one of his scouts, in the neighborhood of Wheeling, our hero took shelter on a stormy evening, in a deserted cabin on the bottom, not far from the present residence of Mr. Hamilton Woods. Gathering a few broken boards he prepared a place on the loft to sleep. Scarcely had he got himself adjusted for a nap, when six Indians entered, and striking a fire, commenced preparing their homely meal. Wetzel watched their movements closely, with drawn knife, determined, the moment he was discovered, to leap into their midst, and in the confusion endeavor to escape. Fortunately, they did not see him, and soon after supper the whole six fell asleep. Wetzel now crawled noiselessly down, and hid himself behind a log, at a convenient distance from the door of the cabin. At early dawn, a tall savage stepped from the door, and stretching up both hands in a long, hearty yawn, seemed to draw in new life from the pure, invigorating atmosphere. In an instant, Wetzel had his finger upon the trigger, and the next moment the Indian fell heavily to the ground, his life's blood gushing upon the young grass brilliant with the morning dew drops. The report of his rifle had not ceased echoing through the valley ere the daring borderer was far away, secure from all pursuit.

When about twenty-five years of age, Lewis entered the service of Gen. Harmar, commanding at Marietta. His new duties growing distasteful, he took leave of absence, and visited his friends in the neighborhood of Wheeling. Shortly afterwards, however, he returned to duty, and was chiefly employed in the capacity of scout. It was whilst thus engaged that an affair occurred, which changed the whole current of his life. Of the Indians who visited Marietta, was one of some celebrity, known by the name of George Washington. He was a large, fine-looking savage, and of much influence in his tribe. The time we write of was one of comparative peace, and Gen. Harmar was particularly anxious to preserve the good feeling then subsisting. Wetzel, during one of his scouts, met this Indian and shot him. The act was justly regarded as an outrage, and he was accordingly arrested and placed in close confinement at the fort.

"Wetzel admitted, without hesitation, 'that he had shot the Indian.' As he did not wish to be hung like a dog, he requested the general to give him up to the Indians, as there were a large number of them present. 'He might place them all in a circle, with their scalping knives and tomahawks — and give him a tomahawk, and place him in the midst of the circle, and then let him and the Indians fight it out in the best way they could.' The general told him, 'That he was an officer appointed by the law, by which he must be governed. As the law did not authorize him to make such a compromise, he could not grant his request.' After a few days longer confinement, he again sent for the general to come and see him; and he did so. Wetzel said 'he had never been confined, and could not live much longer if he was not permitted some room to walk about.' The general ordered the officer on guard to knock off his iron fetters, but to leave on his handcuffs, and permit him to walk about on the point at the mouth of the Muskingum; but to be sure to keep a close watch upon him. As soon as they were outside of the fort gate, Lewis began to caper about like a wild colt broken loose from the stall. He would start and run a few yards, as if he were about making an escape, then turn round and join the guard. The next start he would run farther, and then stop. In this way he amused the guard for some time, at every start running a little farther. At length he called forth all his strength, resolution, and activity, and determined on freedom or an early grave. He gave a sudden spring forward, and bounded off at the top of his speed for the shelter of his beloved woods. His movement was so quick, and so unexpected, that the guard were taken by surprise, and he got nearly a hundred yards before they recovered from their astonishment. They fired, but all missed; they followed in pursuit, but he soon left them out of sight. As he was well acquainted with the country, he made for a dense thicket, about two or three miles from the fort. In the midst of this thicket he found a tree which had fallen across a log, where the brush were very close. Under this tree he squeezed his body. The brush were so thick, that he could not be discovered unless his pursuers examined very closely. As soon as his escape was announced, General Harmar started the soldiers and Indians in pursuit. After he had lain about two hours in his place of concealment, two Indians came into the thicket, and stood on the same log under which he lay concealed; his heart beat so violently he was afraid they would hear it thumping. He could hear them hallooing in every direction, as they hunted through the brush. At length, as the day wore away, Lewis found himself alone in the friendly thicket. But what should he do? His hands were fastened with iron cuffs and bolts, and he knew of no friend on the same side of the Ohio to whom he could apply for assistance. He had a friend who had recently put up a cabin on the Virginia side of the Ohio, who, he had no doubt, would lend him any assistance in his power. With the most gloomy foreboding of the future, a little after night-fall, he left the thicket and made his way to the Ohio. He came to the river about three or four miles below the fort. He took this circuit, as he expected guards would be set at every point where he could find a canoe. How to get across the river was the all-important question. He could not make a raft with his hands bound. He was an excellent swimmer, but was fearful he could not swim the Ohio with his heavy iron handcuffs. After pausing some time, he determined to make the attempt. Nothing worse than death could happen; and he would prefer drowning than again falling into the hands of Harmar and his Indians. Like the illustrious Caesar in the storm, he would trust the event to fortune; and he plunged into the river. He swam the greater part of the distance on his back, and reached the Virginia shore in safety; but so much exhausted that he had to lay on the beach some time before he was able to rise. He went to the cabin of his friend, where he was received with rapture. A file and hammer soon released him from his iron handcuffs."

Information having reached General Harmar of Wetzel's whereabouts, he sent a party of men in a canoe to take him. As the boat neared the Virginia shore, Wetzel, with his friend, and several other men, posted themselves on the bank and threatened to shoot the first man who landed. Unwilling to venture farther, the party returned, and Lewis made his way homeward, having been furnished by his kind friend with gun, ammunition, tomahawk, blanket, &c.

Exasperated at the escape of Wetzel, General Harmar offered a large reward for his apprehension, and at the same time despatched a file of men to the neighborhood of Wheeling, with orders to take him dead or alive. The detachment was under the command of a Captain Kingsbury, who, hearing that Wetzel was to be at Mingo Bottom on a certain day, marched thither to execute his orders. We will let an eye-witness finish the story: —

"A company of men could as easily have drawn old Horny out of the bottomless pit, as take Lewis Wetzel by force from the neighborhood of the Mingo Bottom. On the day that Captain Kingsbury arrived, there was a shooting match at my father's, and Lewis was there. As soon as the object of Captain Kingsbury was ascertained, it was resolved to ambush the captain's barge, and kill him and his company. Happily, Major McMahon was present, to prevent this catastrophe, and prevailed on Wetzel and his friends to suspend the attack till he would pay Captain Kingsbury a visit, and perhaps he would prevail with him to return without making an attempt to take Wetzel. With a great deal of reluctance they agreed to suspend the attack till Major McMahon should return. The resentment and fury of Wetzel and his friends were boiling and blowing, like the steam from a scape-pipe of a steamboat. 'A pretty affair, this,' said they, 'to hang a man for killing an Indian, when they are killing some of our people almost every day.' Major McMahon informed Captain Kingsbury of the force and fury of the people, and assured him that if he persisted in the attempt to seize Wetzel, he would have all the settlers in the country upon him; that nothing could save him and his company from a massacre, but a speedy return. The captain took his advice, and forthwith returned to Fort Harmar. Wetzel considered the affair now as finally adjusted." In this, however, he was mistaken. His roving disposition never permitted him to remain long in one place. Soon after the transactions just recorded, he descended the river to Limestone (Maysville); and while there, engaged in his harmless frolicking, an avaricious fellow, named Loller, a lieutenant in the army, going down the river with a company of soldiers for Fort Washington, landed at Maysville, and found Wetzel sitting in a tavern. Loller returned to his boat procured some soldiers, seized Wetzel, and dragged him aboard of the boat, and without a moment's delay pushed off, and that night delivered him to General Harmar at Fort Washington, where he again had to undergo the ignominy of having his hands and feet bound with irons, "The noise of Wetzel's capture — and captured, too, for only killing an Indian — spread through the country like wild-fire. The passions of the frontiermen were roused up to the highest pitch of fury. Petitions for his release were sent from the most influential men to the general, from every quarter where the story had been heard. The general at first paid but little attention to these; at length, however, the settlements along the Ohio, and some of the back counties, were preparing to embody in military array, to release him by force of arms. General Harmar, seeing the storm that was approaching, had Wetzel's irons knocked off, and set him at liberty.

Wetzel was once more a free man. He returned to his friends, and was caressed by young and old, with undiminished respect. The vast number of scalps which he had taken, proved his invincible courage, as well as his prowess in war; the sufferings and persecutions by which he had been pursued by General Harmar, secured for him the sympathy of the frontiermen. The higher he was esteemed, the lower sank the character of General Harmar with the fiery spirits on the frontier."

Had Harmer possessed a tithe of the courage, skill, and indomitable energy of Wetzel, the gallant soldiers under his command, in the memorable and disastrous campaign against the Miamis, might have shared a very different fate.

Shortly after his return from Kentucky, a relative from Dunkard Creek invited Lewis home with him. The invitation was accepted, and the two leisurely wended their way along, hunting and sporting as they travelled. On reaching the home of the young man, what should they see, instead of the hospitable roof, a pile of smoking ruins. Wetzel instantly examined the trail, and found that the marauders were three Indians and one white man, and that they had taken one prisoner. That captive proved to be the betrothed of the young man, whom nothing could restrain from pushing on in immediate pursuit. Placing himself under the direction of Wetzel, the two strode on, hoping to overhaul the enemy before they had crossed the Ohio. It was found, after proceeding a a short distance, that the savages had taken great care to obliterate their trail; but the keen discernment of Wetzel, once on the track, and there need not be much difficulty. He knew they would make for the river by the most expeditious route, and therefore, disregarding their trail, he pushed on, so as to head them at the crossing-place. After an hour's hard travel, they struck a path, which the deer had made, and which their sagacity had taught them to carry over knolls in order to avoid the great curves of ravines. Wetzel followed the path because he knew it was in almost a direct line to the point at which he was aiming. Night coming on, the tireless and determined hunters partook of a hurried meal, then again pushed forward, guided by the lamps hung in the heavens above them, until, towards midnight, a heavy cloud shut out their light and obscured the path. Early on the following morning, they resumed the chase, and descending from the elevated ridge, along which they had been passing for an hour or two, found themselves in a deep and quiet valley, which looked as though human steps had never before pressed its virgin soil. Travelling a short distance, they discovered fresh footsteps in the soft sand, and upon close examination, the eye of Wetzel's companion detected the impress of a small shoe with nail-heads around the heel, which he at once recognized as belonging to his affianced. Hour after hour the pursuit was kept up; now tracing the trail across hills, over alluvion, and often detecting it where the wily captors had taken to the beds of streams. Late in the afternoon, they found themselves approaching the Ohio, and shortly after dark, discovered, as they struck the river, the camp of the enemy on the opposite side, and just below the mouth of Captina. Swimming the river, the two reconnoitered the position of the camp, and discovered the locality of the captive. Wetzel proposed waiting until day-light before making the attack, but the almost frantic lover was for immediate action. Wetzel, however, would listen to no suggestion, and thus they awaited the break of day. At early dawn, the savages were up and preparing to leave, when Wetzel directed his companion to take good aim at the white renegade, while he would make sure work of one of the Indians. They fired at the same moment, and with fatal effect. Instantly the young man rushed forward to release the captive; and Wetzel reloading, pursued the two Indians, who had taken to the woods, to ascertain the strength of the attacking party. Wetzel pursued a short distance, and then fired his rifle at random, to draw the Indians from their retreat. The trick succeeded, and they made after him with uplifted tomahawks, yelling at the height of their voices. The adroit hunter soon had his rifle loaded, and wheeling suddenly, discharged its contents through the body of his nearest pursuer. The other Indian now rushed impetuously forward, thinking to dispatch his enemy in a moment. Wetzel, however, kept dodging from tree to tree, and, being more fleet than the Indian, managed to keep ahead until his unerring gun was again loaded, when turning, he fired, and the last of the party lay dead before him.

Soon after the occurrence just narrated, our hero determined to visit the extreme south, and for that purpose engaged on a flat-boat about leaving for New Orleans. Many months elapsed before his friends heard anything of his whereabouts, and then it was to learn that he was in close confinement at New Orleans, under some weighty charge. What the exact nature of this charge was, has never been fully ascertained, but it is very certain he was imprisoned and treated like a felon for nearly two years. The charge is supposed to have been of some trivial character, and has been justly regarded as a great outrage. It was alleged at the time of his arrest, to have been for uttering counterfeit coin; but this being disproved, it was then charged that he had been guilty of illicit connection with the wife of a Spaniard. Of the nature of these charges, however, we know but little, and it may therefore be unsafe to say more. He was finally released by the intervention of our government, and reached home by way of Philadelphia, to which city he had been sent from New Orleans. Mr. Rodefer says he saw him immediately after his return, and that his personal appearance had undergone great change from his long confinement. He remained but two days on Wheeling creek after his return — one at his mother's, and the other at Captain Bennett's, (the father of Mrs. Rodefer). Many of the older citizens have told us that they saw him during this brief visit, and conversed freely with him about the infamous manner he had been treated. Our venerable friend, Jacob Keller, Esqr., who now owns the old Bennett farm, says he saw him, and gathered many particulars of his imprisonment.

From the settlement he went to Wheeling, where he remained a few days, and then left again for the south, vowing vengeance against the person whom he believed to have been accessory to his imprisonment, and in degrading his person with the vile rust of a felon's chain. During his visit to Wheeling, he remained with George Cookis, a relative. Our informant says she met him there, and heard Mrs. Cookis plague him about getting married, and jocularly asked whether he ever intended to take a wife. "No," he replied, "there is no woman in this world for me, but I expect there is one in heaven."

After an absence of many months, he again returned to the neighborhood of Wheeling; but whether he avenged his real or imaginary wrongs upon the person of the Spaniard alluded to, the biographer, at this time, has not the means of saying. His propensity to roam the woods was still as great as ever, and soon after his return an incident occurred which showed that he had lost none of his cunning while undergoing incarceration at New Orleans. Returning home from a hunt, north of the Ohio, somewhat fatigued and a little careless of his movements, he suddenly espied an Indian in the very act of raising his gun to fire. Both immediately sprung to trees, and there they stood for an hour, each afraid of the other. What was to be done? To remain there during the whole day, for it was then early in the morning, was out of the question. Now it was that the sagacity of Wetzel displayed itself over the child-like simplicity of the savage. Cautiously adjusting his bear-skin cap to the end of his ram-rod, with the slightest, most dubious and hesitating motion, as though afraid to venture a glance, the cap protruded. An instant, a crack, and off was torn the fatal cap by the sure ball of the ever vigilant savage. Leaping from his retreat, our hero rapidly advanced upon the astonished Indian, and ere the tomahawk could be brought to its work of death, the tawny foe sprang convulsively into the air, and straightening as he descended, fell upon his face quite dead.

Wetzel was universally regarded as one of the most efficient scouts and most practised woodmen of his day. He was frequently engaged by parties who desired to hunt up and locate lands, but were afraid of the Indians. Under the protection of Lewis Wetzel, however, they felt safe, and thus he was often engaged for months at a time. Of those who became largely interested in western lands was John Madison, brother of James, afterwards President Madison. He employed Lewis Wetzel to go with him through the Kanawha region. During their expedition they came upon a deserted hunter's camp, in which were concealed some goods. Each of them helped himself to a blanket, and that day in crossing little Kanawha they were fired upon by a concealed party of Indians, and Madison killed.

General Clark, the companion of Lewis in the celebrated tour across the Rocky Mountains, had heard much of Lewis Wetzel in Kentucky, and determined to secure his services in the perilous enterprise. A messenger was accordingly sent for him, but he was reluctant to go. However, he finally consented, and accompanied the party during the first three months travel, but then declined going any further, and returned home. Shortly after this, he left again on a flatboat, and never returned. He visited a relative named Phillip Sikes, living about twenty miles in the interior from Natchez, and there made his home until the summer of 1808, when he died,

The personal appearance of this distinguished borderer was very remarkable. He was five feet ten inches in height, very erect, broad across the shoulders, an expansive chest, and limbs denoting great muscular strength. His complexion was very dark, and eyes of the most intense blackness, wild, rolling, and "piercing as the dagger's point;" emitting, when excited, such fierce and withering glances, as to cause the stoutest adversary to quail beneath their power. His hair was of raven jetness, and very luxuriant, reaching, when combed out, below his knees. This would have been a rare scalp for the savages, and one for which they would at any time have given a dozen of their best warriors.

When Lewis Wetzel professed friendship, he was as true as the needle to the pole. He loved his friends and hated their enemies. He was a rude, blunt man, of few words before company, but with his friends, not only sociable, but an agreeable companion. Such was Lewis Wetzel; his name and fame will long survive, when the achievements of men vastly his superior in rank and intellect, will slumber with the forgotten past.

ANDREW POE.

A MOST formidable and fearful man was the vanquisher of "Big-Foot." Every body has heard of the fight between the huge Wyandott chief and Poe, but, unfortunately, the credit has always been given to the wrong man. Dr. Doddridge started the error; and every writer upon western history for nearly thirty years, has insisted that Adam Poe killed "Big-Foot."

Unwilling to strip the laurel from the brow of any man, but pledged to do justice to all, and give honor where honor is due, it now devolves upon us to say that it was not "Adam" but Andrew Poe who accomplished the wonderful feat we are about to record.

Of those who settled at an early day on the Ohio, near the extreme upper corner of Virginia, were two brothers, Andrew and Adam Poe. They were born near the present town of Frederick, Maryland, and emigrated to the west in 1774. Adam was the elder by some five years; he lived to the age of ninety-three, and died in 1840.

These brothers were "backwoodsmen" in every sense of the word. They were shrewd, active and courageous, and having fixed their abodes on the frontier of civilization, determined to contest inch by inch with the savages, their right to the soil, and their privilege to live. In appearance they were tall, muscular and erect, with features indicating great strength of character. Andrew, in the general contour of his face, differed somewhat from that of his brother, while the freshness of his color indicated a better degree of health than the sallow complexion of the other. Both, however, were endowed with an unusual degree of strength, and woe to the man who dared engage in single combat with either. Early in the fall of 1781, there was an occurrence on the Ohio which stamped the character of one as a man of no ordinary make. The place of combat was near the mouth of Tomlinson's run, and about two miles below Yellow creek. A few months since we visited the spot, and obtained from a member of the family the particulars of that celebrated conflict, which we now give.

During the summer of 1781, the settlements in the region indicated, suffered not a little from Indian depredation. At length it was ascertained that a party of six warriors had crossed the river and committed sundry outrages; among the rest, killing a defenceless old man in his cabin. The people became aroused, and it was at once determined to raise a force and intercept the retreat of the savages.

Eight determined spirits at once volunteered, and placing themselves under Captain Andrew Poe, as he was then called, were ready for action in five minutes' notice. Early on the following morning, they found the trail of the enemy, and detected among the footprints those of a celebrated chief called Big-Foot, who was distinguished for his daring, skill, eloquence, and immense size. He stood, literally, like the tall man of Tarsus, a head above his peers; for he is said to have been nearly, or quite seven feet in height, and large in proportion. The feet of this giant were so large as to gain for him the name of Big-Foot. Andrew Poe, delighted at the prospect of testing his strength with so renowned a chief, urged the pursuit with unabated zeal, until brought within a short distance of the enemy.

"For the last few miles, the trail had led up the southern bank of the Ohio, where the footprints in the sand were deep and obvious; but when within a few hundred yards of the point at which the Indians were in the habit of crossing, it suddenly diverged from the stream, and stretched along a rocky ridge, forming an obtuse angle with its former direction. Here Andrew halted for a moment, and directed his brother and the other young men to follow the trail with proper caution, while he still adhered to the river path, which led through a cluster of willows directly to the point where he supposed the enemy to lie. Having examined the priming of his gun, he crept cautiously through the bushes until he had a view of the point of embarcation. Here lay two canoes, empty and apparently deserted. Being satisfied, however, that the Indians were close at hand, he relaxed nothing of his vigilance, and quickly gained a jutting cliff, which hung over the canoes. Hearing a low murmur below, he peered cautiously over, and beheld the object of his search. The gigantic Big-Foot lay below him, in the shade of a willow, and was talking in a low, deep tone to another warrior, who seemed a mere pigmy by his side. Andrew cautiously drew back and cocked his gun. The mark was fair, the distance did not exceed twenty feet, and his aim was unerring. Raising his rifle slowly and cautiously, he took a steady aim at Big-Foot's breast, and drew the trigger. His gun flashed. Both Indians sprung to their feet with a deep interjection of surprise, and for a single second all three stared upon each other. This inactivity, however, was soon over. Andrew was too much hampered by the bushes to retreat, and setting his life upon the cast of the die, sprung over the bush which had sheltered him, and summoning all his powers, leaped boldly down the precipice, and alighted upon the breast of Big-Foot with a shock which bore him to the earth. At the moment of contact, Andrew had also thrown his right arm around the neck of the smaller Indian, so that all three came to the earth together.

"At that moment, a sharp firing was heard among the bushes above, announcing that the other parties were engaged, but the trio below were too busy to attend to anything but themselves. Big-Foot was for an instant' stunned by the violence of the shock, and Andrew was enabled to keep them both down. But the exertion necessary for that purpose was so great, that he had no leisure to use his knife. Big-Foot quickly recovered, and without attempting to rise, wrapped his long arms around Andrew's body, and pressed him to his breast with the crushing force of a boa constrictor! Andrew, as we have already remarked, was a powerful man, and had seldom encountered his equal; but never had he yet felt an embrace like that of Big-Foot. He relaxed his hold of the small Indian, who sprung to his feet. Big-Foot then ordered him to run for his tomahawk, which lay within ten steps, and kill the white man while he held him in his arms. Andrew, seeing his danger, struggled manfully to extricate himself from the folds of the giant, but in vain. The lesser Indian approached with his uplifted tomahawk, but Andrew watched him closely, and as he was about to strike, gave him a kick so sudden and violent, as to knock the tomahawk from his hand, and send him staggering back into the water. Big-Foot uttered an exclamation in a tone of deep contempt at the failure of his companion, and raising his voice to its highest pitch, thundered out several words in the Indian tongue, which Andrew could not understand, but supposed to be a direction for a second attack. The lesser Indian now again approached, carefully shunning Andrew's heels, and making many motions with his tomahawk, in order to deceive him as to the point where the blow would fall. This lasted for several seconds, until a thundering exclamation from Big-Foot compelled his companion to strike. Such was Andrew's dexterity and vigilance, however, that he managed to receive the tomahawk in a glancing direction upon his left wrist, wounding him deeply, but not disabling him. He now made a sudden and desperate effort to free himself from the arms of the giant, and succeeded. Instantly snatching up a rifle, (for the Indian could not venture to shoot, for fear of hurting his companion,) he shot the lesser Indian through the body. But scarcely had he done so, when Big Foot arose, and placing one hand upon his shoulder, and the other upon his leg, threw him violently upon the ground. Before his antagonist could spring upon him, he was again upon his feet, and stung with rage at the idea of being handled so easily, he attacked his gigantic antagonist with a fury which, for a time, compensated for inferiority of strength. It was now a fair fist fight between them, for in the hurry of the struggle, neither had leisure to draw their knives. Andrew's superior activity and experience as a pugilist, gave him great advantage. The Indian struck awkwardly, and finding himself rapidly dropping to the leeward, he closed in with his antagonist, and again hurled him to the ground. They quickly rolled into the river, and the struggle continued with unabated fury, each attempting to drown the other. The Indian being unused to such violent exertion, and having been much injured by the first shock in his stomach, was unable to exert the same powers which had given him such a decided superiority at first — and Andrew seizing him by the scalp-lock, put his head under water, and held it there, until the faint struggle of the Indian induced him to believe that he was drowned, when he relaxed his hold, and attempted to draw his knife. The Indian, however, to use Andrew's own expression, 'had only been possoming!' He instantly regained his feet, and in his turn, put his adversary under.

"In the struggle, both were carried out into the current beyond their depth and each was compelled to relax his hold and swim for his life. There was still one loaded rifle upon the shore, and each swam hard in order to reach it, but the Indian proved the most expert swimmer, and Andrew seeing that he should be too late, turned and swam out into the stream, intending to dive and thus frustrate his enemy's intention. At this instant, Adam having heard that his brother was alone in a struggle with two Indians, and in great danger, ran up hastily to the edge of the bank above, in order to assist him. Another white man followed him closely, and seeing Andrew in the river, covered with blood, and swimming rapidly from shore, mistook him for an Indian, and fired upon him, wounding him dangerously in the left shoulder. Andrew turned, and seeing his brother called loudly to him to 'shoot the Indian upon the shore.' Adam's gun, however, was empty, having just been discharged. Fortunately, Big-Foot had also seized the gun with which Andrew had shot the lesser Indian, so that both were upon an equality. The contest now was who should beat loading, the Indian exclaiming, 'Who load first, shoot first!' Big-Foot got his powder down first, but in the excitement of drawing the ramrod out, it slipped through his fingers and fell in the river. The noble savage now feeling that all was over, faced his foe, pulled open the bosom of his shirt, and the next instant received the ball of his adversary fair in his breast. Adam alarmed for his brother, who was scarcely able to swim, threw down his gun and rushed into the river, in order to bring him ashore — but Andrew more intent upon securing the scalp of Big-Foot as a trophy, than upon his own safety, called loudly upon his brother to leave him alone, and scalp the big Indian, who was endeavoring to roll himself into the water, from a romantic desire, peculiar to the Indian warrior, of securing his scalp from the enemy. Adam, however, refused to obey, and insisted upon saving the living, before attending to the dead. Big Foot, in the meantime, had succeeded in reaching the deep water before he expired, and his body was borne off by the waves, without being stripped of the ornament and pride of an Indian warrior."

The death of Big-Foot was a severe blow to his tribe, and is said to have thrown them all into mourning. He was an able and noble chief, and often rendered signal service to the whites by reclaiming prisoners from the stake, and otherwise averting the doom which his tribe seemed determined to visit upon their captives.

Poe recovered from his wounds, and lived until within about twenty years. We have recently seen a gentleman, who often witnessed Poe go through the "fight," and he declares the scene was the most thrilling he ever beheld. He says the old man would enter into the spirit of the conflict, and with dilated pupil, contracted muscle, and almost choked with foaming saliva, go through every motion and distinct feature of that terrible fight. He describes the appearance of these pantomime exhibitions as most painfully interesting, and declares, that the old man would be as much exhausted after the performance as though the scene had been actual.

Andrew Poe was certainly an extraordinary man, and the impress of his character is still visible in the region where he lived. An incident is related as occurring shortly before his death, which strongly marked the character of the man. Among his cattle, was a fierce and powerful young bull, endangering the life of any one who went near him. Poe, however, then a man of advanced age, would visit his stockyard, regardless of the animal in question, until he supposed it knew him. On one occasion, the refractory animal made at Poe, and before he could get out of reach, received a severe wound from one of its horns. So exasperated was this singular man, that he went at once to his house, armed himself with a tomahawk, and, despite the entreaties of his family, returned to the yard, and driving all the cattle out but the one alluded to, faced it, and with a menacing scowl, laid hold of the right horn. The animal plunged, and attempted to break loose, but Poe held on, and at every favorable opportunity, struck him with the pipe end of his tomahawk. In this way, he repeated his blows until finally the animal sunk dead at his feet.

Mr. Poe, during his whole life, was a most active and useful man. He lived about one mile from Hookstown, Pa., where many of his descendants still reside.

# CHAPTER III. COLONEL WILLIAM CRAWFORD.

The fate of this unfortunate officer has excited, and will continue to excite, so long as the history of the west shall be read, the most painful interest and the liveliest sympathy. We do not propose at this time to give a lengthy sketch of his life and services, but simply to notice a few points in his personal history.

Col. Crawford was a native of Berkeley county, Virginia. He was born in 1732 — a year memorable as giving birth to Washington and Marion. He early gave promise of much talent and energy of character. At the age of twenty-six, he raised a company, and joined Washington's regiment in the expedition of Gen. Forbes against Fort DuQuesne. His fine military bearing at that time attracted the attention and commanded the esteem of Washington. On the breaking out of the Revolution, by his own indomitable energy, he enrolled a regiment, and received, in consideration of his great personal effort, a colonel's commission in the Colonial army.

His first visit to the west was in 1767, and two years after, he removed his family. The place selected for his home was on the Youghiogheny river, where the town of Connellsville, Fayette county, Pennsylvania, now stands. His house was one of the first in the valley of the Youghiogheny, and it was always open to those who thought proper to give him a call. His hospitality, generosity, and uniform kindness were subjects of general remark. Of those who early shared the hospitalities of his roof, was Washington. We find by his journal of a tour to the west in 1770, frequent reference to Col. Crawford, who proved one of his most devoted friends. He seems to have enjoyed himself finely, and passed the time most pleasantly. A sister of the gallant colonel commanded not a little of the distinguished guest's attention, and were we disposed, now that Time has flung his many colored veil over all, could call upon Fancy with her pallette and brush, and paint a scene in that western cabin, but our limits forbid.

During this visit of Washington, he remained several days, and then, accompanied by Col. Crawford, proceeded to Fort Pitt, thence in company with others to the Great Kanawha, and after a pretty thorough exploration, returned to the Youghiogheny. Most of the lands belonging to Washington in the west were located by Col. Crawford. We have frequently heard the old surveyors along the Ohio say that they often met with his "corners." Some of the earliest surveys within the present limits of Brooke, Ohio, and Marshall counties, Virginia, were made by Colonel C. We sincerely regret the scarcity of material for a suitable memoir of this meritorious, but most unfortunate officer. His papers and records were never preserved; his family became scattered; "most of his contemporaries have followed him to the land of spirits, and very little else than a few brief stories remain to tell of his virtues and his fame." Passing over many of his years of usefulness to the west, we come to the fearful catastrophe. Colonel Crawford had frequently led expeditions against the Indians, but on the occasion of which we are about to speak, he, at first, absolutely declined to go. It seemed as though he had a presentiment of the fate which was to befall him. At length, however, he yielded to the importunities of his friends, and accompanied the men to the place of rendezvous. It is even asserted that after his selection as commander, he was reluctant to accept. Having noticed elsewhere the progress of the army, and its disastrous defeat, it now alone remains to finish the sad story by giving the particulars of the terrible death of its commanding officer. As these have been most faithfully narrated by Dr. Knight, the fellow-prisoner of Colonel Crawford, and an eye-witness to the whole terrible scene, we will follow his account. A retreat having been determined on, the whole army moved off in the silence of the night, hoping thereby to avoid pursuit. But the ever vigilant enemy noticed the movement, and instantly pursuit was given.

"We had not got a quarter of a mile from the field of action, when I heard Col. Crawford calling for his son John, his son-in-law Major Harrison, Major Rose and William Crawford, his nephews, upon which I came up and told him I believed they were before us. He asked, 'Is that the doctor?' I told him it was. He then replied, that they were not in front, and begged of me not to leave him; I promised him I would not.

"We then waited, and continued calling for these men till the troops had passed us. The colonel told me his horse had almost given out, that he could not keep up with the troops, and wished some of his best friends to remain with him: he then exclaimed against the militia for riding off in such an irregular manner, and leaving some of the wounded behind, contrary to his orders. Presently there came two men riding after us, one of them an old man, the other a lad. We inquired if they had seen any of the above persons, and they answered they had not.

"By this time there was a very hot firing before us, and, as we judged, near where our main body must have been. Our course was then nearly south-west, but changing it, we went north about two miles, the two men remaining in company with us. Judging ourselves to be now out of the enemy's lines, we took a due east course, taking care to keep at the distance of fifteen or twenty yards apart, and directing ourselves by the north star.

"About day-break Col. Crawford's and the young man's horses gave out, and they left them. We pursued our journey eastward, and about two o'clock fell in with Capt. Biggs, who had carried Lieut. Ashly from the field of action, who had been dangerously wounded. We then went on about the space of an hour, when a heavy rain coming up, we concluded it was best to encamp, as we were encumbered with the wounded officer. We then barked four or five trees, made an encampment and a fire, and remained there all night. Next morning we again prosecuted our journey, and having gone about three miles found a deer which had been recently killed. The meat was sliced from the bones and bundled up in the skin with a tomahawk lying by it. We carried all with us, and in advancing about one mile further, espied the smoke of a fire. We then gave the wounded officer into the charge of the young man, desiring him to stay behind, whilst the colonel, the captain and myself, walked up as cautiously as we could toward the fire. When we came to it, we concluded, from several circumstances, some of our people had encamped there the preceding night. We then went about roasting the venison, and when just about to march, observed one of our men coming upon our tracks. He seemed at first very shy, but having called to him he came up and told us he was the person who had killed the deer, but upon hearing us come up, was afraid of Indians, hid in a thicket, and made off. Upon this we gave him some bread and roasted venison, proceeded together on our journey, and about two o'clock came upon the paths by which we had gone out. Capt. Biggs and myself did not think it safe to keep the road, but the colonel said the Indians would not follow the troops farther than the plains, which we were then considerably past. As the wounded officer rode Capt. Biggs' horse, I lent the captain mine; the colonel and myself went about one hundred yards in front, the captain and the wounded officer in the centre, and the two young men behind. After we had travelled about one mile and a half, several Indians started up within fifteen or twenty steps of the colonel and I. As we at first discovered only three, I immediately got behind a large black oak, made ready my piece and raised it up to take sight, when the colonel called to me twice not to fire; upon that one of the Indians ran up to the colonel and took him by the hand. The colonel then told me to put down my gun, which I did. At that instant one of them came up to me, whom I had formerly seen very often, calling me doctor, and took me by the hand. They were Delaware Indians of the Wingenim tribe. Capt. Biggs fired amongst them, but did no execution. They then told us, to call these people and make them come there, else they would go and kill them, which the colonel did, but they four got off and escaped for that time. The colonel and I were then taken to the Indian camp, which was about half a mile from the place where we were captured. On Sunday evening, five Delawares, who had posted themselves at some distance further on the road, brought back to the camp, where we lay, Capt. Biggs and Lieut. Ashly's scalps, with an Indian scalp which Capt. Biggs had taken in the field of action: they also brought in Biggs' horse and mine; they told us the two other men got away from them.

"Monday morning, the tenth of June, we were paraded to march to Sandusky, about thirty-three miles distant; they had eleven prisoners of us and four scalps, the Indians being seventeen in number.

"Colonel Crawford was very desirous to see a certain Simon Girty, who lived among the Indians, and was on this account permitted to go to town the same night, with two warriors to guard him, having orders at the same time to pass by the place where the colonel had turned out his horse, that they might, if possible, find him. The rest of us were taken as far as the old town, which was within eight miles of the new.

"Tuesday Morning, the eleventh, Colonel Crawford was brought out to us on purpose to be marched in with the other prisoners. I asked the colonel if he had seen Mr. Girty? He told me he had, and that Girty had promised to do everything in his power for him, but that the Indians were very much enraged against the prisoners, particularly Captain Pipe, one of the chiefs; he likewise told me that Girty had informed him that his son-in-law, Colonel Harrison, and his nephew, William Crawford, were made prisoners by the Shawanese, but had been pardoned. This Captain Pipe had come from the towns about an hour before Colonel Crawford, and had painted all the prisoners' faces black.

"As he was painting me, he told me I should go to the Shawanese towns and see my friends. When the colonel arrived he painted him black also, told him he was glad to see him, and that he would have him shaved when he came to see his friends at the Wyandot town. When we marched, the colonel and I were kept between Pipe and Wyngenim, the two Delaware chiefs, the other nine prisoners were sent forward with a party of Indians. As we went along we saw four of the prisoners lying by the path tomahawked and scalped, some of them were at the distance of half a mile from each other. When we arrived within half a mile of the place where the colonel was executed, we overtook the five prisoners that remained alive; the Indians had caused them to sit down on the ground, as they did, also the colonel and myself, at some distance from them; I was there given in charge to an Indian fellow to be taken to the Shawanese towns.

"In the place where we were now made to sit down, there was a number of squaws and boys, who fell on the five prisoners and tomahawked them. There was a certain John McKinley amongst the prisoners, formerly an officer in the 13th Virginia Regiment, whose head an old squaw cut off, and the Indians kicked it about upon the ground. The young Indian fellows came often where the colonel and I were, and dashed the scalps in our faces. We were then conducted along toward the place where the colonel was afterwards executed. When we came within half a mile of it, Simon Girty met us, with several Indians on horseback; he spoke to the colonel, but as I was about one hundred and fifty yards behind, could not hear what passed between them.

"Almost every Indian we met struck us either with sticks or their fists. Girty waited till I was brought up, and then asked. Was that the doctor? I answered him Yes, and went towards him, reaching out my hand, but he bid me begone, and called me a damned rascal; upon which the fellow who had me in charge, pulled me along. Girty rode up after me and told me I was to go to the Shawanese towns.

"When we came to the fire, the colonel was stripped naked, ordered to sit down by the fire, and then they beat him with sticks and their fists. Presently after, I was treated in the same manner. They then tied a rope to the foot of a post about fifteen feet high, bound the colonel's hands behind his back, and fastened the rope to the ligature between his wrists. The rope was long enough either for him to sit down or to walk round the post once or twice and return the same way. The colonel then called to Girty, and asked if they intended to burn him? Girty answered, Yes. The colonel said he would take it all patiently. Upon this, Captain Pipe, a Delaware chief, made a speech to the Indians, consisting of about thirty or forty men, and sixty or seventy squaws and boys.

"When the speech was finished, they all yelled a hideous and hearty assent to what had been said. The Indian men then took up their guns and shot powder into the colonel's body, from his feet as far up as his neck. I think not less than seventy loads were discharged upon his naked body. They then crowded about him, and to the best of my observation, cut off his ears: when the throng had dispersed a little, I saw the blood running from both sides of his head in consequence thereof.

"The fire was about six or seven yards from the post to which the colonel was tied; it was made of small hickory poles, burnt quite through in the middle, each end of the poles remaining about six feet in length. Three or four Indians, by turns, would take up, individually, one of these burning pieces of wood and apply it to his naked body, already burned black with the powder. These tormentors presented themselves on every side of him, so that which ever way he ran round the post they met him with the burning fagots and poles. Some of the squaws took broad boards, upon which they would put a quantity of burning coals and hot embers and throw them on him, so that in a short time he had nothing but coals of fire and hot ashes to walk upon.

"In the midst of these extreme tortures he called to Simon Girty, and begged of him to shoot him: but Girty making no answer, he called to him again. Girty then, by way of derision, told the colonel he had no gun, at the same time turning about to an Indian who was behind him, laughed heartily, and by all his gestures seemed delighted at the horrid scene.

"Girty then came up to me and bade me prepare for death. He said, however, I was not to die at that place, but to be burnt at the Shawanese towns. He swore by G—d I need not expect to escape death, but should suffer it in all its extremities.

"Colonel Crawford at this period of his suffering, besought the Almighty to have mercy on his soul, spoke very low, and bore his torments with the most manly fortitude. He continued in all the extremities of pain for an hour and three quarters or two hours longer, as near as I can judge, when at last being almost spent, he lay down on his belly; they then scalped him and repeatedly threw the scalp in my face, telling me 'That was my great captain's.' An old squaw (whose appearance every way answered the ideas people entertain of the devil) got a board, took a parcel of coals and ashes and laid them on his back and head after he had been scalped; he then raised himself upon his feet and began to walk round the post; they next put a burning stick to him as usual, but lie seemed more insensible of pain than before."

Colonel Crawford was about fifty years of age, when he suffered at the stake. His son-in-law and nephew were executed about the same time; John escaped. What became of the other members of his family cannot satisfactorily be ascertained. A daughter was raised by Colonel Shepherd, of Wheeling creek, and married a Mr. Thornburg. At her marriage, Col. S. gave her one hundred acres of land, lying near the present town of Triadelphia.

The death of Col. Crawford cast a gloom over the whole west, and cannot be contemplated, at this late day, without an involuntary shudder.

## CAPTAIN SAMUEL BRADY.

Of the many brave spirits who started into existence at the first drum-tap of the Revolution, but few have become better known, or more respected in the west, than the gallant Brady, captain of the spies.

At a very early age, this devoted partizan gave indications of future usefulness; exhibiting in all his movements a spirit and a purpose to do and dare, which marked him as a man of no ordinary character, and proved him fit for almost any emergency.

Brady was emphatically the Marion of the west. Like the Chevalier Bayard, he was "without fear and without reproach." A bolder or braver man never drew a sword or fired a rifle; and these marked elements of his nature rendered him the terror of the Indian warrior, whether on the scout or in the wigwam, for he felt himself alike insecure from the noiseless vengeance of the "leader of the spies." No man stood higher in the esteem of the hardy settlers, and no name could inspire more of confidence and of safety, than that of Samuel Brady. During the whole of the fierce, protracted, and sanguinary war which ravaged the frontier settlements of Virginia and Pennsylvania, from 1785 to 1794, no man could so quiet the trembling and fear-stricken settlers as Captain Brady. His presence, backed by the band of devoted followers who always stepped in his footprints, was felt as security everywhere. The fond mother, who in after years related to her children the many thrilling incidents of frontier life which she witnessed and passed through, never failed, as she thanked her Heavenly Father for having protected her little innocents from the scalping-knife and tomahawk, to express her heartfelt gratitude to him who had been the instrumentality of saving her all from savage barbarity.

Devoted as this man was to the interests of the west, and sacrificing as he did, almost everything but life, it is a burning shame that his memory should have been so long neglected, and that some public recognition of his services has not been made. It is a reflection upon our gratitude and patriotism, that while whole galleries are to be found of men whose services in behalf of their country were not to be compared with those of Brady, live upon canvas and in marble, not one single bust or portrait of the gallant leader of the spies is anywhere to be found. And what is still worse, his remains lie in an humble burial ground without even a stone, bearing the most simple inscription to mark the spot from the undistinguished mass around.

Samuel Brady was born at Shippensburgh, Pennsylvania, in 1756. His father, John Brady, was made a captain in the Colonial army, for his services in the old French and Indian wars. The family, at an early day, moved to the Susquehanna. On the breaking out of the Revolution, Samuel joined a volunteer company, and marched to Boston. The patriotic fervor of the youth, prompted the commander to offer young Brady a commission; but his father objected, thinking he was too young, saying, "First let him learn the duties of a soldier, and then he will better know how to act as an officer."

"In 1776, Samuel Brady was appointed a first lieutenant. He continued with the army, and was in all the principal engagements until after the battle of Monmouth, when he was promoted to a captaincy, and ordered to the west under Colonel Brodhead. On their march, he had leave to visit his friends in Northumberland county. His father, in 1776, had accepted a captaincy in the 12th Pennsylvania regiment, been badly wounded at the battle of Brandywine, and was then at home. Whilst there, he heard of his brother's death, who had been murdered by the Indians on the 9th of August, 1778. He remained at home until 1779, and then rejoined his regiment at Pittsburgh. During the same year, his father was murdered by the Indians; and then it was that our hero swore vengeance against the whole race. Terribly, too, did he keep that vow."

In 1781, the Indians became very troublesome in the settlements above Pittsburgh. Washington, as we have elsewhere noticed, knew very well that the only guaranty of safety was to strike the enemy at home. With this view, he directed Colonel Brodhead to send some suitable person to their towns, who could ascertain their strength, resources, etc. Colonel Brodhead's keen military eye saw in Brady the very man for the service, and giving him the necessary instructions, the gallant soldier started on his perilous mission, accompanied by John Williamson and one of the Wetzels. These men were so completely disguised as Indians, that it would almost have defied the skill and cunning of a genuine chief to detect the deception. After a hurried march, they reached the Indian town at Upper Sandusky, shortly after dark. Brady posted his men, then entered the town, and after a thorough reconnoitre rejoined his companions, and commenced a rapid retreat. His keen eye had caught a lurking suspicion in some of those whom he met, and it was deemed important to get beyond their reach as rapidly as possible. With scarcely a moment's intermission, the three travelled all night, and stopping a few minutes in the morning, discovered the Indians were in pursuit. Increasing their movements, and adopting the precaution of travelling upon logs and avoiding direct routes, the trio were soon beyond immediate danger. The remainder of that day, all of that night, and part of the third day, passed without any cause of apprehension. Fatigued and hungry, (their sole diet since leaving home having been parched com and jerked venison) the party concluded to take a rest. Williamson stood guard while the others slept. Brady, at all times a great snorer, on this occasion gave vent to sounds, that, in the language of Williamson, "were enough to alarm all the Indians between here and Sandusky." Thinking a change of position might stop the nasal artillery, Williamson turned Brady, and then resumed his seat by the fire. Scarcely had he seated himself, when he detected the stealthy tread of a savage. Looking attentively in the direction of the sound, he saw an Indian cautiously approach, and waiting until he came nearly up, the guard took steady aim and fired. One convulsive spring, a heavy fall, and deep groan, were all that could be seen or heard. His companions sprang to their feet and moved rapidly off, to avoid an attack; but this was the only Indian, and the three travelled on without further attempt at molestation. According to the account furnished by one of the family, of which we shall have occasion frequently to avail ourselves during this notice, —

"The map furnished by General Brodhead was found to be defective. The distance was represented to be much less than it really was. The provisions and ammunition of the men were exhausted by the time they had readied the Big Beaver, on their return. Brady shot an otter, but could not eat it. The last load was in his rifle. They arrived at an old encampment, and found plenty of strawberries, which they stopped to appease their hunger with. Having discovered a deer-track, Brady followed it, telling the men he would perhaps get a shot at it. He had gone but a few rods when he saw the deer standing broadside to him. He raised his rifle and attempted to fire, but it flashed in the pan. He sat down, picked the touch-hole, and then started on. After going a short distance the path made a bend, and he saw before him a large Indian on horseback, with a child before and its mother behind, and a number of warriors marching in the rear. His first impulse was to shoot the Indian on horseback, but as he raised the rifle he observed the child's head to roll with the motion of the horse. It was fast asleep, and tied to the Indian. He stepped behind the root of a tree, and waited until he could shoot the Indian, without danger to the child or its mother.

"When he considered the chance certain, he fired, and the Indian, child, and mother, all fell from the horse. Brady called to his men, with a voice that made the forest ring, to surround the Indians, and give them a general fire. He sprung to the fallen Indian's powder horn, but could not pull it off. Being dressed like an Indian, the woman thought be was one, and said 'Why did you shoot your brother?' He caught up the child, saying, 'Jenny Stoop, I am Captain Brady; follow me, and I will secure you and your child.' He caught her hand in his, carrying the child under the other arm, and dashed into the brush. Many guns were fired at him, but no ball touched, and the Indians, dreading an ambuscade, were glad to make off. The next day he arrived at Fort M'Intosh, with the woman and her child. His men had got there before him. They had heard his war-whoop, and knew they were Indians he had encountered, but having no ammunition, had taken to their heels and run off."

"The incursions of the Indians had become so frequent, and their outrages so alarming, that it was thought advisable to retaliate upon them the injuries of war, and carry into the country occupied by them, the same system with which they had visited the settlements. For this purpose an adequate force was provided, under the immediate command of General Brodhead, the command of the advance guard of which was confided to Captain Brady.

"The troops proceeded up the Alleghany river, and had arrived near the mouth of Redbank creek, now known by the name of Brady's Bend, without encountering an enemy, Brady and his Rangers were some distance in front of the main body, as their duty required, when they suddenly discovered a war party of Indians approaching them. Relying on the strength of the main body, and its ability to force the Indians to retreat, and anticipating, as Napoleon did in the battle with the Mamelukes, that when driven back they would return by the same route they had advanced on, Brady permitted them to proceed without hindrance, and hastened to seize a narrow pass, higher up the river; where the rocks, nearly perpendicular, approached the river, and a few determined men might successfully combat superior numbers."

In a short time the Indians encountered the main body under Brodhead, and were driven back. In full and swift retreat they pressed on to gain the pass between the rocks and the river, but it was occupied by Brady and his Rangers, who failed not to pour into their flying columns a most destructive fire. Many were killed on the bank, and many more in the stream. Cornplanter, afterwards the distinguished chief of the Senecas, but then a young man, saved himself by swimming. The celebrated war-chief of this tribe, Bald-Eagle, was of the number slain on this occasion.

"The army moved onward, and after destroying all the Indians' corn, and ravaging the Kenjua flats, returned to Pittsburgh.

"Shortly after Captain Brady's return from Sandusky, he was observed one evening by a man of the name of Phouts, sitting in a solitary part of the fort, apparently absorbed in thought. Phouts approached him, pained to the bottom of his honest heart to perceive that the countenance of Brady bore traces of care and melancholy. He accosted him, however, in the best English he had, and soothingly said, 'Gabtain, was ails you?' Brady looked at him a short time without speaking; then resuming his usual equanimity, replied, 'I have been thinking about the red skins, and it is my opinion there are some above us on the river. I have a mind to pay them a vist. Now, if I get permission from the general to do so, will you go along?' Phouts was a stout thick Dutchman of uncommon strength and activity. He was also well acquainted with the woods. When Brady had ceased speaking, Phouts raised himself on tiptoe, and bringing his heels hard down on the ground, by way of emphasis, his eyes full of fire, said, 'By dunder und lightnin, I would rader go mit you, Gabtain, as to any of te finest weddins in tis guntry.' Brady told him to keep quiet, and say nothing about it, as no man in the fort must know any thing of the expedition but General Brodhead. Bidding Phouts call at his tent in an hour, he then went to the general's quarters, whom he found reading. After the usual topics were discussed, Brady proposed for consideration, his project of ascending the Alleghany, with but one man in company; stating his reasons for apprehending a descent from that quarter by the Indians. The general gave his consent, at parting took him by the hand in a friendly manner, advising him how to proceed, and charging him particularly to be careful of his own life, and that of the men or man whom he might select to accompany him. So affectionate were the general's admonitions, and so great the emotion he displayed, that Brady left him with tears in his eyes, and repaired to his tent, where he found Phouts deep in conversation with one of his pet Indians.

"He told Phouts of his success with the general, and that, as it was early in the light of the moon, they must get ready and be off betimes.

"They immediately set about cleaning their guns, preparing their ammunition, and having secured a small quantity of salt, lay down together, and slept soundly until about two hours before daybreak. Brady awoke first, and stirring Phouts, each took down the 'deadly rifle,' and whilst all but the sentinels were wrapped in sleep, they left the little fort, and in a short time found themselves deep buried in the forest. That day they marched through woods never traversed by either of them before; following the general course of the river they reached a small creek that put in from the Pittsburgh side; it was near night when they got there, and having no provision, they concluded to remain there all night.

"Next morning they started early and travelled all day; in the evening the espied a number of crows hovering over the tops of the trees, near the bank of the river. Brady told Phouts that there were Indians in the neighborhood, or else the men who were expected from Susquehanna at Pittsburgh were there encamped, or had been some time before.

"Phouts was anxious to go down and see, but Brady forbade him; telling him at the same time, 'We must secrete ourselves till after night, when fires will be made by them, whoever they may be.' Accordingly, they hid themselves among fallen timber, and remained so till about ten o'clock at night. But even then they could still see no fire. Brady concluded there must be a hill or thick woods between him and where the crows were seen, and decided on leaving his hiding place to ascertain the fact; Phouts accompanied him. They walked with the utmost caution down towards the river bank, and had gone about two hundred yards, when they observed the twinkling of a fire, at some distance on their right. They at first thought the river made a very short bend, but on proceeding further discovered that it was a fork or branch of the river, probably the Kiskeminetas. Brady desired Phouts to stay where he was, intending to go himself to the fire, and see who was there; but Phouts refused, saying, 'No, by George, I vill see too.'

They approached the fire together, but with the utmost caution; supposing it to be an Indian encampment, much too large to be attacked by them.

"Resolved to ascertain the number of the enemy. Captain Brady and his brave comrade went close up to the fire, and discovered an old Indian sitting beside a tree near the fire, either mending or making a pair of moccasins.

"Phouts, who never thought of danger, was for shooting the Indian immediately; but Brady prevented him. After examining carefully around the camp, he was of opinion that the number by which it was made had been large, but that they were principally absent. He determined on knowing more in the morning; and forcing Phouts away, retired a short distance to await the approach of day. As soon as it appeared they returned to the camp, but saw nothing, except the old Indian, a dog, and a horse.

"Brady wished to see the country around the camp, and understand its features better; for this purpose he kept at some distance from it, and examined about, till he got on the river above it. Here he found a large trail of Indians, who had gone up the Alleghany; to his judgment it appeared to have been made one or two days before. Upon seeing this he concluded to go back to the camp, and take the old Indian prisoner.

"Supposing the old savage to have arms about him, and not wishing to run the risk of the alarm the report of a rifle might create, if Indians were in the neigborhood, Brady determined to seize the old fellow single handed, without doing him further 'scath,' and carry him off to Pittsburgh. With this view, both crept toward the camp again, very cautiously. When they came so near as to perceive him, the Indian was was lying on his back, with his head towards them.

"Brady ordered Phouts to remain where he was, and not to fire, unless the dog should attempt to assist his master. In that case he was to shoot the dog, but by no means to hurt the Indian. The plan being arranged, Brady dropped his rifle, and, tomahawk in hand, silently crept towards the old man, until within a few feet, then raising himself up, he made a spring like a panther, and with a yell that awakened the echoes round, seized the Indian, hard and fast by the throat. The old man struggled a little at first, but Brady's was the gripe of a lion; holding his tomahawk over the head of his prisoner, he bade him surrender, as he valued his life. The dog behaved very civilly; he merely growled a little. Phouts came up, and they tied their prisoner. On examining the camp they found nothing of value, except some powder and lead, which they threw into the river. When the Indian learned that he was to be taken to Pittsburgh, and would be kindly treated, he showed them a canoe, which they stepped into with their prisoner and his dog, and were soon afloat on the Alleghany.

"They paddled swiftly along for the purpose of reaching the mouth of the run on which they had encamped coming up; for Brady had left his wiping rod there. It was late when they got to the creek's mouth. They landed, made a fire, and all laid down.

"As soon as daylight appeared, the captain started to where they left some jerk hanging on the evening before, leaving Phouts in charge of the prisoner and his canoe. He had not left the camp long, till the Indian complained to Phouts that the cords upon his wrist hurt him. He had probably discovered that in Phout's composition there was a much larger proportion of kindness than of fear. The Dutchman at once took off the cords, and the Indian was, or pretended to be, very grateful.

"Phouts was busied with something else in a minute, and had left his gun standing by a tree. The moment the Indian saw that the eye of the other was not upon him, he sprung to the tree, seized the gun, and the first Phouts knew was that it was cocked, and at his breast. The trigger was pulled, but the bullet whistled harmless past him, taking with it a part of his shot-pouch belt. One stroke of the Dutchman's tomahawk settled the Indian forever, and nearly severed the head from his body.

"Brady heard the report of the rifle, and the yell of Phouts; and supposing all was not right, ran instantly to the spot, where he found the latter sitting on the body of the Indian, examining the rent in his shot-pouch belt. 'In the name of Heaven,' said Brady, 'what have you done!' 'Yust look, Gabtan,' said the fearless Dutchman, 'vat dis d—d black b—h vas apout;' holding up to view the hole in his belt. He then related what has been stated with respect to his untying the Indian, and the attempt of the latter to kill him. They then took off the scalp of the Indian, got their canoe, took in the Indian's dog, and returned to Pittsburgh, the fourth day after their departure."

Beaver valley was the scene of many of Captain Brady's stirring adventures. We have recently visited some of the interesting localities celebrated as Brady's theatre of action, and heard from many of the older citizens their accounts of his thrilling exploits. They speak in unbounded terms of admiration of his daring and success; his many hair-breadth escapes by "field and flood;" and always concluded by declaring that he was a greater man than Daniel Boon or Lewis Wetzel, either of whom, in the eyes of the old pioneers, were the very embodiment of dare-devilism.

The following, illustrating one of Brady's adventures in the region referred to, we give from a published source. In one of his trapping and hunting excursions, he was surprised and taken prisoner by a party of Indians who had closely watched his movements.

"To have shot or tomahawked him would have been but a small gratification to that of satiating their revenge by burning him at a slow fire, in presence of all the Indians of their village. He was therefore taken alive to their encampment, on the west bank of the Beaver river, about a mile and a half from its mouth. After the usual exultations and rejoicings at the capture of a noted enemy, and causing him to run the gauntlet, a fire was prepared, near which Brady was placed, after being stripped, and with his arms unbound. Previous to tying him to the stake, a large circle was formed around of Indian men, women, and children, dancing and yelling, and uttering all manner of threats and abuses that their small knowledge of the English language could afford. The prisoner looked on these preparations for death, and on his savage foe with a firm countenance, and a steady eye, meeting all their threats with truly savage fortitude. In the midst of their dancing and rejoicing, a squaw of one of their chiefs came near him with a child in her arms. Quick as thought and with intuitive prescience, he snatched it from her and threw it into the midst of the flames. Horror stricken at the sudden outrage, the Indians simultaneously rushed to rescue the infant from the fire. In the midst of this confusion, Brady darted from the circle, overturning all that came in his way, and rushed into the adjacent thicket, with the Indians yelling at his heels. He ascended the steep side of a hill amidst a shower of bullets, and darting down the opposite declivity, secreted himself in the deep ravines and laurel thickets that abound for several miles to the west. His knowledge of the country and wonderful activity, enabled him to elude his enemies, and reach the settlements in safety."

From one of Brady's old soldiers — one of the noble spies, who has not yet answered to the roll-call of death — one who served with him three years, during the most trying and eventful period of his life, we have gathered the facts of the following incident. On one of their scouting expeditions into the Indian country, the spies, consisting at that time of sixteen men, encamped for the night at a place called "Big Shell Camp." Toward morning, one of the guard heard the report of a gun, and immediately communicating the fact to his commander, a change of position was ordered. Leading his men to an elevated point, the Indian camp was discovered almost beneath them. Cautiously advancing in direction of the camp, six Indians were discovered standing around the fire, while several others lay upon the ground apparently asleep. Brady ordered his men to wrap themselves in their blankets, and lie down while he kept watch. Two hours thus passed without anything materially occurring. As day began to appear, Brady roused his men, and posted them side by side, himself at the end of the line. When all were in readiness, the commander was to touch with his elbow the man who stood next to him, and the communication was to pass successively to the farthest end. The orders then were, the moment the last man was touched, he should fire, which was to be the signal for a general discharge. With the first faint ray of light, rose six Indians and stood around the fire. With breathless expectation, the whites waited for the remainder to rise, but failing, and apprehending a discovery, the captain moved his elbow, and the next instant the wild wood rang with the shrill report of the rifles of the spies. Five of the six Indians fell dead, but the sixth, screened by a tree, escaped. The camp being large, it was deemed unsafe to attack it further, and a retreat was immediately ordered.

Soon after the above occurrence, in returning from a similar expedition, and when about two miles from the mouth of Yellow creek, at a place admirably adapted for an ambuscade, a solitary Indian stepped forward and fired upon the advancing company. Instantly, on firing, he retreated toward a deep ravine, into which the savage hoped to lead his pursuers. But Brady detected the trick, and in a voice of thunder ordered his men to tree. No sooner had this been done, than the concealed foe rushed forth in great numbers, and opened upon the whites a perfect storm of leaden hail. The brave spies returned the fire with spirit and effect; but as they were likely to be overpowered by superior numbers, a retreat was ordered to the top of the hill, and thence continued until out of danger.

The whites lost one man in this engagement, and two wounded. The Indian loss is supposed to have been about twenty in killed and wounded.

In concluding this imperfect sketch of one who performed no ordinary part in the settlement of the west, we regret that our means and time have not allowed us to prepare a more full and general biography.

Captain Brady married a daughter of Captain Van Swearengen, of Ohio county, who bore him two children, John and Van S., both of whom are still living. Captain Brady possessed all the elements of a brave and successful soldier. Like Marion, "he consulted with his men respectfully, heard them patiently, weighed their suggestions, and silently approached his own conclusions. They knew his determination only by his actions." Brady had but few superiors as a woodman: he would strike out into the heart of the wilderness, and with no guide but the sun by day, and the stars by night, or in their absence, then by such natural marks as the bark and tops of trees, he would move on steadily, in a direct line toward the point of his destination. He always avoided beaten paths and the borders of streams; and never was known to leave his track behind him. In this manner he eluded pursuit, and defied detection. He was often vainly hunted by his own men, and was more likely to find them than they him.

Such was Brady, the leader of the spies.

GENERAL ANDREW LEWIS.

We greatly regret our inability to give in the present edition, a comprehensive biography of this distinguished man. We were promised through a member of the family, material necessary to prepare the sketch proposed, but having been disappointed, it will be impossible to do more now than present a brief notice of the family, written by a gentleman of the Valley, whose position and relationship enables him to state many interesting facts of family history which otherwise might have escaped attention.

"John Lewis was a native and citizen of Ireland, descended from a family of Huguenots, who took refuge in that kingdom from the persecutions that followed the assassination of Henry IV. of France. His rank was that of an esquire, and he inherited a handsome estate, which he increased by industry and frugality, until he became the lessee of a contiguous property, of considerable value. He married Margaret Lynn, daughter of the laird of Loch Lynn, who was a descendant of the chieftains of a once powerful clan in the Scottish Highlands. By this marriage he had four sons, three of them, Thomas, Andrew, and William, born in Ireland, and Charles, the child of his old age, born a few months after their settlement in their mountain home.

"For many years after the settlement at Fort Lewis, great amity and goodwill existed between the neighboring Indians and the white settlers, whose numbers increased until they became quite a formidable colony. It was then that the jealousy of their red neighbors became aroused, and a war broke out, which, for cool though desperate courage and activity on the part of the whites, and ferocity, cunning and barbarity on the part of the Indians, was never equalled in any age or country. John Lewis was, by this time, well stricken in years, but his four sons, who were grown up, well qualified to fill his place, and to act the part of the leader to the gallant little band, who so nobly battled for the protection of their homes and families. It is not my purpose to go into the details of a warfare, during which scarcely a settlement was exempt from monthly attacks of the savages, and during which Charles Lewis, the youngest son of John, is said never to have spent one month at a time out of active and arduous service. Charles was the hero of many a gallant exploit, which is still treasured in the memories of the descendants of the border riflemen, and there are few families among the Alleghanies where the name and deeds of Charles Lewis are not familiar as household words. On one occasion he was captured by the Indians while on a hunting excursion, and after travelling over two hundred miles barefooted, his arms pinioned behind, and goaded by the knives of his remorseless captors, he effected his escape. While travelling along the bank of a precipice some twenty feet in height, he suddenly, by a strong muscular exertion, burst the cords which bound him, and plunged down the steep into the bed of a mountain torrent. His persecutors hesitated not to follow. In a race of several hundred yards, Lewis had gained some few yards upon his pursuers, when, upon leaping a fallen tree which lay across his course, his strength suddenly failed and he fell prostrate among the weeds which had grown up in great luxuriance around the body of the tree. Three of the Indians sprung over the tree within a few feet of where their prey lay concealed; but with a feeling of the most devout thankfulness to a kind and superintending Providence, he saw them one by one disappear in the dark recesses of the forest. He now bethought himself of rising from his uneasy bed, when lo! a new enemy appeared, in the shape of an enormous rattlesnake, who had thrown himself into the deadly coil so near his face that his fangs were within a few inches of his nose; and his enormous rattle, as it waved to and fro, once rested upon his ear. A single contraction of the eyelid — a convulsive shudder — the relaxation of a single muscle, and the deadly beast would have sprung upon him. In this situation he lay for several minutes, when the reptile, probably supposing him to be dead, crawled over his body and moved slowly away. 'I had eaten nothing,' said Lewis to his companions, after his return, 'for many days; I had no fire-arms, and I ran the risk of dying with hunger, ere I could reach the settlement; but rather would I have died, than made a meal of the generous beast.' During this war, an attack was made upon the settlement of Fort Lewis, at a time when the whole force of the settlement was out on active duty. So great was the surprise, that many of the women and children were captured in sight of the fort, though far the greater part escaped, and concealed themselves in the woods. The fort was occupied by John Lewis, then very old and infirm, his wife, and two young women, who were so much alarmed that they scarce moved from their seats upon the ground floor of the fort. John Lewis, however, opened a port-hole, where he stationed himself, firing at the savages, while Margaret reloaded the guns. In this manner he sustained a siege of six hours, during which he killed upwards of a score of savages, when he was relieved by the appearance of his party.

"Thomas Lewis, the eldest son, labored under a defect of vision, which disabled him as a marksman, and he was, therefore, less efficient during the Indian wars than his brothers. He was, however, a man of learning and sound judgment, and represented the county of Augusta many years in the House of Burgesses; was a member of the convention which ratified the constitution of the United States, and formed the constitution of Virginia, and afterwards sat for the county of Rockingham in the House of Delegates of Virginia. In 1765, he was in the House of Burgesses, and voted for Patrick Henry's celebrated resolutions. Thomas Lewis had four sons actively participating in the war of the Revolution; the youngest of whom, Thomas, who is now living, bore an ensign's commission when but fourteen years of age.

"Andrew, the second son of John Lewis and Margaret Lynn, is the General Lewis who commanded at the battle of Point Pleasant.

"Charles Lewis, the youngest of the sons of John Lewis, fell at the head of his regiment, when leading on the attack at Point Pleasant. Charles was esteemed the most skilful of loved for his noble and amiable qualities as he was admired for his military talents.

"William, the third son, was an active participator in the border wars, and was an officer of the revolutionary army, in which one of his sons was killed, and another maimed for life. When the British force under Tarleton drove the legislature from Charlottesville to Staunton, the stillness of the Sabbath eve was broken in the latter town by the beat of the drum, and volunteers were called to prevent the passage of the British through the mountains at Rockfish Gap. The elder sons of William Lewis, who then resided at the old fort, were absent with the northern army. Three sons, however, were at home, whose ages were seventeen, fifteen and thirteen years. Wm. Lewis was confined to his room by sickness, but his wife, with the firmness of a Roman matron, called them to her, and bade them fly to the defence of their native land. 'Go my children,' said she, 'I spare not my youngest, the comfort of my declining years. I devote you all to my country. Keep back the foot of the invader from the soil of Augusta, or see my face no more.' When this incident was related to Washington, shortly after its occurrence, he enthusiastically exclaimed, 'Leave me but a banner to plant upon the mountains of Augusta, and I will rally around me the men who will lift our bleeding country from the dust, and set her free.'

"I have frequently heard, when a boy, an anecdote related by an old settler, somewhat to this effect: — The white, or wild clover, is of indigenous growth, and abounded on the banks of the rivers, etc. The red was introduced by John Lewis, and it was currently reported by their prophets, and believed by the Indians generally, that the blood of the red men slain by the Lewises and their followers, had dyed the trefoil to its sanguine hue. The Indians, however, always did the whites the justice to say, that the Red man was the aggressor in their first quarrel, and that the white men of Western Virginia had always evinced a disposition to treat their red brethren with moderation and justice."

Andrew Lewis, with four of his brothers, were in the expedition of Braddock, and exhibited marked courage and caution. Samuel commanded the company, and acquitted himself with great ability. Andrew Lewis was twice wounded at the siege of Fort Necessity. After the amnesty, and as the Virginians were marching off, an Irishman became displeased with an Indian, and "cursing the copper-headed scoundrel," elevated his gun to fire. At that moment, Major Lewis, who, crippled, was passing along, raised his staff and knocked up the muzzle of the Irishman's rifle, thus doubtless preventing a general massacre.

Major Lewis was made prisoner at Grant's defeat, and his bearing on that occasion (elsewhere noticed) on discovering the treachery of Grant, was a true characteristic of the man.

Washington, at an early day, formed an exalted opinion of General Lewis's ability as a military commander. On the breaking out of the Revolution, he recommended him to Congress "as one of the major-generals of the American army — a recommendation which was slighted, in order to make room for General Stephens. It is also said, that when Washington was commissioned as commander-in-chief, he expressed a wish that the appointment had been given to General Lewis. Upon this slight in the appointment of Stephens, Washington wrote General Lewis a letter, which is published in his correspondence, expressive of his regret at the course pursued by Congress, and promising that he should be promoted to the first vacancy. At his solicitation, Lewis accepted the commision of brigadier-general, and was soon after ordered to the command of a detachment of the army stationed near Williamsburg. He commanded the Virginia troops when Lord Dunmore was driven from Gwynn's Island, in 1776, and announced his orders for attacking the enemy by putting a match to the first gun, an eighteen-pounder, himself.

"General Lewis resigned his command in 1780, to return home, being seized ill with a fever. He died on his way, in Bedford county, about forty miles from his own house, on the Roanoke, lamented by all acquainted with his meritorious services and superior qualities.

"'General Lewis,' says Stuart, in his Historical Memoir, 'was upwards of six feet high, of uncommon strength and agility, and his form of the most exact symmetry. He had a stern and invincible countenance, and was of a reserved and distant deportment, which rendered his presence more awful than engaging. He was a commissioner with Dr. Thomas Walker, to hold a treaty, on behalf of the colony of Virginia, with the six nations of Indians, together with the commissioners from Pennsylvania, New York, and other eastern provinces, held at Fort Stanwix, in the province of New York, in the year 1768. It was then remarked by the governor of New York, that "the earth seemed to tremble under him as he walked along." His independent spirit despised sycophantic means of gaining popularity, which never rendered more than his merits extorted.'"

GENERAL DANIEL BRODHEAD.

It has with much truth been said, "that the history of the Revolution, is not written, and cannot be, till the biographies of the men who made the Revolution are complete." This is eminently true of the great struggle in the west. The conflict here was with the tomahawk and scalping knife, united to the arm of scientific warfare. It was one in which the remorseless savage stole upon the infant settlements in the stillness of the night, and dealt death in all the horrid forms of his peculiar and revolting warfare. It was a war terrible indeed to man, but more terrible still to gentle woman, and most terrible to helpless infancy.

To defend the country against the ravages of such war, required men of iron nerve and determined will. To lead on these men to victory and success, demanded others of no ordinary character. But there were men fitted to the task; men able, ready, and willing to lead and to strike. It was to the energy of this defence; the skill, bravery, and consummate judgment of these able officers, and experienced frontier soldiers, that the west was saved from the diabolical system of subjugation, meditated by the British ministry.

One of the men most prominent in this defence, and one who contributed greatly towards breaking down the power of the savage, and humbling the dominion of Britain, was Daniel Brodhead, the subject of this memoir.

Prefacing our sketch with a brief notice of Gen. Brodhead's immediate ancestry, we will proceed to notice such of the more important features of his history, as will be most interesting, and come more directly within the range of our work.

Daniel Brodhead, the great-grandfather of the subject of this notice, was born in Yorkshire, England. He was a Captain in the service of Charles II., and by that monarch ordered to America with the expedition under Col. Richard Incolls. On the surrender of New Amsterdam, by Stuyversant, he was sent to Albany, and was one of the witnesses to the treaty with the Indians in 1664. He died in 1670, leaving three sons, Daniel, Charles, and Richard. The last of these was the father of Daniel Brodhead, the subject of our notice.

Daniel, or Gen. Brodhead, as we will now call him, married Elizabeth Depue, daughter of Samuel Depue, one of the earliest settlers in the neighborhood of Stroudsburg, Pennsylvania. He had one son and a daughter by this marriage, and their descendants are scattered throughout the State, embracing some of the most extensive and respectable families in the commonwealth.

Gen. Brodhead a second time married, the last wife being the widow of Gen. Mifflin.

General Brodhead was a man of acknowledged ability and great energy of character. He early gave indications of much promise, and foreshadowed the career of honor and usefulness, which he afterwards run. Scarcely had the news of the battle of Lexington ceased agitating the people, ere Captain Brodhead mustered a company, and marched to the defence of the seaboard. He joined Sullivan, and at the battle of Long Island, his brave "Pennsylvania Riflemen" literally cut their way through the ranks of the enemy.

In the fall of 1777, information having been given that the Indians meditated a united attack upon the settlements along the upper Susquehanna, vigorous efforts were made to resist them. In the spring of 1778, Fort Muncy was evacuated, as well as Antis' and Horn's forts above, the inhabitants taking refuge at Sunbury. The savages destroyed Fort Muncy, but did not penetrate near Sunbury, their attention having been directed to the memorable descent upon Wyoming. Shortly after this Col. Brodhead was ordered to Pittsburgh to relieve General Mcintosh, in command of the western division of the army. His appointment was communicated in a very complimentary letter, which is herewith in part given:

Head-Quarters, Middle Brook,

5th March, 1778.

"Sir: — Brigadier-General Mcintosh having requested from Congress leave to retire from the command of the westward, they have, by a resolve of the 20th February, granted his request, and directed me to appoint an officer to succeed him. From my opinion of your abilities, your former acquaintance with the back country, and the knowledge you must have acquired upon this last tour of duty, I have appointed you to the command in preference to a stranger, as he would not have time to gain the necessary information between that of his assuming the command and the commencement of operations.

"As soon as Congress had vested me with the superintendence and direction of affairs to the westward. I gave General Mcintosh orders to make the preparations and inquiries contained in my letters of the 31st January and 15th February last. Copies of these letters he will deliver to you, and will inform you how far he hath proceeded in the several matters recommended to him; and will likewise communicate to you, what measures he may have taken, and what orders may have been given towards the completion of the remainder.

"I had desired General Mcintosh to come down after he had put the matters recommended to him in a proper train, and to bring down a list of such stores and other necessaries as might be wanting for the expedition. But I do not see how there will be a possibility of your doing this. Had Gen. Mcintosh come down, you would have been fully competent to carrying on the preparations; but if you quit the post, I apprehend there will be no officer left of sufficient weight and ability. This is an opinion which

I would wish you to keep to yourself, because it might give offence to officers in all other respects very worthy of the stations they fill.

"I must, therefore, desire you to remain at Fort Pitt, and you shall be, from time to time, fully informed of everything necessary for your government.

"I have desired General Mcintosh, in case you should be absent, to send to you by a special messenger wherever you may be; and I must desire you to repair to Fort Pitt with the utmost expedition, as you will, notwithstanding every exertion, find the time, which you have for the execution of the business, full short for its completion.

"I am, sir,

"Your most ob't. and h'ble. serv't.,

"(Signed), G. Washington.

"Colonel Brodhead."

He again wrote to him, under date of 22d same month, that an incursion into the country of the Six-nations was in preparation, and that in connection therewith, it might be advisable to have a force ascend the Alleghany to Kittaning, thence to Venango, and having fortified both points, to strike the Mingoes and Munceys on French creek, and thus greatly to aid General Sullivan in the decisive blow which he was to give by his march up the Susquehanna. He further directed Col. Brodhead to notify the western Indians, that in the event of any troubles on their part, the whole force of the United States should be turned against them. On the 21st of April, however, these orders were countermanded, and Col. B. directed to prepare a rod for the savages north and west of the Ohio, and especially to learn the best time for attacking Detroit. Whether this last advise came too late or was withdrawn again, we have no means of ascertaining. Brodhead proceeded, as at first directed; marched up the Alleghany, destroyed the Indians' crops, burned their towns, etc.

The immediate effect of this prompt and energetic movement on the part of the western commander was to bring the Delawares, Wyandotts, ShaAvanese, &c., to a treaty of peace at Fort Pitt in the month of September, to which reference has already been made.

It had long been apparent to Washington and the Board of War, that the possession of Detroit and Niagara by the British, enabled them to exert a controlling influence over most of the Indian tribes occupying the north-west; and thus greatly to annoy the frontier settlements of Pennsylvania and Virginia.

Col. Brodhead, soon after assuming the duties of commander of the western division, clearly saw the absolute necessity of striking an effective blow against these two strong-holds of the British. In a letter to Washington, dated Fort Pitt, January 23d, 1781, he writes thus: "The whole of my present force very little exceeds three hundred men, and many of them are unfit for such active service as is necessary here. I hope your excellency will be pleased to enable me to take Detroit the ensuing campaign; for until that and Niagara fall into our hands, there will be no rest for the innocent inhabitants, whatever sums may be expended on a defensive plan."

Previous to this, Washington, in a letter to Col. B., dated April 21, 1779, in reply to his request to fit out such an expedition, directed him to make the necessary preparations; but, on the 4th of January following, wrote to countermand the order, in consequence of the operations in South Carolina and his inability to reinforce Fort Pitt, in case of disaster. Feb. 4th, 1780, he again declined a compliance with Colonel B.'s renewed and urgent solicitation, on the ground that his regular troops would all be needed to co-operate with our French allies. The want of provisions too, at that time, was greatly felt, which Washington alluding to, adds, "You must therefore, of necessity, confine yourself to partizan strokes, which I wish to see encouraged. The State of Virginia is very desirous of an expedition against Detroit, and would make great exertions to carry it into execution. But while the enemy are so formidable to the southward, and are making such strides in that quarter, I fear it will require a greater force of men and supplies to check them than we, since the defeat near Cambden, shall be able shortly to draw together."

The desire of Col. B. to undertake the reduction of Detroit, was thus regretfully declined by the commander-in-chief, and the wishes of Virginia, and indeed the whole country, disappointed.

In the spring of 1781, Colonel Brodhead led an expedition against the Indian towns on the Muskingum; a full account of which having been elsewhere given in this volume, it will be unnecessary to notice further now.

Near the mouth of Broken-straw creek, a tributary of the Alleghany, stood the Indian town of Buckaloon. In 1781, Colonel Brodhead attacked this strong-hold of the enemy, and after a hard siege, finally routed the savages and burned the town.

We regret our inability to notice in detail all his expeditions. They were numerous and extensive enough to fill a volume. No better officer could have been selected for the arduous post of commander of the western-division of the army. It required a man bold, cautious and sagacious, and Col. Brodhead was the very embodiment of all these. He proved himself admirably qualified for the most trying situations, and acquitted himself with distinction, and to the entire satisfaction of the commander-in-chief. In November, 1781, with the consent of Washington, he relinquished the post into the hands of Col. John Gibson, a gallant Virginian, who had done active duties on the frontier.

Colonel Brodhead negotiated during his residence in the west, two important treaties; the one was concluded July 22, 1779, with deputies of the Cherokee nation. In this treaty, intimations were given out of a native representation in Congress, and a new Indian confederacy with the Delawares as the head.

Congress passed Colonel Brodhead a unanimous vote of thanks for the highly satisfactory manner in which he had discharged his duties on the western frontier.

General Brodhead received many marks of distinction from the State of Pennsylvania. He was surveyor-general for many years, and filled other places of honor and profit. He was a large, robust man, kind, generous and amiable. He died at Milford, Pa., November 15, 1809, at the age of seventy-three. The portrait which accompanies this memoir is from a miniature now in possession of his great-grandson, Henry Johnson, Esq., a prominent member of the bar in northern Pennsylvania.

JESSE HUGHES.

One of the most active, daring and successful Indian hunters in the mountain region of Virginia, was Jesse Hughes. He has not inappropriately been styled the Wetzel of that portion of the state, and, in many respects, certainly was not undeserving of that distinctive appellation. Jesse Hughes possessed in an eminent degree the rare constituents of courage and energy. These qualities, so essential in those days of savage warfare, gained for him the confidence of the sturdy men by whom he was surrounded, and often induced them to select him for the post of leader in their various expeditions against the enemy. Many are the tales of adventure which the people of West-Fork and Little Kanawha relate of this notable personage. A few of these we have collected and now give.

Hughes was a native of the region to which his operations were chiefly confined. He was born on the head-waters of the Monongahela, and grew to manhood amid the dangers and privations which the people of that section of Virginia endured during the long years of a border warfare. Early learning that the rifle and tomahawk were his principal means of maintenance and defence, he became an adept in their use, and refused to acknowledge a superior anywhere. Passionately devoted to the wood, he became invaluable to the settlements as hunter and scout. A man of delicate frame, but an iron constitution, he could endure more fatigue than any of his associates, and thus was enabled to remain abroad at all seasons without inconvenience or detriment. Many were the threatened blows which his vigilance averted, and numerous the lives of helpless settlers his strong arm was reached forth to save. The recollection of his services and devotion is still cherished with a lively feeling of admiration by the people of the region with which his name is so intimately associated.

The following incidents illustrative of his career, we derive from sources entitled to every credit. The one which immediately follows, is from an old and intimate friend of Hughes, (Mr. Renick of Ohio,) to whom it was communicated by the hero himself, and afterwards confirmed by Mr. Harness, who was one of the expedition. The time of the incident was about 1790.

No Indian depredations had recently occurred in the vicinity of Clarksburgh, and the inhabitants began to congratulate themselves that difficulties were finally at an end.

"One night a man hearing the fence of a small lot, he had a horse in, fall, jumped up and running out saw an Indian spring on the horse and dash off. The whole settlement was alarmed in an hour or two, a company of twenty-five or thirty men were paraded, ready to start by daylight. They took a circle outside of the settlement, and soon found the trail of apparently eight or ten horses, and they supposed, about that many Indians. The captain (chosen before Hughes joined the company) called a halt, and held a council to determine in what manner to pursue them. The captain and a majority of the company were for following on their trail: Hughes was opposed, and he said he could pilot them to the spot where the Indians would cross the Ohio, by a nearer way than the enemy could go, and if they reached there before the Indians, could intercept them and be sure of success. But the commander insisted on pursuing the trail. Hughes then tried another argument: he pointed out the danger of trailing the Indians:

insisted that they would waylay their trail, in order to know if they were pursued, and would choose a situation where they could shoot two or three and set them at defiance; and alarming the others, the Indians would out-travel them and make their escape. The commander found that Hughes was like to get a majority for his plan, in which event he (the captain) would lose the honor of planning the expedition. Hughes, by some, was considered too wild for the command, and it was nothing but jealousy that kept him from it, for in most of their Indian excursions, he got the honor of the best plan, or did the best act that was performed. The commander then broke up the council by calling aloud to the men to follow him and let the cowards go home, and dashed off full speed, the men all following. Hughes knew the captain's remark was intended for him, and felt the insult in the highest degree, but followed on with the rest. They had not gone many miles until the trail ran down a ravine where the ridge on one side was very steep, with a ledge of rock for a considerable distance. On the top of this cliff two Indians lay in ambush, and when the company got opposite they made a noise of some kind, that caused the men to stop: that instant two of the company were shot and mortally wounded. They now found Hughes' prediction fully verified, for they had to ride so far round before they could get up the cliff, that the Indians with ease made their escape.

"They all now agreed that Hughes' plan was the best, and urged him to pilot them to the river where the Indians would cross. He agreed to do it; but was afraid it might be too late, for the Indians knew they were pursued and would make a desperate push. After leaving .some of the company to take care of the wounded men, they put off for the Ohio river, at the nearest point, and got there on the next day shortly after the Indians had crossed. The water was still muddy, and the rafts that they crossed on were floating down the opposite shore. The men now were unanimous for returning home. Hughes soon got satisfaction for the insult the captain had given him: he said he wanted to find out who the cowards were; that if any of them would go, he would cross the river and scalp some of the Indians. They all refused. He then said if one man would go with him, he would undertake it; but none would consent. Hughes then said he would go and take one of their scalps, or leave his own.

"The company now started home, and Hughes went up the river three or four miles, keeping out of sight of it, for he expected the Indians were watching them to see if they would cross. He there made a raft, crossed the river, and encamped for the night. The next day he found their trail, and pursued it very cautiously, and about ten miles from the Ohio found their camp. There was but one Indian in it, the rest were out hunting. The Indian left to keep camp, in order to pass away the time, got to playing the fiddle on some bones that they had for the purpose. Hughes crept up and shot him, took his scalp, and made the best of his way home."

The following characteristic anecdote goes far to illustrate the great discernment and instantaneous arrangement of plans, of this shrewd and skilful Virginia hunter.

It is a general belief that the Indian is exceedingly cunning; unrivalled in the peculiar knowledge of the woods, and capable, by the extraordinary imitative faculties which he possesses, to deceive either man, beast, or fowl. This is true to a certain extent; but still, with all his natural sagacity and quick perception of a native woodman, the Indian warrior falls short of the acquired knowledge of a well trained hunter, as the following case serves to illustrate. Jesse Hughes was more than a match at any time for the most wary savage in the forest. In his ability to anticipate all their artifices, he had but few equals, and fewer still, superiors. But, to the incident.

"At a time of great danger from the incursions of the Indians, when the citizens of the neighborhood were in a fort at Clarksburgh, Hughes one morning, observed a lad very intently fixing his gun. 'Jim,' said he, 'what are you doing that for?' 'I am going to shoot a turkey that I hear gobbling on the hill-side,' said Jim. 'I hear no turkey,' said the other. 'Listen,' said Jim: 'there, didn't you hear it? listen again.' 'Well,' says Hughes, after hearing it repeated, 'I'll go and kill it.' 'No you won't,' said the boy, 'it is my turkey; I heard it first.' 'Well,' said Hughes, 'but you know I am the best shot. I'll go and kill it, and give you the turkey!' The lad demurred but at length agreed. Hughes went out of the fort on the side that was furthest from the supposed turkey, and passing along the river, went up a ravine and cautiously creeping through the bushes behind the spot, came in whence the cries issued, and, as he expected, espied a large Indian sitting on a chestnut stump, surrounded by sprouts, gobbling, and watching if any one would come from the fort to kill the turkey. Hughes shot him before the Indian knew of his approach, took off the scalp, and went into the fort, where Jim was waiting for his prize. 'There now,' says Jim, 'you have let the turkey go. I would have killed it if I had gone.' 'No,' says Hughes, 'I didn't let it go;' and, taking out the scalp, threw it down. 'There, take your turkey, Jim, I don't want it.' The lad was overcome, and nearly fainted, to think of the certain death he had escaped, purely by the keen perception and good management of Jesse Hughes."

Jesse Hughes, as we have already stated, was often of invaluable service to the settlements along the upper Monongahela, by advising them of the approach of Indians. On one occasion, a considerable body of the common enemy attacked a fort near Clarksburg, and but for the energy and fearlessness of Hughes might have reduced the frail structure, and massacred every one within it. This daring man boldly went forth for succor, and succeeded in reaching a neighboring station in safety. Immediately, a company of men left to relieve the besieged; when the Indians, fearing the superior numbers, retreated in haste.

Hughes' scouting expeditions were not always confined to the extreme upper regions of the Monongahela. He often visited the stations lower clown, and spent much of his time at Prickett's fort, also at the stockade where Morgantown now stands, and many other settlements in the neighborhood. He was a great favorite; and no scouting party could be complete, unless Jesse Hughes had something to do with it. We regret that our limits will not allow us to give more incidents in his very eventful life.

A SKIRMISH.

This incident, which was inadvertently omitted in its proper place, is now given as not without interest to most readers of our local history.

One of the earliest settlers below Grave creek was John Baker. In 1775 he made an improvement on what is now known as Cresap's bottom. During the Dunmore war. Baker, with most of the settlers below Wheeling, resorted to the fort erected at that point; but in 1781, the settlement having become considerably strengthened by new additions, it was determined to erect a place of defence in the neighborhood, and accordingly, some additions were made to the house of Baker, and the whole protected by a stout stockade. Into this the settlers retreated on the renewal of hostilities in 1782.

Several years, however, passed without anything occurring at "Baker's Station," as it was called, worthy of special remark. At length, in 1791, an incident took place not unworthy of notice. Indications of the enemy became manifest, and strong apprehensions began to be entertained that Indians were about. In order to satisfy themselves, five experienced hunters were sent over the river to scout. These were Isaac McKeon, John McDonald, John Bean, Miller, and a Dutchman, named Shopto. They crossed opposite the station, and proceeded up to the mouth of Captina, (one mile,) and were moving cautiously along, when a heavy fire was opened upon them, killing Miller on the spot, and dangerously, wounding McDonald, who was made prisoner. The others ran in the direction of the station, calling for help as they approached; and so close upon them were the Indians, that they shot McKeon after he had reached the beach opposite the fort. Shopto and Bean escaped by swimming.

Of the men collected at the station was Lieutenant Abraham Enochs, of the Ohio county militia, and he proposed at once to head a company and go in pursuit. Eighteen men, including all the efficient force of the station, at once joined the gallant officer, and at once left on their perilous duty. Enochs led his men up the Virginia side to a point above the mouth of the creek, and then crossing the river, proceeded directly over the hill to the creek, instead of pursuing the bottom.

As the whole party were descending to a small stream which empties into the creek, about two miles above its mouth, they were fired upon by a large body of Indians, and John Baker (son of the proprietor of the station) severely wounded in the right thigh. The men were thrown into great confusion by this unexpected fire, and it was with the utmost difficulty they could be rallied. But Enochs, who possessed great intrepidity, as well as much tact as a commander, restored something like order, and cried to his men to rout the Indians from their covert. Leading them on with a shout of defiance, and a cry of confident victory, the bold and gallant officer, like Brunswick's fated chieftain,

"Rushed to the field, and foremost, fighting fell,"

He received at the first onset a rifle ball in his breast, and fell dead on the spot.

The death of their leader, and a simultaneous outbreak of a new body of Indians, so disconcerted the rest of the men, that they gave but one fire, and then broke in a disordered and general rout, amid the shouts and terrible war-whoops of the savage. Every man retreated for himself, most of them making their way to Grave creek.

Of those wounded, was George McColloch, who received a rifle ball in his ancle. Ray Vennam one of the party, took him on his shoulder and carried him some distance, but

Shopto, Bean, and four old men, were all the male adults left. These were ordered not to leave the fort until the expedition returned. McColloch, finding that they would be overtaken, entreated the other to take care of himself. Vennam concealed McColloch behind a log, and made his way to the fort. That night a man's plaintive cry was heard from the opposite shore, and on Vennam saying it was George McColloch, those in the fort said no, it was an Indian. Vennam, however, was firm in his opinion that it was his friend, and accordingly went over in a canoe to get McColloch. lie had made his way that far on one foot.

On the following day a body of men from Grave creek, with most of the fugitives from the battle, went over to the scene of disaster. Baker, who had crawled under a rock, was dead, and, together with Enochs, scalped. Their remains, together with those who fell in the morning, were carried to the fort and decently interred. They lie in the rude burial place at the head of Cresap's bottom.

Of the men engaged in this affair, it is impossible to collect any other names than those of Enochs, Baker, McColloch, Hoffman, Bean, Sutherland, Dobbins, Vennam and McArthur. The latter, Duncan McArthur, afterwards Governor of Ohio, then a young man, had but recently gone to the station. He thus early evinced much of that true courage and great energy of mind and character which afterwards so distinguished him.

According to Mr. McIntyre, young McArthur cried out, as they ascended the bank, to "surround them," but the Indians having the advantage, spread themselves and would have prevented this even had the whites kept together.

NOTE A.

The original way of spelling this name was Whetzell, or Whitzell. The pronunciation was Whet-zell. We have several signatures of Jacob Wetzel, who was sheriff of Ohio county, all of which are spelt with an "h." Considerable difficulty was created in the Virginia Legislature, at the time of forming the county of "Wetzel," as to the proper orthography. An examination of the files in the land office, induced the committee to adopt that followed by ourselves.

In this decision they were clearly correct. During the past summer, the author, after examining various papers in possession of friends of the family, was shown an old account book, belonging to Mr. John Rodefer, Sr., an aged and respectable citizen of Belmont county, Ohio, and by marriage, a relative of the Wetzels This account book is in the hand-writing of Mr. Rodefer, and was made at the time he lived in the neighborhood of the Wetzels, on Wheeling creek. There are a number of entries in the name of "Wetzel," or in German, as it is written, "Watzal." He said that was the manner in which the family wrote it, and that for some time after coming to the west, noticed the name in various places upon old books and papers in possession of the family, and that it was invariably written, "Watzal," or in English, Wetzel. Regarding this as conclusive, we have adopted the style.

The signatures of Jacob Wetzel, to which allusion has been made, were not executed by that person, as we are informed by Mr. Rodefer, but by a deputy. This is doubtless correct, as we notice the name spelled differently, in different places.

# A NOTE TO THE READER

WE HOPED YOU LOVED THIS BOOK. IF YOU DID, PLEASE LEAVE A REVIEW ON AMAZON TO LET EVERYONE ELSE KNOW WHAT YOU THOUGHT.

WE WOULD ALSO LIKE TO THANK OUR SPONSORS **WWW.DIGITALHISTORYBOOKS.COM** WHO MADE THE PUBLICATION OF THIS BOOK POSSIBLE.

**WWW.DIGITALHISTORYBOOKS.COM** PROVIDES A WEEKLY NEWSLETTER OF THE BEST DEALS IN HISTORY AND HISTORICAL FICTION.

SIGN UP TO THEIR NEWLSETTER TO FIND OUT MORE ABOUT THEIR LATEST DEALS.

Made in the USA
Columbia, SC
31 May 2024

36423474R00190